SCHOOLS COUNCIL WORKING PAPER 75

Primary practice
a sequel to *The practical curriculum*

Methuen Educational

First published 1983 for the Schools Council
Newcombe House, 45 Notting Hill Gate, London W11 3JB
by Methuen Educational
11 New Fetter Lane, London EC4P 4EE
Reprinted 1984

Filmset in Monophoto Times
by Northumberland Press Ltd, Gateshead
Printed in Great Britain by
Richard Clay (The Chaucer Press) Ltd
Bungay, Suffolk

British Library Cataloguing in Publication Data
Primary practice.—(Schools Council working papers; 75)
1. Education, Elementary—England and Wales—Curricula
I. Series
372.19'0942   LB1564.G7

ISBN 0–423–51260–9

Contents

Acknowledgements

The Schools Council and the publishers are grateful to the following for permission to reproduce copyright material: the Centre for the Teaching of Reading, University of Reading School of Education, for extracts from *The Literacy Schedule* by Mrs Joan Dean; the Controller, HM Stationery Office, for extracts from *Physical Development* by the Assessment of Performance Unit (DES, 1983), extracts from *Science in Primary Schools*, a discussion paper produced by the HMI Science Committee (DES, 1983), an extract from *Mathematics 5–11: a Handbook of Suggestions* (HMI Matters for Discussion Series, HMSO, 1979), an extract from *Primary Education in England*, a survey by HM Inspectors of Schools (HMSO, 1978), and extracts from *A View of the Curriculum* (HMI Matters for Discussion Series, HMSO, 1980); Croom Helm Ltd, for an extract from *Organising Learning in the Primary School Classroom* by Mrs Joan Dean (1983); Frederick Warne Ltd, for extracts from *Music with Everything* by Margaret Hope-Brown (1973); Mr Gordon Elliot, for an extract from *Self-evaluation and the Teacher* (1980); Hertfordshire County Council, for an extract from *Agreed Syllabus of Religious Education* (1981); the States of Jersey Education Committee, for extracts from *Routes to the Way Ahead* (1980).

Introduction: the year 2000

Today's schoolchildren will be young adults in 2000 A D. Many of them will live into the second half of the twenty-first century.

It is already almost half way from man's first landing on the moon to the end of the century. Not one of today's primary schoolchildren was alive in 1969 when Neil Armstrong took that 'giant stride for mankind'. For every one of them, the first moon landing is history. For every one of their teachers it must be among the major landmarks of their lifetime.

We have just passed another landmark. Britain is the first country to claim to have a microcomputer in every secondary school. By the time this book is published we shall be well on the way to having a micro in every primary school. The silicon chip is already transforming our factories, offices and household appliances. We can hardly imagine what changes it may now bring to the content and practice of primary education.

What we can be sure of, is this. Our own age is one of extreme turbulence. The structure of established industries like coal, iron and steel, textiles and transport, patterns of employment, world trade and banking, the pattern of family life, and social customs, are in ferment. Television by satellite and information by cable are only two among the most obvious changes our children will need to take in their stride. Already, improved communications and large-scale movements of people have greatly extended our knowledge of other cultures, bringing both opportunities for enrichment and the risk of conflict.

Educating the young has always been a heavy responsibility. It is now more daunting than ever before. Fortunately, we are better equipped to tackle this task, professionally, than ever before. We understand more about how children develop, how they learn, and how they are sometimes prevented from learning. We are beginning to see how to match teaching and learning to their stages of development. We have marvellous insights into the working of the brain's two hemispheres. The left hemisphere handles words and numbers, while the right remembers shapes and tunes. The left processes information sequentially; the right can absorb many different impressions simultaneously. One is rational and analytic, the other intuitive and imaginative. We see now how important it is to develop

11

both hemispheres, since even in science, the most rational of human activities, new insights are characteristically intuitive, and equally characteristically are described in scientific papers by rational arguments. Most significant creative activities depend on the collaborative work of the left and right cerebral hemispheres.[1] Both have to be nurtured.

We shall need these insights to discharge our responsibilities for today's children. To talk of preparing for the twenty-first century may seem too dramatic. Perhaps the task has to be dramatized. The proximity of the year 2000 – startlingly near for a somewhat middle-aged working party – should jerk us into taking an objective view of what schooling is all about.

It is not too hard to suggest some of the questions we ought to consider.

1. What should children know and be able to do at the end of the first major stage in their education? What knowledge, skills, concepts and attitudes should primary schools seek to instil?
2. How should schools organize their work
   to take account of the latest research on the learning processes of young children,
   ensure balance and coherence in the curriculum without overloading it,
   and ensure progression and continuity between each successive stage of education?
3. How can primary schools help each of their pupils to move forward with a firm basis for lifelong education and personal development?
4. What are the best forms of cooperation between primary schools and their pupils' families, the local community and other community services?
5. What are the role and responsibilities of teachers and headteachers in primary schools? What initial and in-service training do they need?

Our suggestion that it might be helpful to approach these questions with the needs of the year 2000 in mind is a formidable challenge. It is an invitation to consider what qualities will be valued in an uncertain future, to try in so far as we are able to make our children's education future-proof.

That means reviewing and rethinking what happens in schools. This collection of papers is intended to help in that process, by raising issues and giving examples of current practice.

We see these papers as a sequel to *The Practical Curriculum*. *The Practical Curriculum* was a collection of working papers for practising teachers. As it took shape the working party began to think that it might be the first of a series, in which other volumes dealt in greater depth with particular stages or areas of the curriculum. We have already published one sequel, on post-16 courses.[2] This volume is about primary education. Like *The Pract-*

ical Curriculum it is designed in the first instance for practising teachers. Each of the chapters takes one major issue, and suggests ways in which schools might approach it. After discussing some contrasting approaches to setting aims, we go on in Chapter II to consider different ways of describing the curriculum. This leads on to the question of what objectives to set and what standards to aim at in different areas of the curriculum. There are six short chapters about how to approach these questions in science; mathematics; language and literacy; studying people past and present; imagination, feeling and sensory expression; and personal and social development. Chapter IX discusses the contribution topic work can make to cohesion in the curriculum. Chapter X is about the contribution which pupil assessment and record-keeping can make to progression and continuity. In Chapter XI we turn to organization and planning, and discuss in particular the use of specialists, the problems of small schools, resources for learning, and the potential contributions of parents and others outside the school. How schools can best cooperate with agencies such as the psychological, welfare, social and health services may depend on local circumstances. Chapter XII is about evaluation and staff development. In each chapter we have tried to suggest questions which groups of teachers might like to take further.

We believe that examining the issues raised in these papers will help teachers to make better primary schools. Clear thinking, sound planning and good management all have a part to play in this process.

We hope these papers will provide a useful framework for agreeing what needs to be done.

I. A primary school's aims: contrasting approaches

Schools should set out in writing the aims which they pursue.[1]

If you're not sure where you're going, you're liable to end up some place else – and not even know it.[2]

Our logical left hemisphere tells us this advice is right. You do need to know where you are going. But setting aims is difficult. It calls on skills which some talented and creative people seem not to have. As the Plowden Report said, 'some of the head teachers who were considered by H M Inspectors to be most successful in practice were least able to formulate their aims clearly and convincingly'.[3]

However successful they may be, these heads do add to their own difficulties. If their aims are not explicit it is difficult to see how other people can understand, accept or support them. A school's success depends on many contributions, and we believe it is more likely to be successful if it has explicit aims which many people inside and outside the school support wholeheartedly.

Writing aims is hard and time-consuming. Securing agreement and support for a set of aims is even harder, and takes much longer. It may be helpful to take a short cut, to borrow someone else's aims, to take a set 'off the peg' as it were, even if the fit leaves something to the imagination. If this is how you choose to start there are several possible sources of help.

As we said in *The Practical Curriculum*, 'There is no better general statement of the aims of education than that of the Warnock Report: "first, to enlarge a child's knowledge, experience and imaginative understanding, and thus his awareness of moral values and capacity for enjoyment; and secondly, to enable him to enter the world after formal education is over as an active participant in society and a responsible contributor to it, capable of achieving as much independence as possible".'[4]

The Department of Education and Science suggested a somewhat more detailed set of aims in both *A Framework for the School Curriculum* and *The School Curriculum*:

15

  i to help pupils to develop lively, enquiring minds, the ability to question and argue rationally and to apply themselves to tasks, and physical skills;
  ii to help pupils to acquire knowledge and skills relevant to adult life and employment in a fast-changing world;
  iii to help pupils to use language and numbers effectively;
  iv to instil respect for religious and moral values, and tolerance of other races, religions, and ways of life;
  v to help pupils to understand the world in which they live, and the interdependence of individuals, groups and nations;
  vi to help pupils appreciate human achievements and aspirations.[5]

These aims are couched in very general terms, like those *The Practical Curriculum* suggested. They were:

  i to acquire knowledge, skills and practical abilities, and the will to use them;
  ii to develop qualities of mind, body, spirit, feeling and imagination;
  iii to appreciate human achievements in art, music, science, technology and literature;
  iv to acquire understanding of the social, economic and political order, and a reasoned set of attitudes, values and beliefs:
  v to prepare for their adult lives at home, at work, at leisure, and at large, as consumers and citizens; . . .
  vi to develop a sense of self-respect, the capacity to live as independent, self-motivated adults and the ability to function as contributing members of co-operative groups.[6]

Aims such as these may seem too broad and vague to be of any great practical help to practising teachers. That is to ask too much of them. They should be considered only as starting points in the planning process. As *The Practical Curriculum* said, more specific aims are needed for each school, each year and each class. In setting its whole school aims, for example, a primary school might wish each of its pupils to learn

  i to read fluently and accurately, with understanding, feeling and discrimination;
  ii to develop a legible style of handwriting and satisfactory standards of spelling, syntax, punctuation and usage;
  iii to communicate clearly and confidently in speech and writing, in ways appropriate for various occasions and purposes;
  iv to listen attentively and with understanding;
  v to learn how to acquire information from various sources, and to record information and findings in various ways;
  vi to apply computational skills with speed and accuracy;
  vii to understand the applications of mathematical ideas in various situations in home, classroom, school and local area;

viii to observe living and inanimate things, and to recognize characteristics such as pattern and order;

ix to master basic scientific ideas;

x to investigate solutions and interpret evidence, to analyse and to solve
problems;

xi to develop awareness of self and sensitivity to others, acquire a set of
moral values and the confidence to make and hold to moral judgements, and develop habits of self-discipline and acceptable behaviour;

xii to know about geographical, historical and social aspects of the local
environment and the national heritage, to be aware of other times and
places, and to recognize links between local, national and international events;

xiii to acquire sufficient control of self or of tools, equipment and instruments to be able to use music, drama and several forms of arts and
crafts as means of expression;

xiv to develop agility and physical coordination, confidence in and
through physical activity, and the ability to express feeling through
movement.

In deciding its own aims, a primary school might make a list like that and
work systematically through it, amending, discarding and adding, to make
a list of its own. From time to time the school might ask itself two questions:
first, whether its own list was compatible with the more general aims we
quoted earlier, and if not how the school would wish to amend the general
statement; and second, what teaching and activities the school would
provide in order to achieve these aims, and how it would know whether
they had been achieved.

This approach to aim-setting might be called the 'aims to practice'
approach. It keeps the ultimate aims of education in focus, and helps to
ensure that more practical immediate objectives support the wider aims.

Aims to practice

This kind of approach seemed particularly important to the Schools Council teams responsible for the Science 5/13 Project. The introduction to this
project, *With Objectives in Mind*, shows how it might work. The two
examples below show how two teachers tried to relate interesting opportunities for experiential learning to their overall objectives. Other teachers
may find it helpful to look at some of their own lessons with a similarly
critical eye.

An experienced teacher of children aged seven to nine years in a country school,
planning a morning's walk with her class to a nearby wood, chose carefully the part

of the wood to be visited. Walking in the wood was not a new experience for the children, but on this day the teacher made sure that there would be opportunity to notice and explore fresh and exciting features. This time they walked through some dense parts of the wood and also through large green clearings which, in itself, encouraged the children to question why there were green spaces, why certain trees had fallen, why some trees were taller than others, how much taller they were and why it was so much wetter under the trees than in the clearings. It rained on the day she took them; the teacher commented afterwards 'I recommend a wet, dripping wood for the greatest interest', and she went on in her notes 'The children were allowed to collect anything they wished – provided that they had some reason for the collection.' These collections included rotting wood, fungi, leaf mould, a large saturated log, rocks and fossils, and many other things, all of which were very thoroughly observed or used later in the classroom, as would be expected since the children had definite purposes for what they gathered. They brought something else back too, because, again in the teacher's words, 'This walk resulted in good free-expression writing about the "feel" of the wood that day. Children who usually said little had lots to say in the class discussion.'

The second example comes from a teacher's account of working with the unit 'Time' during pilot trials:

We were lucky with the weather this week and were able to do some [more] work with shadow sticks on the playground. When groups of children went out to have a look at shadows on the playground they noticed that the length and position of the shadow at a particular time of the day were not identical to the length and position that the shadow had been when previous work had been done. As a result of looking at these shadows, discussion followed on the movement of the sun. From these discussions much work was done on time of the day, day and night, and seasons. Groups of children devised experiments to try to explain the movement of the sun. After this, discussion followed and some book research.[7]

From simple observation and recording of shadows these children made considerable progress towards an appreciation of quite complex relationships. Of course this particular situation was not arranged in order to start work on day and night and the seasons, neither was this exact development suggested in the unit. But what was suggested in the unit was that teachers might keep in mind various objectives, one of which was awareness of factors in the environment that change with the passage of time and ability to investigate these factors.

This teacher saw, in the situation he described, an opportunity to work towards this objective, and, being mentally prepared to take advantage of it, he encouraged progress in a useful direction. Perhaps this opportunity for making progress may have been missed had he not had the objective in mind: we cannot tell. We only know that, in this case, he did think it helped; which supports our view that objectives have a value in encouraging progression in work.

Despite its value the approach from aims to practice is far from easy, as one series of discussions showed. When twelve headteachers were asked to give their aims for their school as far as reading and language were concerned, only three mentioned writing, and two listening. Some of their aims were so general – 'our aims are to make sure all children are literate when they leave school and to encourage their use of language to the best of their abilities' or 'parents want their children to be literate and this is one of the general aims of the school'[8] – that they seem unlikely to have had much influence on the work of the school.

Practice to aims

Another approach is to start from what the school is already doing and try to decide what aims are implied by current practice. This 'practice to aims' approach ensures that the exercise is rooted in the realities of school life, and it is moreover a necessary part of the critical self-evaluation that must take place before any change is made. The experience of one school which volunteered to take part in a school development programme shows how this might happen. Many of the staff felt a need for help in mathematics and the head was concerned about the lack of music in the school. These two areas were therefore chosen for review. They posed very different problems. 'Mathematics has been more documented than any other curriculum area; nothing has been written down about music and it has never been discussed at staff meetings,' wrote the head. The staff's work on music was included in a wider review of the school's work in creative arts. 'The creative arts group tended to move into action more quickly as there is no stated policy for them; ... assessing current practice was also difficult as many staff felt they did very little music with their class.' This review of existing practice, or non-practice, led the review group to ask for help in running a series of workshops on music for non-specialists.[9]

At another infants' school the staff decided to review arts and craft. A neighbouring head with experience as a course tutor agreed to work with the staff. She and a staff group began by viewing slides showing art work in their own and other schools. This led to some discussion of how the work was organized in other schools, and how materials were stored. The review team realized that their own school had insufficient storage space, and asked their authority's help in converting a cloakroom area into a store. They then turned to art displays in the school hall and corridor. These displays would be a means of creating unity in the school, and the staff agreed on the common theme, nursery rhymes. Only at that rather late stage did aims begin to emerge from their review of what the school was doing.[10]

Practice to aims, and aims to practice, are therefore complementary. We hope schools can find time to try them both. Among the most challenging aims are 'to help pupils to develop lively enquiring minds', from *The School Curriculum*, and 'to develop a sense of self-respect', from *The Practical Curriculum*. The two aims have this in common: they are both to do with the kind of people our pupils will become. That is something which concerns teachers greatly. They know their contribution is limited, that home, community, friends and the media may have greater influence. They know, too, that how they teach, and what is taught through the hidden curriculum of values implied by relationships within the school, may contribute as much to their pupils' personal development as what they teach. The link between what is taught to a child, and what kind of adult that child becomes, is so subtle and intricate that it has to be approached from both ends. Teachers have to ask two questions at the same time: 'What do we need to do to develop the qualities we esteem?' and 'What qualities are likely to arise from what we are doing?' Attacking the problem from both ends gives the best chance of a sensible match between aims and practice.

An example may help to illustrate this. Most schools would put developing self-confidence and self-esteem fairly high among their aims, though not all do so explicitly. Most teachers do have various ways of achieving these aims, by encouraging their pupils and helping them to make an acknowledged contribution to the communal life of the school. Teachers make a point of praising children, displaying their work, enrolling them as monitors, and helping them to take part in concerts, fetes, sporting events and other activities.

These activities are much more important than they may seem at first. This is because they convey many hidden messages. The behaviour and work of those who are praised is reinforced, though it may perhaps be those whose behaviour and work is less good who most need support and reinforcement. Those whose work is displayed, who help as monitors or take part in activities, may blossom. Others may have few opportunities to blossom. The problem for teachers is to ensure that all their pupils are helped to develop self-confidence and self-esteem.

The children who find ordinary school work easy have many successes to build on. It is those who find the formal curriculum difficult who may most need other opportunities for personal development.

Teachers may also need to provide some sort of balance to other cultural differences which originate outside school. They need to ask, for example, whether girls and boys have equal opportunities for access to the curriculum as a whole and in particular for activities such as using construction kits, home play, craft work and outdoor play.

It may also be helpful to ask whether there is any justification for differences, where they occur, in the way girls and boys are treated and the kind of tasks they are asked to do. Is it likely for example for girls and boys to be praised equally for such qualities as neatness, or courage, or equally likely for girls and boys to be asked to lift and to carry heavy objects, or to carry messages?

We believe teachers would find it illuminating and helpful to take a careful look at their practice in matters like these, and to ask what aims can be inferred from what they actually do and say.

Many of the activities which help to build self-confidence and self-esteem contribute also to other aims. They may well involve listening, talking or writing, calculating, sorting and classifying, planning, working with other people, or service to a wider community. Just as a single aim can be pursued in many ways, so a single activity can contribute to several aims. The important thing is to make aims and practice consistent with each other.

To some extent that is a problem for each teacher to tackle personally. It is also a problem for the staff as a whole. They need to pull together if their work is to be effective. That means supporting and working to achieve the same aims, and adopting consistent practices throughout a school.

Such agreement between a school and individual teachers is by no means universal. There are of course some natural differences between the teachers of children of different ages. These differences should where possible reflect only the stage of development their pupils have reached. At the beginning and end of the primary stage there are differences in emphasis between nursery teachers and secondary teachers. 'For nursery teachers the most important aims have to do with children's ability to get along with other children, become more independent, substitute verbal expression for aggression, explain ideas and convey information and develop an easy relationship with staff. Next comes a group of aims concerned with personal, physical, intellectual and social skills.'[11]

Not surprisingly, secondary teachers with an active interest in primary education have different priorities. They tend to believe that the intellectual aspect of development is the most important, and to emphasize formal skills in arithmetic, spelling and legible writing.[12]

In primary schools there is likely to be a similar divergence between teachers of reception classes and teachers of older juniors. It might be difficult for a reception teacher to subscribe wholeheartedly to a set of school aims written with only the 11-year-old leavers in mind. Those responsible for drawing up a school's aims should bear in mind that the top juniors are more than twice as old, and twice as experienced, as the reception class.

A school's overall aims should be framed in a way which wins the support of all the staff. The immediate objectives for each class should differ from each other provided they are consistent with each other.

Securing active commitment to a set of agreed aims may be among a headteacher's most difficult tasks. It is certainly one of the most important. The teaching staff of a school share professional knowledge and expertise, and many values and attitudes. In these respects they are likely to have a high level of agreement. In other respects they may differ. They reflect also the diverse attitudes and values of the whole community, and may not agree about what knowledge, skills, concepts, values and attitudes to foster. In any school the teachers may legitimately hold differing views about the school's aims. There seemed indeed in one study of a dozen schools to be very little general agreement among the staff of any of the schools.[13] In those circumstances the head has to work hard to achieve sufficient agreement among the staff to ensure that each child has a coherent education. In such a context the retirement or resignation of one or two teachers in a staff of ten or twelve and the arrival of newcomers might make a considerable change in the staff's collective views. These factors underline the importance to a school of the skills needed in obtaining agreement, understanding, acceptance and active support for its aims.

These skills are needed both inside the school and in the community it serves. For a school to flourish it needs the support of parents, governors, and others too. Negotiating their support demands tact and patience. Success in this adds greatly to a school's strength.

Aims need to be relevant as well as realistic. They should reflect a school's position in time and place. That means regular revision to take account of changes outside the school. One obvious and pervasive change in contemporary Britain is that our society has become multicultural and multiracial. Six years ago in 1977 the Green Paper *Education in Schools* said 'the curriculum should reflect a sympathetic understanding of the different cultures and races that now make up our society'.[14] Our understanding of the needs has been much enlarged since then, by our realization that social and linguistic barriers to learning may have led to a disproportionate number of West Indian children being referred to special schools, by the Scarman report on the Brixton riots, by the increasing contribution of black people in such fields as law, medicine, commerce, theatre and television, the selection of black people to represent England at cricket, football and athletics, and many other happenings. Our aims need rethinking in the light of our developing perception of the issues, and our increasing national commitment to eliminate discrimination on grounds of race, sex or handicap.

These general principles need the support of more detailed objectives related to a school's day-to-day work.

Teachers may find it helpful to ask themselves, for example, whether the curriculum in their school includes examples drawn from a wide range of cultures, and gives sufficient weight to the contribution of minority groups to developments in history, and in art, science and other fields. Particularly in areas where there are few if any representatives of ethnic minority groups, it may be more difficult for teachers to appreciate the importance of including in materials about contemporary Britain a fair proportion of references to ethnic minorities. More is needed than just a fair proportion of references, though this in itself is a useful criterion. Ethnic and cultural diversity should be presented as an enriching, valued element in our society.

The key issue is whether applying these principles would require changes in practice. Reviewing the formal curriculum is a necessary step. So too is reviewing the school's everyday practice, its hidden curriculum. Applying these principles to the formal curriculum will be effective only if the school ethos is hospitable to diversity, and the school has a clear and unambiguous policy for dealing with overt discrimination in the classroom, on the playground and at the school gate.

It is also possible to appreciate better now another of the Green Paper's points. 'We also live in a complex, interdependent world, and many of our problems in Britain require international solutions. The curriculum should therefore reflect our need to know about and understand other countries.'[15]

Perhaps as a nation we should go further. Our awareness of other countries, particularly of the Third World, the Middle East and the European Community, is perhaps a little keener than it was even six years ago. We are certainly more conscious now of living in a complex and interdependent world.

Schools need sensitive antennae to detect changes like these, and sensitivity in adapting and updating their aims in response to them. In these fast-moving times the need is for constant review. At the very least perhaps schools should agree to let no set of aims run for more than five years without review.

Points to consider and discuss

1. How do your own school's aims compare with those quoted on pages 16–17?
2. Does the curriculum and teaching in your own school meet the school's stated aims?
3. Can you find examples in your own school where it has paid to work from aims to practice, from practice to aims?
4. Did the teachers described on pages 17 and 18 make the most of their opportunities?

5. Have you reviewed your aims and practice to take account of the suggestions on pages 22–3 for the treatment of ethnic and cultural diversity?
6. What more can you do to provide opportunities for each of your pupils to succeed and develop self-esteem?
7. Are there aims which all the staff should support and matters where disagreement is acceptable?
8. What steps have you taken to acquire the skills needed to contribute effectively to obtaining agreement, understanding, acceptance and active support for your school's aims? Is this a question only for heads?

II. Describing the curriculum

Do the words commonly used to describe the curriculum match present-day requirements? One or two fairly recent examples will help to illustrate how important this is. Some of our older school buildings still have engraved in stone words like 'Manual'. Terms like 'nature study', 'singing', 'Bible knowledge', 'cookery' and 'arithmetic' are no longer adequate descriptions of what we are trying to achieve. Terms like 'boys' crafts' and 'girls' crafts' imply views and judgements which are no longer acceptable.

These examples show how an outdated vocabulary might influence a school's thinking about the curriculum. This would not matter if the curriculum itself were static and unchanging. At times when society itself changed little an education based on the transmission of traditional skills, and described in traditional terms, was sufficiently up to date to prepare young people for adult life. In today's fast-changing times young people need some knowledge and understanding of new technologies, and almost certainly the ability to cope with technologies as yet unknown.

That is why the curriculum needs to be updated constantly, and why the language used to describe the curriculum needs updating too, to ensure that it promotes and does not inhibit necessary change.

The curriculum as subjects

For many purposes a conventional approach to describing the curriculum is likely to be helpful. This approach, common in secondary schools, and therefore of great importance to primary schools, is through the use of subject titles. Their use in secondary schools reflects the remarkable success mankind has had in describing, classifying and investigating many aspects of the environment. Young people need to understand the ways in which most forms of human knowledge are collected and organized. School subject titles correspond to this system of classification.

Their use in primary schools is less appropriate. Young children have little experience, and limited ability to generalize. The range and depth of their generalizations increase with experience, and they acquire the ability to handle more complex ideas and form concepts only as they reach the later stages of their primary education. Young children need many varied experiences and the opportunity to explore and learn from these experiences in ways which lead them gradually to understand how adults usually organize knowledge.

This adult systematization of knowledge is so fundamental to our civilization that it has underpinned most recent thinking about the content of

Table 1

	A	B	C	D	E
1.	English	Language	English	English	
2.	Arithmetic	Mathematics	Mathematics	Mathematics	
3.	R I	Religion	Spiritual and moral development	R E	
4.	History	History	History	History	Social abilities including
5.	Geography	Geography	Geography	Geography	
6.	Nature study	Natural science	Science	Science	
7.	PT	PE	PE	PE	
8.	Art, craft (boys) needlework (girls)	Art, craft and needlework	Art, craft, needlework, homecraft handicraft	Art and craft	Aesthetic education including
9.	Music	Handwriting Music	Music	Music	
10.			Foreign language	Foreign language	

A. *Handbook of Suggestions for the Consideration of Teachers and Others Concerned in the Work of Public Elementary Schools* (1905)
B. *Primary Education* (1959)
C. *Half Our Future* (1963)
D. *Children and Their Primary Schools* (1967)

the curriculum. The unanimity is so marked, one wonders why there ever was concern about the core and basics.

The evidence in many official documents, from the 1905 *Handbook* to our own document *The Practical Curriculum* in 1981, is of consistency in theory, and stability in practice. Some of these documents are summarized in Table 1. The table shows remarkable consistency in the nine main

E (cont'd)	F	G	H	I
Language and literacy	Language	English	English	English
Mathematics	Mathematics	Mathematics	Mathematics	Mathematics
RE		RE	RE	RE
History		History and social studies	History and social studies	History and social studies
Geography		Geography	Geography	Geography
Science: experimental and observational	Science	Science	Science	Science
PE	PE	PE, including movement, dance and games	PE	PE, including games
Art and craft	Aesthetics: appreciation of form, colour, texture and sound	Art, craft	Art and craft	Art, craft, design and technology, home economics
Music		Music, drama	Music	Music
		Foreign language (but only in exceptionally favourable circumstances)		

E. *Primary Education in England: a Survey by HM Inspectors of Schools*
F. APU from *Record Keeping in Primary Schools* (Schools Council Research Studies)
G. *A View of the Curriculum* (HMI)
H. *The School Curriculum* (DES)
I. *The Practical Curriculum* (Schools Council)

elements recommended for inclusion in the curriculum for top juniors. Only in the 1960s did a tenth element, a foreign language, make a fleeting appearance among the main recommendations.

In practice, too, there is remarkable stability. This stability seems to go back almost to the priority given to basic skills by the system of payment by results. Schools may still tend to concentrate on teaching basic skills, to the exclusion of other elements of the curriculum. Unhappily for children taught in this way, the teaching of skills in isolation does not produce the best results.[1] Skills have to be applied effectively if they are to be learned thoroughly. A broad curriculum can and should be planned to provide many opportunities for using and practising skills in reading, writing and calculating. Planned in the right way, a broad curriculum is likely to help children to master these fundamental skills.

The general educational progress of children and their competence in the basic skills appear to have benefited where they were involved in a programme of work that included art and craft, history and geography, music and physical education, and science, as well as language, mathematics and religious and moral education, although not necessarily as separate items on a timetable.[2]

Such a statement amply confirms our everyday experience that when children are fired by some new experience, they talk, and write, and draw, and count, as if possessed.

Not all schools do provide a broad curriculum. The HMI primary survey suggests that the provision of observational and experimental science is lacking in many schools[3] and the provision of religious education, physical education, music, art and craft is often poorly structured, undemanding and limited in range.[4] Where this is so, schools may be failing to provide their pupils with important and necessary opportunities to develop their imagination and sensory perceptions. Some schools, even primary schools, operate a system of options which may deprive pupils of important skills. For example, in one school the junior girls made aprons while the boys made lampshades, and in another the girls sewed and knitted while the boys painted and made collage pictures.[5] In other schools young girls and boys followed separate programmes of physical education. Instead of thus reinforcing traditional differences between the sexes, schools might adopt positive policies for achieving equal opportunities for both sexes. This might mean providing, for example, compensatory opportunities to stimulate boys' language and girls' mechanical development.

Describing the curriculum in terms of subjects should make it possible to discover whether each child is following a broad curriculum. If any are not doing so, their teacher should try to establish whether this is because the school lacks the necessary resources, expertise or imagination, or because of some deliberate decision.

Curriculum as process

In suggesting that possibility we have touched on other possible ways of describing the curriculum. One is to consider what skills and qualities today's young people are likely to need now and in their adult lives. Do they include, for example, such qualities as:

1. Communication skills, through whatever medium is most appropriate to the message and the intended audience, e.g. language, mathematics, symbols, graphics, movement, sound;
2. Study skills, the ability to work and learn independently, the ability to organize information through themes, formulae or concepts;
3. Ability to work from written technical instructions;
4. Ability to define problems and find solutions to them, to plan, and to make decisions;
5. Practical and technical skills;
6. Personal and social qualities including coping skills and adaptability, ability to work cooperatively with others, sensitivity, imagination and creativity, self-esteem, and a sense of moral values.

Whether a school decides on these or other skills and qualities to aim at we need to establish how schools can help to develop the chosen skills. Most seem to be the kind of abilities which come at least as much through practice as through formal instruction. It might be helpful therefore to describe the curriculum in terms of the opportunities it gives to practise and acquire these skills and qualities.

Curriculum as the study of problems

When considering the qualities needed for adult life some people see an important link with the explosion of knowledge. The amount of information now available is so vast that children cannot possibly learn more than a small proportion of it. Selecting what is to be learned is even more important than it was in the past, and teachers can help by focusing on what seem likely to be the most pressing issues of the twenty-first century. They include such matters as computer literacy, rights and duties in a democratic society, consumer education, Third World studies, conservation, energy and pollution, and peace studies. Some would go so far as to suggest that the curriculum should consist entirely of issues like these. It might certainly be helpful to try describing the existing curriculum in those terms, so that schools can judge whether the issues are treated adequately.

One of the most pressing current issues is our response to the emergence of a multicultural, multi-ethnic society in Britain. Some teachers may be able to present diversity in a practical and positive way, well within the experience and understanding of their pupils. Two examples show what can be done.

One infant school with twenty-one nationalities represented among its 170 pupils tries to include songs, stories, dances, pictures, models and ornaments from all cultures so that the children are reassured, and helped to learn from one another.

A junior school with about 200 pupils from a dozen different ethnic groups has library books in each of the languages represented. The music room has instruments from many parts of the world, and these are often played by parents or friends; wallcharts show the words and tunes of simple national songs which the children sing in the appropriate language. Lessons in meteorology include the making of simple thermometers, rain gauges, sunshine and humidity records, and weather data from the daily newspapers is used to chart the weather in Cyprus, Egypt, Turkey, Hong Kong Ireland, Portugal, Bermuda, New York and elsewhere. Studies of water included four stories about great floods: The Great Deluge (from ancient Greece), The Flood (Babylonia), Noah's Ark (from Israel) and Irraweka (from the West Indies). In these ways its ethnic diversity enriches the school's curriculum, and extends its pupils' knowledge and experience.

These examples show how valuable ethnic diversity can be. Schools without that strength will have to find other ways of tackling this issue, perhaps through radio, television and the press, exchange visits with other schools, or the study of regional diversity.

Curriculum as areas of knowledge and experience

The need to select from a growing mass of information is acknowledged also in numerous attempts to identify key areas of knowledge and experience. This way of describing the curriculum tries to identify the main ways in which people know and experience reality, and to ensure that what is taught in schools includes the main areas and strikes a reasonable balance between them.

Table 2 summarizes several different attempts to describe the main areas of knowledge and experience. They were prepared for different purposes and do not necessarily use words in precisely the same way as each other. With those reservations in mind teachers may find it helpful to consider whether their pupils are having, and should have, opportunities to enter each of these areas of knowledge and experience. A further question of great importance is whether these lists omit any important aspect of the curriculum. Neither of the two more theoretical analyses makes any specific mention, for example, of language and communication, or physical

Table 2 Areas of knowledge and experience

1.	2.	3.	4.
Philosophy			
Moral judgement and awareness	Moral education	Ethical	
Human studies	Humanities and social science	Social and political	Social abilities, including history, geography and religious education
Religious understanding		Spiritual	
Formal logic and mathematics	Mathematics	Mathematical	Mathematics
Physical sciences	Physical and biological sciences	Scientific	Experimental and observational science
Aesthetic experiences	Expressive and creative arts	Aesthetic and creative	Aesthetic education including art and craft, music and physical education
		Physical	
		Linguistic	Language and literacy
P. H. Hirst and R. S. Peters, *The Logic of Education*, Routledge & Kegan Paul, 1970.	D. Lawton, *Social Change, Educational Theory and Curriculum Planning*, University of London Press, 1973.	DES, *Curriculum 11–16*. HMSO, 1977.	HMI, *Primary Education in England*, HMSO, 1978.

education and expression. And none of the four refers in any way to technological understanding, experience and capability. The fact that English has no single words to describe this area of knowledge and experience, whereas both French and German have, is sometimes thought to indicate the low regard we British have for technology, and a longstanding weakness in our system of education. Whatever the validity of this line of thought, it does illustrate the importance of subjecting approaches like these to critical examination.

The curriculum through a child's eyes

Writing mainly for teachers, we have naturally described the curriculum in ways which might help adults to decide how to structure the curriculum and what to include in it. None of this would mean very much to very young children. They know school as a place where there are things to learn, to do and to make, things to play with, things to look at, to touch, to smell and perhaps to taste, things to listen to, people to talk with and people to play with. For most children the richness and variety of the school experience greatly enlarges the experiences from which they have already learned much at home. They need support and guidance in exploring further and help in making sense of their experiences.

Particularly for young pupils, each of a school's aims may be pursued in many ways. Skills for observation may be fostered by looking at plants, or rocks, or buildings, or places. Practical problems arise in craft and geography as well as science and mathematics. Opportunities for listening, talking, reading, writing, illustrating and calculating arise whatever the topic. Language, mathematics and science across the curriculum correspond to the realities of everyday life.

The examples which follow describe quite ordinary activities undertaken by half a dozen classes. Readers may find it helpful to consider how these activities relate to the different ways of describing the curriculum mentioned in this chapter.

1. A class of top juniors visited Oliver Cromwell's birthplace in Huntingdon as part of their work on the Pilgrim Fathers. They heard the story of the *Mayflower*, used atlases to identify places in the United Kingdom, the Netherlands and North America, marked the route on a roneoed sketch map, measured it and calculated the distance travelled. They discussed their visit, then wrote and illustrated imaginative accounts of their experiences as a Pilgrim Father.
2. Another similar class from an outer London suburb, not long grown out of a rural village, visited a nearby new town. They compared the

houses, schools and civic buildings in their own area with those of the new town, considered the relative number of flats, and the provision of car parks and open spaces, and referred to population statistics. They drew up shopping lists, and compared prices in the two areas. When they visited the new town they were given money to buy their own lunch. Some discovered that by combining they would each get a better lunch.

3. At harvest time a class of infants were working on seasonal changes, harvesting crops and fruit picking. They considered the mystery of growth, the place of thanksgiving. Each pupil brought an apple or pear to school. They compared the apples and pears by weight, and by girth, making pictorial bar charts to show their findings. They split each fruit in half, along the core, noting the symmetry of pips and flesh around the stalk. Then they painted pictures of the halved fruit, and mounted each picture on a card. The pictures were displayed on the wall in a regular array, four cards high and seven wide. Each pupil's picture could then be identified by a number pair, as the third along and second up, fourth along and third up, and so on.

4. Mathematical concepts can be introduced into other kinds of work, with equal success. As part of their health education a class of juniors discovered their own birth weights and lengths, displayed these on a bar chart and discovered that most of them were much the same. Their chart illustrated the ideas of range and mode. They compared their birth and their present measurements, mapped their birthplaces, and measured the distance from their present homes.

5. Arrangements were made to extend an inner city school's playground by acquiring a neighbouring disused factory site. The first proposal to extend the hard play area was amended in consultation with the head and staff, who brought in pupils, parents and local residents. An imaginative scheme for landscaping and planting the site was eventually agreed, and funded jointly by the LEA and Manpower Services Commission. Much of the work was done voluntarily by pupils, parents and residents. The children planned, measured, recorded, worked and observed, helping to create a beautiful area where they and future generations can study plants and living creatures.

6. Two boys in a reception class had difficulty getting a bin of plastic balls out of the PE cupboard; they said the cupboard needed tidying. With their teacher, the class agreed what had to be done and did it. They had to empty the cupboard, sort its contents into piles, sweep the cupboard and clean the container boxes, decide where to put things, label boxes, count things, mend broken things, and make a list of contents. All this required skills in communicating, counting, sorting,

judging space, and working together, and the class had the satisfaction of having solved a tricky problem.

It is sometimes hard to know how to classify activities like these. They do not slot neatly into any of the formal systems of describing the curriculum mentioned in this chapter, though they do contribute to several elements of the curriculum and several aspects of a child's development. Experiences like these can provide much lively, interesting material. Teachers need to be able to use these undifferentiated experiences as ways of leading children to an understanding of the concepts implied by subjects, problems, processes and areas of experience.

More detailed objectives

To do this successfully means working to more detailed objectives. Indeed, more detailed objectives will be needed whatever approach a school adopts to describing the curriculum.

The first task is to define each area of the curriculum precisely enough for teachers to be able to plan programmes of work and decide on appropriate ways of assessing their pupils' learning. Sometimes the curriculum is defined at least in part by someone outside the school. Teachers may work to local authority guidelines or self-assessment schedules, or be guided by the authors and publishers of textbooks or work schemes, or the setters of tests and examinations for which all the pupils prepare. If the curriculum is decided in one of these ways by people outside the school, teachers have to make a special effort to understand its underlying logic and make it their own. Whatever the contribution from outside, it is still necessary for a school to think out its own programmes of work. Sometimes headteachers take this responsibility themselves, but the task of putting together the overall programme may fall to a subject coordinator, the whole staff, or teachers as individuals. The approach is quite likely to be different in different areas of the curriculum. Religious education is required for example to follow an agreed syllabus adopted by the local education authority, and mathematics is often based on a series of published books or workcards, but will still require a school programme. In social studies or art the programme is more often devised inside the school. Teachers may find it helpful to consider why their school has chosen one approach in some areas of the curriculum and other approaches in other areas. Whatever the source of the programme of work and whoever actually puts it into writing, it must be considered and discussed by every teacher if they are to make it their own and see where each teacher's work fits into the total pattern.

Other important questions have to do with the terms used in defining each area of the curriculum. It may be defined in terms of knowledge to be retained and skills mastered; content to be covered, activities undertaken, or experiences undergone; understandings, values and attitudes to be fostered. Agreeing the terms to be used in defining part of the curriculum leads to statements about the kinds of progress children are expected to make, and how their progress is to be assessed.

In some areas of the curriculum it may perhaps be appropriate to look only for progress in acquiring theoretical knowledge and extending cognitive skills. In others it may be appropriate just to provide as many experiences as time permits. In reality it is far more likely that teachers will be looking for progress of many kinds, in acquiring knowledge and skills, in understanding concepts, or in developing powers of expression in art and craft, music and movement, writing and speaking, and sensitivity of response to poetry and drama, music and art, to other people, and moral issues.

Some of these kinds of progress are readily measured by objective criteria, and proceed hierarchically from one grade to another. We can take it as read, for example, that anyone who can swim 1000 metres can swim all shorter distances, that anyone who can run a mile in four minutes could manage it in five or six, or that anyone who can apply the four rules to fractions could manage whole numbers.

Other kinds of progress are not as easily measured by objective criteria, and do not proceed so clearly from one level to another. Is Botham or Gower the better batsman, Lymeswold or Cheddar the better cheese? Writers of good prose do not usually go on to become writers of good poetry, or vice versa. There is no clear line of progression from skill in calculation to a grasp of mathematical concepts, or from an encyclopaedic knowledge of historical facts to an understanding of issues.

The point we are trying to illustrate is that there are important differences in the terms used to define the different areas of the curriculum and the ways in which it is possible to assess pupils' progress in these areas. These differences have important implications for teachers in discussing objectives, assessment and planning.

Our first example is drawn from Science 5/13.[6] We put this first because that project's approach to primary science is based on a precise statement of aims and objectives, rooted firmly in what is known about children's growth and development. That must be our starting point.

In some areas of the curriculum, notably mathematics, the logic of the subject provides a framework for the school curriculum. More than most, mathematics is an area of knowledge which becomes steadily and progressively more difficult; and because mathematics is a logical system, capability can be assessed objectively and accurately. Mathematics is the most evidently hierarchical of all school subjects, and the one in which mastery of concepts, knowledge and skills is most easily measured. For these reasons there is a great deal of readily available guidance on mathematics.

In other areas of the curriculum it is more difficult to recognize a clear hierarchy whether in exercising skills or understanding concepts. It is also more difficult to find objective ways of measuring achievement, particularly when the achievement is a work of imagination or art, an emotional or sensory response, or a sense of judgement or values. We have tried to illustrate some of these difficulties which arise in defining the curriculum in such areas as science; mathematics; language and literacy; the study of people past and present; imagination, feeling and sensory expression; and personal and social development. Our hope is that these notes will help teachers to work out their own ways of defining the curriculum, deciding objectives and setting standards.

Points to consider and discuss

1. Does every child in your school follow a broad curriculum including all the nine elements listed in Table 1 (pages 26–7)?
2. Has your school a coherent strategy for practising and developing each of the qualities mentioned on page 29? What evidence have you that they are being acquired? Could you provide more or better opportunities?
3. Does the curriculum in your school provide adequately for learning about some important current problems?
4. How do you describe the curriculum in your school? If you describe it as a number of areas of knowledge and experience, or in any other ways mentioned in this chapter, are you happy with the result?
5. Can you identify activities or pieces of work which contribute to each of your school's stated aims? To what extent do you feel you succeed in achieving them?
6. Have you written down your detailed objectives for each area of the curriculum, and for major activities undertaken by the pupils? What kinds of progress do these objectives imply? Is this the kind of progress you really believe in?

III. Science

What we have tried to do in this and the next five chapters is to illustrate some of the issues which arise in defining various areas of the curriculum. We have put science first for two reasons: because it ought to be a major area of the curriculum and is much neglected, and because there is to hand a clear statement of the aims and objectives which might shape a primary science programme.

There is clear evidence that more and better science is needed. 'The H M I report *Primary Education in England*, 1979, found that few primary schools visited had effective programmes for the teaching of science. More recently the A P U reports have shown that although few schools admitted to no science, few gave more than 5 per cent of the time to it. In junior and junior and infant schools, among the goals for science only 29 per cent listed understanding of basic science concepts, only 8 per cent familiarity with the correct use of simple science equipment, only 9 per cent the ability to plan experiments.'[1]

The reasons for this state of affairs are not clear. Lack of suitable guidance is not among them. There are to hand clear statements of possible aims and objectives and well-conceived suggestions for materials to use and activities to undertake.

Starting from what is known about children's growth and development the Science 5/13 team prepared most useful tables of the attitudes, interests and abilities children are likely to show at each stage. The tables provide a splendid framework for mapping the levels of interest and skill children should acquire as they develop. Their interest and relevance extend to other areas of the curriculum as well as science, so they are included as Appendix A to these papers. The following conclusions about what might be expected of most infants have been taken from the main tables. Infant teachers will probably find this a very handy summary, useful both as a framework for their work in most areas of the curriculum, and a basis for checking their own knowledge and experience of young children. Following Piaget, the project team believe that most children of this age move from an essentially intuitive mode of thought to the early stage of concrete thought. The tables distinguish between a transitional stage, and the early stage of concrete thought.

Table 3

Transition from intuition to concrete operations. Infants generally.	Concrete operations. Early stage.
The characteristics of thought among infant children differ in important respects from those of children over the age of about seven years. Infant thought has been described as 'intuitive' by Piaget: it is closely associated with physical action and is dominated by immediate observation. Generally, the infant is not able to think about or imagine the consequences of an action unless he has actually carried it out, nor is he yet likely to draw logical conclusions from his experiences. At this early stage the objectives are those concerned with active exploration of the immediate environment and the development of ability to discuss and communicate effectively: they relate to the kind of activities that are appropriate to these very young children, and which form an introduction to ways of exploring and of ordering observations.	In this Stage, children are developing the ability to manipulate things mentally. At first this ability is limited to objects and materials that can be manipulated concretely, and even then only in a restricted way. The objectives here are concerned with developing these mental operations through exploration of concrete objects and materials – that is to say, objects and materials which, as physical things, have meaning for the child. Since older children, and even adults, prefer an introduction to new ideas and problems through concrete example and physical exploration, these objectives are suitable for all children, whatever their age, who are being introduced to certain science activities for the first time.

Attitudes, interests and aesthetic awareness

Willingness to ask questions. Willingness to handle both living and non-living material. Sensitivity to the need for giving proper care to living things. Enjoyment in using all the senses for exploring and discriminating. Willingness to collect material for observation or investigation.	Desire to find out things for oneself. Willing participation in group work. Willing compliance with safety regulations in handling tools and equipment. Appreciation of the need to learn the meaning of new words and to use them correctly. Awareness that there are various ways of testing out ideas and making observations.

Transition from intuition to concrete operations. *Infants generally.*	*Concrete operations.* *Early stage.*
	Interest in comparing and classifying living or non-living things. Enjoyment in comparing measurements with estimates. Awareness that there are various ways of expressing results and observations. Willingness to wait and to keep records in order to observe change in things. Enjoyment in exploring the variety of living things in the environment. Interest in discussing and comparing the aesthetic qualities of materials.

Observing, exploring and ordering observations

Appreciation of the variety of living things and materials in the environment. Awareness of changes which take place as time passes. Recognition of common shapes – square, circle, triangle. Recognition of regularity in patterns. Ability to group things consistently according to chosen or given criteria.	Awareness of tne structure and form of living things. Awareness of change of living things and non-living materials. Recognition of the action of force. Ability to group living and non-living things by observable attributes. Ability to distinguish regularity in events and motion.

Developing basic concepts and logical thinking

Awareness of the meaning of words which describe various types of quantity. Appreciation that things which are different may have features in common.	Ability to predict the effect of certain changes through observation of similar changes. Formation of the notions of the horizontal and the vertical. Development of concepts of conservation of length and substance. Awareness of the meaning of speed and of its relation to distance covered.

Table 3 (cont'd)

Transition from intuition to concrete operations. Infants generally.	Concrete operations. Early stage.

Posing questions and devising experiments or investigations to answer them

Ability to find answers to simple problems by investigation. Ability to make comparisons in terms of one property or variable.	Appreciation of the need for measurement. Awareness that more than one variable may be involved in a particular change.

Acquiring knowledge and learning skills

Ability to discriminate between different materials. Awareness of the characteristics of living things. Awareness of properties which materials can have. Ability to use displayed reference material for identifying living and non-living things.	Familiarity with sources of sound. Awareness of sources of heat, light and electricity. Knowledge that change can be produced in common substances. Appreciation that ability to move or cause movement requires energy. Knowledge of differences in properties between and within common groups of materials. Appreciation of man's use of other living things and their products. Awareness that man's way of life has changed through the ages. Skill in manipulating tools and materials. Development of techniques for handling living things correctly. Ability to use books for supplementing ideas or information.

Communicating

Ability to use new words appropriately. Ability to record events in their sequences. Ability to discuss and record impressions of living and non-living things in the environment.	Ability to tabulate information and use tables. Familiarity with names of living things and non-living materials. Ability to record impressions by making models, painting or drawing.

Transition from intuition to concrete operations. *Infants generally.*	*Concrete operations.* *Early stage.*
Ability to use representational symbols for recording information on charts or block graphs.	

Appreciating patterns and relationships

Awareness of cause–effect relationships.	Development of a concept of environment. Formation of a broad idea of variation in living things. Awareness of seasonal changes in living things. Awareness of differences in physical conditions between different parts of the Earth.

Interpreting findings critically

Awareness that the apparent size, shape and relationships of things depend on the position of the observer.	Appreciation that properties of materials influence their use.

These tables suggest that even young children have the capacity to develop some simple scientific skills and acquire some elementary scientific ideas. In the first instance children need practice in aspects of scientific thinking such as observing, pattern-seeking, explaining, experimenting, communicating, and applying their ideas and knowledge to new problems. They need opportunities of developing these skills in four main areas, the study of living things and their environment, materials and their characteristics, energy and its interaction with materials, and forces and their effects. Schools need a programme of work in each of these areas to ensure that children have an opportunity to develop skills, knowledge and concepts in a systematic way. 'For example some 6-year-old children tested their ideas on lifting weights with a lever by changing the position of a block of wood under a plank until they could lift their teacher by pressing on the other end of the plank with one foot. Some 9- and 10-year-olds examined the relationship much more systematically by hanging weights from a strip of peg board pivoted by placing a knitting needle horizontally through one of the holes and holding it in a clamp. In this way they determined the mathematical relationship involved.'[2]

Important relationships exist between science and other areas of the curriculum. Observing, pattern-seeking, explaining, experimenting, communicating and applying ideas and knowledge to new problems are valuable skills, though they may be applied in somewhat different ways, in mathematics, language, the study of people, art, craft and design, music and movement, dance and physical education, religious and moral education. There are specific links, too, between work in different areas.

Practical enquiry by children in groups or as a class involves debate and discussion as well as reading and writing. Science gives opportunity for the development of language based on first-hand experience. Children's language is extended through use in a variety of forms aimed at particular audiences, as well as for dealing with reference and general reading texts. Often there is a demand for the application of mathematical skills such as computation and the construction and interpretation of graphs. Science may start from or lead to the study of historical events or characters. 'Movement and physical education can include good examples of force or friction. Transport is a common topic in primary schools and a knowledge of science would help teachers to offer children a deeper understanding of its history, its development and its use. A study of canals in Britain may lead to an investigation into the shapes of boats that travel in restricted waterways, or into the operation of locks. The question "How was the water maintained in the canals?" could give rise to some practical experiments as well as to some research in schools or local library.'[3]

Important though these connections are, there is one very much more important issue. Within the science programme the work in each of the main lines of development must be sequential if the pupils are to make sense of what they study. The following example shows one approach to creating a sequential programme on living things.

In this example sixteen statements are made about living things. They are not in any particular order nor are they necessarily the only statements that might be made for the purpose of primary schools. Obviously the same ideas might have been stated differently. The object is simply to assemble a list of knowledge and ideas and then to look at it in the light of the different age groups and ability levels within the primary schools.

1. Living things depend on each other in various ways.
2. Mammals are warm-blooded.
3. There are certain requirements of food, air and water that are different for different kind of living things.
4. Plants take up substances from both the air and the soil and respond to light.
5. Many living things have adapted their lifestyle to seasonal changes.

6. Man makes use of animals and plants to provide both food and other raw materials.
7. Water is essential to life. It makes up a large proportion of living things.
8. The life cycle of any living thing is repeated in each generation.
9. Young living things need additional care and protection if they are to grow into healthy adults.
10. Some animals eat plants and some eat other animals but all animals ultimately depend on green plants for food.
11. Living things are usually well suited in form and function to the environment in which they are found.
12. There are many different plants and animals which between them show a variety of ways of carrying out life processes.
13. Green plants can make food, animals cannot.
14. All living things produce waste materials in carrying out life processes.
15. Most living things take in oxygen from the air or from the water in which they live.
16. Living things produce offspring of the same 'species' as themselves.

Looking at the list it is possible to associate particular statements with particular years in the primary phase (5–11) and particular levels of activity. Clearly some statements can be approached at a variety of levels and will be returned to in later years but it is important that the latter treatments embody greater complexity of ideas and make greater demand on thinking and grasp of concepts and not merely further 'drill' on the same material.

Year	Statements		Activity
1 (reception)	2, 5, 6, 9		Children may have opportunities to observe and handle classroom pets. Their attention will be drawn to the characteristics of mammals. Most infant classes draw attention to seasonal changes (seed time and harvest in particular) and where food and clothes come from. Farming is another idea commonly mentioned.
2	3, 1, 9, 12	Infant	Pupils can discover that seeds will grow if they are provided with water. Other things are also needed for complete development of the plant. Baby animals can be observed or shown on film or videotape and their needs discussed. At the same time interdependence is illustrated. They can begin to look at the variety of living things.

Year	Statements		Activity
3	7, 8, 10, 16		The abundance of water creatures and the need of both plants and animals for water are easy to illustrate. Given a variety of experience of living things, statement 8 can be grasped almost without emphasis. Food needs of various animals, including man, illustrate 10. Experience of living things and their offspring begins the understanding of 16.
4	5, 12, 14	Lower junior	More systematic ideas of leaf fall, hibernation, and migration can be introduced. Ideas on the variety of plants and animals and their styles can be developed. The cycle of life processes can be made more specific. (At the same time any of statements 1, 2, 3, 6, 7, 8, 9, 10 may well be touched on again.)
5	3, 15		It is possible now to look more closely at the different needs of living things, including oxygen as one essential element.
6	4, 5, 8	Upper junior	More specific experiments carried out with plants to illustrate statement 4. The extent of adaptation to seasonal changes can be developed.
7	11, 13, 15, 16		The ideas of adaptation to environment can be made more specific. Experiments can illustrate the food production of plants, and the production and use of oxygen. The idea of species can be introduced. Reproduction and heredity are also possible topics.

In many of the later years, work on or at least reference to statements that have been met before will be included. The groupings given are no more than a skeletal outline of a sequence of work and are intended to do no more than illustrate the principle. At the same time an 11-year-old boy who had grasped the essential features of these sixteen statements, who had been presented with the evidence underlying them, and had carried out observations and experiments himself to illustrate them, would have a useful knowledge of living things.[4]

Very often, however, schools have no means of ensuring that pupils do follow a sequential programme of work. There is neither a scheme of work nor detailed records of what individual pupils have done. As a result

it is not unusual to find the same topic covered at the same intellectual level in different years, or topics chosen without regard to each other or to their conceptual difficulty. Sometimes teachers are unaware of the work pupils have covered in the previous year or that they are likely to cover in the succeeding year. Schools often have no general scheme of work for science. A common policy on science education among schools in an area is a rarity.

It is important for the teacher to know in detail the range of work already encountered by each pupil in science, the level at which it has been tackled, and how successful the pupil has been in mastering the ideas and knowledge involved. Every school record should contain information on these three aspects of each pupil's science education. Results of any tests given should also be included. This implies careful assessment and an informative record to be passed on – and used.[5]

If this were to happen secondary schools could build on the work done in primary schools instead of behaving sometimes as if their new arrivals had done no science at all before entering the school. There is a long row to hoe.

The general picture emerging of children's performance is that they seem to be doing better in the general skills which are important in all parts of the curriculum but less well in the skills more specifically related to science activities. The close relationship between the kinds of activities most frequently emphasized in schools and performance of pupils, suggests that high performance in the general skills may be the result of emphasis on activities which promote these. At the same time the low performance in the more science-specific skills may well result from lack of opportunities to develop these skills.[6]

Points to consider and discuss

1. What changes would you wish to make in your school's aims and objectives in science education after comparing it with Appendix A?
2. Does your scheme of work in science give sufficient weight to the four main areas of science mentioned on page 41?
3. Have you reviewed the science your own class does to see whether connections between science and other areas are exploited sufficiently?
4. What detailed records do you keep of the work your pupils do in science, and how do your establish what skills, knowledge and concepts they have learned?
5. Have you discussed your school's science programme with any other

primary or secondary schools, to see what scope there is for cooperation?

6. Is your school's work in science inhibited by lack of reasonably well-qualified and confident teachers or by lack of equipment and materials? Have you discussed these problems with your school's LEA Adviser or Inspector?

IV. Mathematics

The contribution of mathematics in science, technology and engineering and its practical value in everyday life have brought home its importance in the school curriculum. Most primary schools have guidelines for mathematics, many based on external schemes of work, or tests, and a curriculum often defined mainly in terms of skills. There is, too, a great deal of readily available and expert advice on aims and objectives and the relation between mathematical competence and child development.

'We teach mathematics in order to help people to understand things better – perhaps to understand the jobs on which they might later be employed, or to understand the creative achievements of the human mind or the behaviour of the natural world. It is the particular power of mathematics that its central ideas help us to do all of these things.'[1] It 'provides a means of communication which is powerful, concise and unambiguous'.[2]

The general aims [of teaching mathematics] should be to develop:

  i a positive attitude to mathematics as an interesting and attractive subject;
 ii an appreciation of the creative aspects of the subject and an awareness of its aesthetic appeal;
iii an ability to think clearly and logically in mathematics with confidence, independence of thought and flexibility of mind;
 iv an understanding of mathematics through a process of enquiry and experiment;
  v an appreciation of the nature of numbers and of space, leading to an awareness of the basic structure of mathematics;
 vi an appreciation of mathematical pattern and the ability to identify relationships;
vii mathematical skills and knowledge accompanied by the quick recall of basic facts;
viii an awareness of the uses of mathematics in the world beyond the classroom. Children should learn that mathematics will frequently help them to solve problems they meet in everyday life or understand better many of the things they see, and provide opportunities for them to satisfy their curiosity and to use their creative abilities;
 ix persistence through sustained work in mathematics which requires some perseverance over a period of time.

47

Finally there is the over-riding aim to maintain and increase confidence in mathematics, shown by the ability to express ideas fluently, to talk about the subject with assurance and to use the language of mathematics.[3]

Aims such as these provide a useful framework for deciding what activities are appropriate for children of different ages, and what objectives should be set. In deciding their own programmes of work teachers may find it helpful to refer to the more detailed objectives HMI suggested both in *Mathematics 5–11* and *A View of the Curriculum*.

  i The development of appropriate language; qualitative description, the recognition of objects from description; discriminating, classifying and sorting of objects; identifying objects and describing them unambiguously.
 ii The recognition of common, simple mathematical relationships, both numerical and spatial; reasoning and logical deduction in connection with everyday things, geometrical shapes, number arrangements in order, etc.
iii The ability to describe quantitatively: the use of numbers in counting, describing, estimating and approximating.
 iv The understanding of whole numbers and their relationships with one another.
  v The appreciation of the measures in common use; sensible estimation using the appropriate units; the ability to measure length, weight, volume and capacity, area, time, angle and temperature to an everyday level of accuracy.
 vi The understanding of money, contributing to a sense of the value of money, and the ability to carry out sensible purchases.
vii The ability to carry out practical activities involving the ideas of addition, subtraction, multiplication and division.
viii The ability to perform simple calculations involving the mathematical processes indicated by the signs $+$, $-$, $\times$, $\div$ with whole numbers (maintaining rapid recall of the sums, differences and products of pairs of numbers from 0 to 10).
 ix The ability to check whether the result of a calculation is reasonable.
  x The ability to use and interpret simple forms of diagrams, maps and tabulated information.
 xi An appreciation of two- and three-dimensional shapes and their relationships with one another. The ability to recognize simple properties; to handle, create, discuss and describe them with confidence and appreciate spatial relationships, symmetry and similarity.
xii An ability to write clearly, to record mathematics in statements, neatly and systematically.

Before the age of 8 for some, but between the ages of 8 and 11 for most, children should continue to develop in these directions, and progress to:

  i The appreciation of place value, the number system and number notation, including whole numbers, decimal fractions and vulgar fractions. The ability to recognize simple number patterns (odds and evens, multiples, divisions, squares, etc.).

ii The ability to carry out with confidence and accuracy simple examples in the four operations of number, including two places of decimals as for pounds and pence and the measures as used.

iii The ability to approximate.

iv A sound understanding of place value applied to the decimal notation for numbers. The ability to carry out the addition and subtraction of numbers with up to two decimal places and the multiplication and division of such numbers up to and including 9.

v The multiplication and division of numbers with up to two decimal places by 10 and 100.

vi An appreciation of the connections between fractions, decimal fractions and the most common percentages.

vii The ability to use fractions in the sequence $\frac{1}{2}$, $\frac{1}{4}$, $\frac{1}{8}$, $\frac{1}{16}$ or $\frac{1}{3}$, $\frac{1}{6}$, $\frac{1}{12}$, or $\frac{1}{5}$, $\frac{1}{10}$, including the idea of equivalence in the discussion of everyday experiences.

viii An appreciation of the broader aspects of number, such as bases other than 10 and easy tests of divisibility.

ix An ability to read with understanding mathematics from books, and to use appropriate reference skills.

A number of children of this age will be capable of more advanced work, and they should be encouraged to undertake it.[4]

Objectives like these put an emphasis on both skills and understanding. They provide a framework for constructing detailed curricular guidelines, and devising critical assessments of any existing scheme of work, whether it is derived from a textbook or external test or is a school's own scheme.

They also help to clarify the teacher's task. As the Cockcroft Report said,

We conclude this chapter by drawing the attention of those who teach mathematics in schools to what we believe to be the implications of the reasons for teaching mathematics which we have discussed. **In our view the mathematics teacher has the task**

of enabling each pupil to develop, within his capabilities, the mathematical skills and understanding required for adult life, for employment and for further study and training, while remaining aware of the difficulties which some pupils will experience in trying to gain such an appropriate understanding;

of providing each pupil with such mathematics as may be needed for his study of other subjects;

of helping each pupil to develop so far as is possible his appreciation and enjoyment of mathematics itself and his realization of the role which it has played and will continue to play both in the development of science and technology and of our civilization;

above all, of making each pupil aware that mathematics provides him with a powerful means of communication.[5]

The following examples show how four schools tackled the task of planning their work. We do not suggest they are necessarily models to copy. The need is for each school to think out its own scheme, and casting a critical eye over someone else's work may be among the easier ways to start. In discussing these examples it may therefore be helpful to ask whether there are good reasons for their diverging, if they do, from the approach to aims and objectives suggested above.

i In a junior department of a JMI school which was streamed, the mathematics specialist had written a syllabus for each of the four years, subdivided into 'number' and 'topic' mathematics. The topic mathematics dealt with time, length, mass, volume and capacity, shape and area. Recognizing that it would be impossible to cover all the items, she marked with an asterisk those that were considered most important in both number and topic. It was recommended that all the mainstream pupils should cover the priority items but that low attainers should only cover the most basic of these. Each teacher was then expected to select what seemed appropriate for his or her pupils from the rest of the syllabus, although the low attainers were expected to concentrate on the number rather than on the topic work.

ii In one junior school where three of the four years were set for mathematics and where the main objective of the teaching was the acquisition of computational skills, the six sets in each year attempted to pursue the same course because at the end of the year all the children in a given age group took the same test.

iii In an infant school, in order to develop children's basic number concepts such as conservation of number, matching and ordering, teachers were recommended to make use of particular materials which were in the school and to use these first in general play, accompanied by questioning and discussion, and later in specific activities initiated by the teacher such as:

> sorting dolls' house furniture and placing in an appropriate room;
> putting away the dressing-up clothes by placing each garment on a coathanger;
> comparison of the heights of towers built with bricks or Lego.

iv The mathematics curriculum in a JMI school not only indicated mathematical content but also included and stressed creative and investigative work in the subject. One such specified activity, in which pupils aged 10 and 11 were asked to divide equilateral triangles into three parts in many different ways, was observed in progress during the visit of the team. The pupils' initial drawings were simple but enthusiasm to produce more intricate designs led them into questioning and discussion about linear measure, area, angles, rotational symmetry and tessellation.[6]

There are also dangers in using a scheme of work from a textbook or published workcards. Such schemes may not cater adequately for either the most or the least gifted. Teachers need skill and imagination to adapt such schemes to the specific needs of all their pupils. The following examples show how three schools tackled this problem.

i One JMI school used the series Making Sure of Maths throughout the school, with pupils starting the Introductory Book in the top infants' year. All pupils worked systematically through each book, missing out very little and having to correct most of the mistakes which they made.

ii In the fourth-year mixed-ability junior class of a JMI, pupils used the Scottish Primary Mathematics Group scheme, working through each topic as a class. Able children and quick workers were given extension work when they had finished until most of the pupils had also completed the work; the class then moved on to a new topic. The two or three low attainers attempted the same work and usually managed to do the initial tasks but then spent the remaining time struggling with activities which were still in the early part of the topic.

iii A very different example of planning easier work for low attainers within a class topic was found in a mixed-ability second-year junior class. In the first lesson of a topic on fractions all the pupils had been introduced to the idea of $\frac{1}{2}$, some to $\frac{1}{4}$ and a few to $\frac{1}{8}$. This had been done by folding, cutting and colouring paper shapes. In the second lesson the teacher divided the class into groups, each containing pupils of roughly similar ability. Each group had different tasks and within the groups pupils worked either individually or in pairs.

The pupils in one group had coloured gummed paper and were making a variety of shapes and cutting them in half in as many ways as they could find.

Another group was using Scottish Primary Mathematics Group's Stage One Workbook in which the work involved colouring in one half of a variety of shapes, and deciding whether or not shapes which were printed in the book had been divided correctly into halves.

These two groups consisted of pupils who had done only halves in the first lesson. The other groups were experimenting and finding a half of: a ball of plasticine, a bag of beans, a jar of buttons, a jug of water, etc., and were using capacity measures, weighing scales, etc., to do this.

The teacher explained that the more able children would do more experiments, then move on to more formal work, whilst the low attainers would spend longer on the experiments and do just a little recorded work.[7]

Finding a match between the difficulty of learning material and each child's development is among a teacher's most necessary skills. Teachers must be on their guard equally against going too slowly and going too fast. Even at 11 children are generally better at manipulating numbers than handling symbols and understanding concepts.[8] As one of their testers observed, 'Having seen some of the children floundering I am now more than ever convinced that before you can understand in the abstract you've got to spend a lot of time working with concrete material.'

For many children among the most concrete material to hand is what they are doing in other areas of the curriculum. Imagination and time are needed to work out how mathematical skills and ideas can be used in other areas of the curriculum, but the potential benefits are great. The usefulness of mathematics, the relevance of one lesson to another, the limitations of subject boundaries and the value of imagination in finding ways of solving problems are demonstrated in ways children can readily understand.

The following paragraphs show how certain mathematical ideas might be introduced in discussing topics from other areas of the curriculum. Stimulating discussion of the possibilities, and suggesting examples, is one of the things the teacher responsible for mathematics should try to do.

i One class of 7-year-olds in a first school had visited an old windmill; on their return some very interesting historical work had developed on the process of producing bread, from growing the corn, to harvesting, milling, distributing the flour, and baking, and on the types of buildings used by the different people in this chain; but although the children had seen the mechanical apparatus of the mill, and there were pictures of the driving shaft and its cog-wheels in their class-books, no opportunity was taken to fix up some simple cog-wheel apparatus. This was a missed opportunity for setting one scene for the future establishment of the difficult concept of inverse proportion (the smaller cog-wheel moves faster than the large cog-wheel; if the larger wheel has twice as many teeth as the smaller wheel, the larger one goes round once while the smaller one goes round twice).

ii The teacher's alertness to mathematical possibilities is crucial; if a Bible story has used the word 'generations', will the teacher develop a short discussion on 'What is a generation? How many generations since the First World War? How many generations since the first motorcar? Since the invention of the steam train?'

iii Has somebody brought a honeycomb to the nature-table? What is the shape of the cells? How do the cells fit together? Would any other shape do? Can the pupils develop work on tessellations, or shall we just store this example away in our minds, to come back to later when they are ready for further work?

iv A farm visit gives interesting opportunities to introduce such concepts as time, volume and weight: What happens on the farm hour by hour from 6.00 a.m.? If each cow produces nine litres of milk twice a day what does that look like and how nearly does a herd of cows fill a milk tank? If each cow eats, daily, fodder which weighs as much as their teacher, how does the volume of the fodder compare with the size of their teacher?

v Similar questions may arise from considering what we can buy in a baker's shop. Each pupil buys one item, bread, buns, cakes, tarts, meringues, or more unusually, pasta, yeast and other items, which prompt discussion of farming, cooking and food processing here and in other countries. A block graph of the items can be made and questions of counting and relative numbers explored.

In ways like these, admirably illustrated in *Mathematics in Primary Schools*,[9] teachers can foster mathematical skills and concepts from their pupils' everyday experiences. And since children spend more time at home than at school the pupils' parents could be very useful allies. Most parents are anxious to help in their children's education, and many would be delighted if they could be shown how to introduce mathematical ideas at home.

The main problem arising from cross-curricular work is likely to be finding ways of observing and recording each child's contribution and mathematical progress when it is displayed in areas other than mathematics. But at least in mathematics there is a wide measure of agreement about defining the curriculum and what kinds of progress to look for. Other areas of the curriculum present different, and more difficult, problems.

Points to consider and discuss

1. Her Majesty's Inspectors' statement about the general aims of teaching mathematics is quoted on pages 47–8. How do your own school's general aims compare with this statement?
2. How do your own school's more detailed objectives compare with the objectives and standards quoted on pages 48–9?
3. Does consideration of the examples quoted on pages 50–52 suggest any ways in which your school might improve its own planning of work in mathematics?

4. Do you think the schools described on pages 51–2 were as successful as they might have been in their use of published schemes of work?
5. After considering the examples on pages 52–3 can you suggest other ways of introducing work in mathematics to other areas of the curriculum in your own school?
6. Have you found ways of helping interested parents to support the school's work in mathematics?

V. Language and literacy

If mathematics is a powerful means of communication, how much more so is language. Along with upright posture, thumbs and bifocal vision, the human species' development of language is the basis of all human progress, civilization and culture. Through language we learn to think, and add constantly to the sum of human knowledge.

What is most remarkable is that by the time they go to school most children have well-developed skills in language and communication. They have learned by listening and watching to speak and communicate. They often communicate by gestures, signs and drawings as well as words, and we suspect there is scope for schools to develop these non-verbal modes of communication more systematically than many do. The school's acknowledged problem is that some children come to school speaking non-standard English; striking a balance between helping all their pupils to use English which can be generally understood, and maintaining their pupils' trust in parents and friends whose example they have followed, is a task of great delicacy.

Since most children are able to listen and to speak fluently by the time they come to school, teachers feel free to concentrate on the more artificial skills of reading and writing. Recognizing that children have to learn to speak through listening and imitating what they hear, teachers expect them to learn to write through reading and copying what they see. It is no surprise then that reading is the first of the three Rs and that most primary guidelines are for teaching reading. Many of these guidelines are confined to reading, and ignore the other aspects of communication through language. Even in reading itself some of the guidelines are more concerned with recognizing and decoding print than with understanding the meaning of words, phrases and sentences. But most schools do use guidelines for reading, so in this chapter we have concentrated on some of the other aspects of language, literacy and communication.

Reading

In shaping a school's reading programme teachers should have in mind some of the many different uses of reading, and the range of skills that would be appropriate for 11- or 12-year-olds. Children of those ages might wish to use reading in ways like these:

1. reading stories for pleasure, to find out what happened, or to tell other people about the stories;
2. reading poetry, or prose, aloud, for pleasure;
3. reading words for singing;
4. reading continuous prose to extract information from it, to be able to understand it or to explain it to other people;
5. using a dictionary to find out what words mean and how to spell them;
6. using an encyclopaedia or an atlas to look things up;
7. reading books or articles about hobbies, or newspapers for their sports news;
8. working from technical instructions, about construction kits, playing games and so on;
9. reading fact books, like the — *Book of Records*;
10. reading cartoon and joke books.

A school's programme should provide practice in these and other reading skills, and provide appropriately graded work to take children to a reasonable standard by the time they move to secondary schools.

Such a systematic approach to the development of reading skills will form part of a larger programme of language development. Teachers in several authorities have recognized this need and have produced guidelines on a wide range of language skills. One such statement includes detailed objectives for talking, listening, reading and writing.[1]

Talking and speaking

The statement identifies eight different kinds of talking skills and then suggests in greater detail what kinds of activity and what kinds of progression might be appropriate in each. The eight objectives are listed below, together with more detailed suggestions for achieving one of the objectives.

TALKING
Objective 1 A child should be able to vocalize all the phonic symbols
Objective 2 A child should speak clearly
Objective 3 A child should be able to talk about his work and experiences
Objective 4 A child should be able to ask for information so that the listener understands his needs
Objective 5 A child shall respond verbally to questions
Objective 6 A child shall tell a simple story using animation and colourful expression

Objective 7   A child should be able to give simple instructions
Objective 8   A child should be able to talk about his thoughts and feelings ...

Objective 3
A child should be able to talk
about his work and experiences.

STAGE 1
Simple information about self or home – one to one with teacher.

Expansion ideas:
Informal chatting, giving facts about himself, his home, his family, his likes
and dislikes, favourite toys, clothes, meals, etc.

STAGE 2
Talking about the practical activities in class.

Expansion ideas:
a Talking about his drawings, models and paintings
b Talking about shape, colour, texture and size
c Teacher ensuring that many class activities will demand discussion, i.e.,
  Do you think that ...? Can this be ...? How will you ...?

STAGE 3
Class activities which will nurture curiosity and thereby provoke questions from the
child.

Expansion ideas:
a Developing the enquiring mind. Class projects provoking the questions
  How does it ...?
  Why will it ...?
  When will this ...?
  Where shall I ...?
b Out of school visits, walks, etc. – observing, discussion, talking, questioning.

STAGE 4
A child capable of sustained conversation.

Expansion idea:
Creating opportunities and reasons for the sustained conversation.

STAGE 5
A child shall be able to talk extemporarily to a group or class.

Expansion idea:
Children encouraged to talk about their varied work and experiences to the
class/school in a semi-formal way, i.e., News Time in the Infants, progressing
to the talk to the whole school at assembly at Upper Junior level.

These objectives, and the detailed suggestions, show how speech serves several different purposes, such as asking for information, telling stories, giving instructions and expressing thanks. Children need this early introduction to the idea that they may use speech for varied purposes, with varied audiences. An indication of the variety is given in *The Literacy Schedule*,[2] a set of guidelines for work with pupils of about 9 to 16. Although some of the suggestions may lie outside the experience and needs of primary children, the list of twenty possible uses may be a useful starting point for rethinking a primary school's aims and work.

1. Deliver correctly a spoken message with at least three parts to it after an interval of twenty-four hours.
2. Describe something that has happened, getting the details right and getting things in the right order.
3. Read a story aloud to a small group so that they enjoy it.
4. Read aloud to a large group in a large space so that you are heard and understood by everyone.
5. Re-tell a story briefly, getting the details right and putting events in the correct order.
6. Tell a story to a chosen audience making it interesting to listen to.
7. Tell a joke so that other people find it funny.
8. Give directions for getting to a place at least half a mile from the school and including at least six instructions.
9. Explain how to draw a simple diagram to someone whose work you can't see, so that he draws it correctly.
10. Teach a small group how to make something or do something so that they make it or do it correctly.
11. Explain to a small group how something works so that they are able to answer questions on what you have told them.
12. Prepare a short talk on a topic which interests you and deliver it to the class, using notes, but not reading the talk.
13. Prepare a short talk on a given topic and deliver it to a group in a large space, using notes but not reading from them. You must be heard clearly by everyone.
14. Make a three-minute speech with only five minutes' preparation.
15. Prepare and propose a note of thanks.
16. Prepare and propose a motion for a debate.
17. Prepare and propose a toast.
18. Sum up at the end of a debate or discussion.
19. Read prose and poetry aloud to a small group; to a large audience.
20. Use a tape recorder to:
    a record a talk or an interview for a given purpose;
    b compile a programme for a given audience and a given purpose.

Listening

Although most children have a natural capacity to learn by listening, schools can do much to train and develop this capacity. The same group of teachers whose work on talking was mentioned earlier have done similar work on listening skills. The five different kinds of listening skill they have identified, and the activities they suggest for developing one of these skills are listed below.

LISTENING

1. Listening for Operational Instructions
2. Listening as a learning skill within the objectives of other skills
3. Listening and comprehension
4. Listening to assimilate facts
5. Listening for pleasure ...

5. Listening for pleasure

SPECIFIC ACTIVITIES

  i Listening to sound patterns and rhythms – in pitch and time.
    Transfer of training to pre-reading skills where sounds pattern experience is essential.
    Percussion and life patterns (machinery, traffic, waves, sirens, etc.).
  ii Playing sound patterns (music). Simple and complex.
    Pure patterns.
    Patterns with meaning – use of musical instruments, listening to music.
  iii Nursery rhymes and jingles (spoken and sung).
    Memory training through listening.
  iv Simple stories with repetition.
    Encourage activity in repetitive parts (e.g. Gingerbread Man, Goldilocks).
  v Simple stories and songs with action clues.
  vi Use of radio and TV
    Stories and Rhymes
    Let's Move
    Something to talk about.
  vii Descriptive passages – film and music for listening response.
  viii Enjoyable stories – for their own merit with no response required more than the pleasure of participation.
  ix Use of drama: stories for play
    improvised characters and plots with natural spontaneous dialogue
    drama of special events
    drama of sound and movement.
  x Group story-telling – 'taking over the thread'.
  xi Listening to poetry.

Memorizing selected poems.
Poetry spoken by children for children (including older children for younger children).
Choral speaking.
xii Expansion of experience in literature.
Listening to literature *well* read from a wide band of authors and subjects.
xiii Discussing the effect of literature.
Creating dramatic activities in literature.
Allowing children to select personal favourites to read to class.
Using audio-visual aids in literature – TV, radio, film.
Literature as a stimulus for art/craft, imaginative writing, poetry.
xiv Music – listening to music.
xv Listening as participant in discussions and debates.
Decisions to speak and act through having listened.[3]

As the list of five objectives shows, much listening contributes directly to a child's learning. Both at school and later the ability to listen attentively and remember accurately what was heard is a great advantage. The following list suggests skills which young people of about 16 might have acquired, but primary pupils might usefully begin to practise many of these skills.

1. Listen to and repeat correctly:
   a A sentence of at least ten words
   b A list of eight familiar words
   c A list of five unfamiliar words
   d A list of five nonsense words.
2. Listen to a story and retell it after one hearing, getting the order and detail right.
3. Listen to an account of something that happened and retell it after one hearing getting the order and details right.
4. Listen to a speaker or radio programme and make a list of main ideas.
5. Listen to a speaker or radio programme and answer questions on it.
6. Listen to a speaker or radio programme in order to answer questions given in advance.
7. Plan questions which might be answered by listening to a speaker or radio programme.
8. Draw conclusions from the way a person speaks about:
   a his feelings about the subject he is talking about;
   b his feelings and his views about his listeners.
9. Know the ways in which these conclusions could be wrong.[4]

Writing

Writing, as Francis Bacon said, maketh an exact man. It is in writing above all that a person's grasp of many important language skills is tested most. In speaking, manner, tone and gestures add much to the word itself, and if the audience fails to understand, the speaker can try again with other words and other constructions. In writing, the author has to depend on the word itself, and any lapse from reasonable standards of legibility, spelling, vocabulary, syntax and punctuation creates a barrier between writer and reader.

Handwriting

Children need to be able to write clearly and well so that they and other people can read what is written. They may often need to write quite fast. They should therefore learn to:

1. Sit properly to write.
2. Hold the pen or pencil correctly.
3. **a** Form all small letters correctly.
   b Form capitals correctly.
   c Join letters correctly.
4. Complete a page of writing in x minutes writing neatly and legibly.
5. Arrange work well on lined paper.
6. Arrange work well on unlined paper.[5]

Spelling

The vagaries of English spelling are a cause of confusion to natives as well as foreigners. Learning ten spellings a day now seems a somewhat dated way of attacking the problem. However helpful it may be, the approach through rote learning should be supplemented by some understanding of the principles on which spelling is based. The following list of detailed objectives may help in drawing up a primary school spelling programme designed to lead pupils to an understanding of these principles.

1. Know the sound each consonant usually represents.
2. Know the short vowel sounds which are represented by a e i o u.
3. Read and write regular words using this knowledge.
4. Know consonant blends of two and three letters.
5. Know consonant digraphs ch, sh, th.
6. Know the use of the marker e.   *magic e*
7. Read and write regular words using this knowledge.
8. Know the most common spellings of the long vowels – a e i o u.
9. Know the effect on spelling of the position of the sound in the word, e.g. pla*i*n, pla*y*.

10. Read and write regular words using this knowledge.
11. Distinguish (a) vowels and consonants, (b) long and short vowels and know the spelling rules relating to them.
12. Know and use the usual spellings of the vowel sounds oo (long and short), ow, our, aw, ar, er and air.
13. Know and use the spelling rules relating to the use of hard and soft c and g sounds.
14. Know the possible spellings of the consonants.
15. Know the rules for forming plurals.
16. Know the rules for adding prefixes.
17. Know the rules for adding suffixes.
18. Know the less usual spellings of the vowel sounds.[6]

Vocabulary, syntax and punctuation

In trying to strike a reasonable balance teachers may find it helpful to use a checklist of skills and knowledge of the language and correct writing. Schools will need to agree what topics to include in their checklist, when to introduce each skill and what standards of proficiency to aim at. For older juniors schools might wish, for example, to include some of the following points in their checklist.

KNOWLEDGE OF THE LANGUAGE
1. Knowing about different kinds of words, nouns, verbs, adjectives and so on.
2. Being able to make nouns, verbs, adjectives and adverbs from each other.
3. Knowing and being able to use different tenses.
4. Being able to use the different forms of pronouns correctly.

CORRECT WRITING
1. Using capitals correctly.
2. Using simple punctuation marks correctly, e.g. full stop, question mark, quotation marks, apostrophe.
3. Knowing some short ways of writing, e.g. I will and you cannot.
4. Knowing some common abbreviations, e.g. etc. and e.g.

These examples are intended to illustrate the kinds of knowledge and skill teachers might wish to include in their objectives. They may be helpful to teachers who want to review their own guidelines, or create their own development plan for this aspect of language and literacy.

A language programme checklist

In shaping its own development plan for language and literacy one school used a forbidding checklist of twenty-eight questions. Despite its length this list does show most helpfully how varied and complex objectives are in this area of the curriculum. We have therefore quoted it in full, with some suggested amendments of our own in italics. Schools might usefully compare their own objectives for language and literacy with this checklist, and consider whether a similarly detailed list would be helpful in any other area of the curriculum.

1. Are there clear objectives in language development, particularly in the reading programme? What are they?
2. Are children taught syntax, punctuation and spelling at levels appropriate to their age and development?
3. Do the objectives include the development of study skills, notably in seeking and collecting information? How are these fostered?
4. Are the children helped to communicate with people of various ages and backgrounds in ways appropriate to the circumstances?
5. Are children encouraged and helped to find and use books to find answers to their questions?
6. Are children encouraged to borrow library books, and helped in their choice?
7. Is there any opportunity for them to discuss what they have read?
    7(a). Does the school help parents to see how they can contribute in relation to questions 4, 5, 6 and 7?
8. Do the books in use reflect multicultural interests?
    8(a). Do the books in use promote ideas of equality between the sexes?
9. At the early stage how do teachers decide whether children are ready to start on a formal reading scheme or to practise phonics?
10. Are children able to proceed at a pace which matches their interests and abilities, and meets their need for progression and success?
11. Are those with special needs identified, and their difficulties diagnosed early?
12. How do teachers know whether their pupils understand and enjoy the substance of what they are reading?
13. Do the children read fiction, or non-fiction, on their own initiative for pleasure? *Could parents be helped to encourage their children in reading?*
14. Is there time for children to browse and read? Do slow as well as quick workers have time for reading?
15. Do the children have enough time for continuous writing?
16. Are they encouraged to use various modes of expression for communicating ideas, information, stories and impressions?
17. Do they spend much or little time in copying from workbooks or cards? What skills does this develop?
18. Do they children spend much time on exercises and assignments from textbooks or workcards? Are these helpful to teachers as a way of identifying and helping children to overcome their errors?

19. What steps are taken to improve the children's listening skills?
20. What opportunities are there for small-group discussions, particularly of shared experiences?
21. Is poetry an esteemed part of the curriculum? What are the criteria for choosing poems?
22. Are television and radio much used? Does their use contribute seriously to the objectives of the language development programme? *Since most TV watching is at home, could parents be helped to use TV programmes to stimulate discussion?*
23. Is there any conscious attempt to link work in language and art?
24. Are children encouraged to produce handwriting that has aesthetic and decorative value?
25. Is time available for imaginative and dramatic play?
26. Is there a good stock of costumes to stimulate play? *Could the school enlist the help of parents to enlarge the stock?*
27. Are puppets made and used to create simple plays?
28. When is it profitable to join classes together, for story-telling for example?

There is evidence that many schools might improve the relevance, range and quality of their work by examining questions like these systematically.[7] The process should help them to develop a structured and integrated programme for language development.

With language and literacy even more than in mathematics, the scope for listening, talking, reading and writing extends across the whole curriculum, and lasts all day. In one three-class primary school the top class of 9- to 11-year-olds has a teacher who chooses themes and topics which can be followed up at many different levels. By offering the opportunity for individual work within a framework, there is scope both for the slower 9-year-old and the forward 11-year-old. The teacher comments on how the varied learning situations are generated:

I find a sort of rhythm has developed itself running in four- to six-week periods. There is a period of stimulation, perhaps a day or two, perhaps a week, when certain experiences are provided – outside expeditions, or reading from books or watching films, talking or drama work, or most usually a combination of some or all of these. Then there is a discussion among us all, perhaps as one big unit, perhaps in smaller units, of the work that could arise to cover all aspects of the curriculum. Now that the children are accustomed to working in this way I find my role is not so much to supply the initial ideas, but rather to help them turn their own ideas to really good use and follow through and see extensions. What generally seems to happen is that the first follow-up work tends to be done in groups initiated by children or by me, but in any case supervised by me. After that it tends to go off into individual channels, or the groups re-sort themselves. During the day there is a definite flow – sometimes all the class will be together, then move out to groups of individual tasks, come together again, move away and so on.

Although the teacher arrives each day with a flexible plan, she doubts whether she has ever completed a day exactly as planned. To observe her is to understand this, for she works very much from what the children bring to the classroom.[8]

As in mathematics, children acquire confidence in their use of language when they are able to start from what they know. The wider their knowledge and experience the more scope there is for using language in different ways. A curriculum rich in content, and experience, is the best basis for developing language. Much of the language curriculum is likely to be defined rather more in terms of content, activities and experience, and rather less in terms of specific skills and knowledge, than mathematics. It may be harder to devise objective measures of pupil progress in developing powers of expression, sensitivity of response and study skills than it is in formal mathematical processes. This probably means teachers need to devote correspondingly more time to systematic subjective assessments, and accessible records, of their pupils' progress in language.

Points to consider and discuss

1. Do your reading guidelines provide adequately for reading of several different kinds, including those mentioned on page 56?
2. Are satisfactory guidelines for talking, listening and writing in regular use at your school? How do you assess whether the objectives have been reached?
3. How would you adapt for use in your own school the list of possible uses of speech on page 58?
4. Prepare a list of listening skills appropriate as objectives for your own pupils.
5. Does your school use guidelines for teaching, handwriting, spelling, vocabulary, syntax and punctuation? Do they say precisely enough what skills to practise and what standards to aim at in each year of the school?
6. Have you used the checklist on pages 63–4 to review your own language programme? What changes has the review prompted?

VI. The study of people past and present

The *central* theme of social studies is the study of people in society. The *ultimate* aim is to help children develop their understanding of people in society. Like scientific discovery, mathematical invention or original writing, at its highest peak understanding people in society requires imagination, intelligence and maturity. Our task in primary schools is to start children on the road to understanding, knowing well that they will reach different points along the road, as they do in science, in mathematics, in language and other areas. Experience and maturity are perhaps more necessary for a deep understanding of people in society than they are for excellence in certain other areas, but we do not think that makes a case for leaving social studies until children reach adolescence, or later. It does mean, however, that this area of the curriculum raises distinct issues when it comes to agreeing objectives and gauging achievement.

There seem to be three important and interrelated ways of developing an understanding of people in society. They are

First, the exploration of experience, one's own and other people's.
Second, the development of personal abilities, by using imagination, organizing knowledge, using evidence, and communicating.
Third, the exploration of ideas.

History and geography are, for older pupils, the two school subjects which contribute most to understanding people in society through the three kinds of activity we suggested. The subject titles do something, but not enough, to define this area of the curriculum. History is about people's experience through time, and geography about their experience in various places. Random voyages into time and place may excite and stir the imagination but we believe the essential aim of exploration is to map the explored territory so that the explorers can have a general grasp of its main characteristics.

We believe therefore that studies in this area should have as one of their objectives the development of frameworks of historical and geographical understanding. We believe such frameworks will ensure that these studies contribute more to developing the capacities for sympathetic imagination, organizing knowledge and using evidence.

At present such frameworks rarely exist.

Even the older children were seldom being helped towards an appreciation of chronological order. Some were introduced to different periods of history through work on cavemen, the Stone Age, the Vikings and the Romans without being made aware of their relative positions on the historical time scale. Other children started with a study of the Victorians and worked backwards in time. Too much of the work on topics selected by individual teachers or suggested by television programmes was not part of a coordinated school plan and tended to be fragmented and superficial.[1]

The problem is similar to that in other areas of the curriculum. Cavemen and Vikings are abstractions. Their artefacts are not, but they are not always readily accessible. Children need to start from the concrete and the immediate, the here and now, in their social studies. The challenge for teachers is to start at 5 by exploring the 5-year-old's experience, and so extend that experience that at 11 children can assemble their explorations of space and time to make at least a rudimentary and recognizable map of what they have explored.

This means that questions of continuity and progression are a great deal more difficult in social studies than in mathematics or language and literacy.

In those areas questions of continuity and progression are mainly a matter of moving from simple to more complex ideas. There is the same need in this area to move from simple to complex ideas but that does not mean teachers must start with the most ancient peoples known to history, or the simplest communities known to geographers. For all these would be well outside the experience of young children. Their experience must be the starting point.

The immediate environment of home, school and area will offer plenty of scope for exploring space and time. Britain is extraordinarily well mapped, its archaeology well researched and its history well documented. For more immediate knowledge, schools may find it helpful to turn to parents, postmen, milkmen, shopkeepers and others with memories, mementoes and knowledge to fire the imagination.

In the earliest stages teachers may like to start with the environment which all their pupils share, their classroom. For example, first mapping exercises might mean asking the children to make simple plans of their classrooms, showing the teacher's desk, children's desks, cupboards and so on. Plans of the school, its grounds, and neighbouring streets can follow. In social studies, the local community is the best classroom.

One class of 6- and 7-year-olds made a 2 × 1 metre model of the district, and followed that with a simple model of their village. That led to a decision to study their river in greater detail. After an expedition to survey the scene, they agreed to divide into five groups, each with a different task. One was to make a model of the river and neighbouring features, the second to make a collage, a third to collect stones and ask themselves which were light and which heavy, which rough and which smooth, and what colour they were. A fourth group studied flowers and trees, and the fifth made a model of a section of the river.[2]

In other places a similar river visit might have prompted a historical investigation. England and Wales are so varied in features, so rich in their rocks and plants, so rich in historical association that almost any short expedition will provide rich opportunities for study. A simple chart such as the one shown in Figure 1 may help to identify the different kinds of exploration a single location can offer.[3]

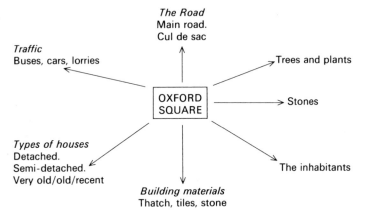

Figure 1

The teacher will need another chart as well, to identify the different kinds of skill to be used and developed in studies of the site (see Figure 2).

This example shows how early experiences can lead equally to work in science, mathematics, language, social studies and expressive arts. Most teachers could probably match this example in their own area.

While out on a walk to collect tadpoles, some children noticed numbers cut into the stonework of some old chapels. They managed to work out that these were dates, showing that the chapels had been built eighty or ninety years previously, before even their grandparents were born. Further search

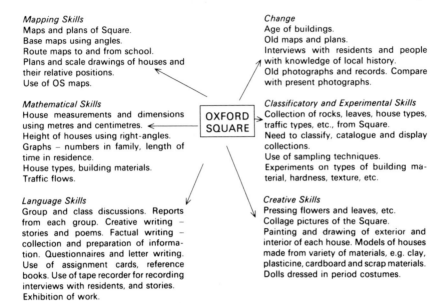

Mapping Skills
Maps and plans of Square.
Base maps using angles.
Route maps to and from school.
Plans and scale drawings of houses and
their relative positions.
Use of OS maps.

Mathematical Skills
House measurements and dimensions
using metres and centimetres.
Height of houses using right-angles.
Graphs – numbers in family, length of
time in residence.
House types, building materials.
Traffic flows.

Language Skills
Group and class discussions. Reports
from each group. Creative writing –
stories and poems. Factual writing –
collection and preparation of information. Questionnaires and letter writing.
Use of assignment cards, reference
books. Use of tape recorder for recording
interviews with residents, and stories.
Exhibition of work.

Change
Age of buildings.
Old maps and plans.
Interviews with residents and people
with knowledge of local history.
Old photographs and records. Compare
with present photographs.

Classificatory and Experimental Skills
Collection of rocks, leaves, house types,
traffic types, etc., from Square.
Need to classify, catalogue and display
collections.
Use of sampling techniques.
Experiments on types of building ma-
terial, hardness, texture, etc.

Creative Skills
Pressing flowers and leaves, etc.
Collage pictures of the Square.
Painting and drawing of exterior and
interior of each house. Models of houses
made from variety of materials, e.g. clay,
plasticine, cardboard and scrap materials.
Dolls dressed in period costumes.

OXFORD SQUARE

Figure 2

revealed many more old buildings, now often closed or converted to some
other use. They found ten disused chapels, twenty shops, two cinemas, a
workmen's hall and several rows of houses.

These discoveries led to their making a plan of New Tredegar, and
plotting the school, their homes, and other important buildings. They made
graphs showing how many lived in each street, how many went to Sunday
School, and the population since 1850. Parents and grandparents began to
send material. Old school photographs of 1896 and 1897 prompted a lively
discussion about the girls' boots and the boys' collars. Textbooks used
between 1900 and 1920 prompted excited comparison with their own
lessons.

One old photograph showed a nearby colliery, and by good fortune a
retired colliery overman who had once won a medal for bravery in saving
two miners was persuaded to tell them about life in the mines in his youth.
At that time most of the men were miners. Now there was no colliery, and
the children listed the jobs their fathers did, and where they worked.

They learned too that the village had once been called White Rose, and
had thatched cottages and stables, before the colliery opened.

More and more material poured in: costumes, an old flat iron which
caused alarm because it had no wires, candlesticks, oil lamps, rubbing

boards, a washing dolly, horse brasses, harness, a coach lamp, photos showing the undertaker and the milkman using horse-drawn vehicles and a phonograph with cylinder. Several children started their own books, on costume, and Grandpa's Time. The school mounted an exhibition for the whole community.

The school's own account of this work ends:

> Looking around the school hall we now see the past unfolded, the children's contributions adding to it. Past and present are united and we have tried to form a link between the generations. Apart from this, the children have become more and more interested. They talk to us much more easily and put forward their own ideas and thoughts. The barriers between subjects have been broken, and the children want to work at each new idea until it is finished, often without any prompting from their teachers. In looking back we hope that perhaps our children will, as they grow, be aware of their heritage and do their small part to preserve it by guarding the treasures around them.[4]

Even schools without these rich resources have plenty of scope for interesting exploratory work. A class of 7-year-olds began to look at the different kinds of house to be found in their neighbourhood. This led them into making maps and models, thinking about the different materials used, the different tradespeople who helped to build the houses, the varied domestic uses of electricity, and how electricity might be used in a model lighthouse or a model theatre.[5] The same starting point, our houses, might lead with other teachers to exploring the memories of parents and grandparents about the homes they had lived in and the facilities they had, and other comparisons between the present and a recent past.

Most schools are quite close to some more ancient building, a castle or a church, a marketplace or much older houses. A quick visit will prompt all sorts of questions about the thickness of the walls, the materials, the reason for the building being there, the people who have lived or worshipped there.[6]

Just as each teacher needs a clear idea of what skills are to be developed through each topic, so the teacher needs to know where the whole course of studies is taking the children, what kind of framework of historical and geographical understanding the children are going to acquire.

It is not so long since the kings and queens of England and the capes, bays and highest peaks in Britain provided all the framework thought necessary in history or geography. Modern teachers are more likely to aim at developing certain skills, and understanding a few key ideas.

Table 4 suggests skills and personal qualities which schools might wish their top juniors to have. The table comes from a book on curriculum planning in history, geography and social science, but the suggested skills and personal qualities would be appropriate in other areas as well.[7]

Table 4

Skills			Personal qualities
Intellectual	Social	Physical	Interests, attitudes, values
1. The ability to find information from a variety of sources, in a variety of ways. 2. The ability to communicate findings through an appropriate medium. 3. The ability to interpret pictures, charts, graphs, maps, etc. 4. The ability to evaluate information. 5. The ability to organize information through concepts and generalizations. 6. The ability to formulate and test hypotheses and generalizations.	1. The ability to participate within small groups. 2. An awareness of significant groups within the community and the wider society. 3. A developing understanding of how individuals relate to such groups. 4. A willingness to consider participating constructively in the activities associated with these groups. 5. The ability to exercise empathy (i.e. the capacity to imagine accurately what it might be like to be someone else).	1. The ability to manipulate equipment. 2. The ability to manipulate equipment to find and communicate information. 3. The ability to explore the expressive powers of the human body to communicate ideas and feelings. 4. The ability to plan and execute expressive activities to communicate ideas and feelings.	1. The fostering of curiosity through the encouragement of questions. 2. The fostering of a wariness of overcommitment to one framework of explanation and the possible distortion of facts and the omission of evidence. 3. The fostering of a willingness to explore personal attitudes and values to relate these to other people's. 4. The encouraging of an openness to the possibility of change in attitudes and values. 5. The encouragement of worthwhile and developing interests in human affairs.

Case Study 1   Discovering rocks: a case study developed by forty children (ages 8–9 years)
(School situated in a rural/urban area)

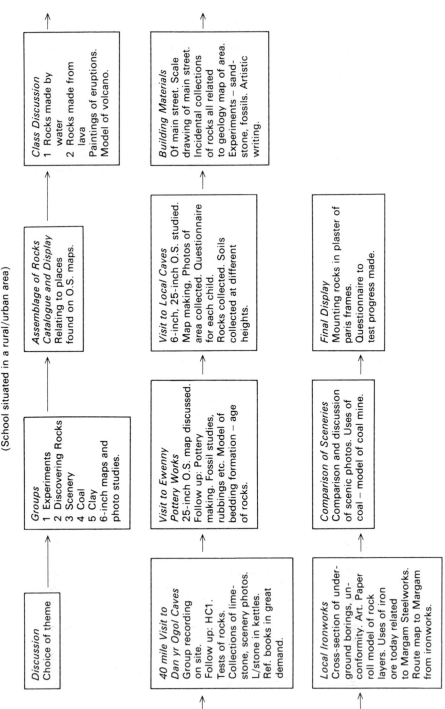

Discussion
Choice of theme

Groups
1 Experiments
2 Discovering Rocks
3 Scenery
4 Coal
5 Clay
6-inch maps and photo studies.

Assemblage of Rocks
Catalogue and Display
Relating to places found on O.S. maps.

Class Discussion
1 Rocks made by water
2 Rocks made from lava
Paintings of eruptions.
Model of volcano.

40 mile Visit to Dan yr Ogol Caves
Group recording on site.
Follow up: HC1.
Tests of rocks.
Collections of limestone, scenery photos.
L/stone in kettles.
Ref. books in great demand.

Visit to Ewenny Pottery Works
25-inch O.S. map discussed.
Follow up: Pottery making. Fossil studies, rubbings etc. Model of bedding formation – age of rocks.

Visit to Local Caves
6-inch, 25-inch O.S. studied.
Map making. Photos of area collected. Questionnaire for each child.
Rocks collected. Soils collected at different heights.

Building Materials
Of main street. Scale drawing of main street.
Incidental collections of rocks all related to geology map of area. Experiments – sandstone, fossils. Artistic writing.

Local Ironworks
Cross-section of underground borings, unconformity. Art. Paper roll model of rock layers. Uses of iron ore today related to Margam Steelworks. Route map to Margam from ironworks.

Comparison of Sceneries
Comparison and discussion of scenic photos. Uses of coal – model of coal mine.

Final Display
Mounting rocks in plaster of paris frames.
Questionnaire to test progress made.

Figure 3

Any teacher planning a topic in local studies, history or geography might usefully ask which of these skills the chosen topic would promote. Figure 3 explains the work to be done in a case study, but it does not refer explicitly to the skills the teacher hopes to develop.[8]

Another useful check is to ask how a topic can be used to help children understand one of several key ideas. Some teachers recognize seven such ideas. Four of them, communication, power, values and belief, and conflict and consensus, are matters of great interest and concern to historians, geographers and students of society. The other three, similarity and difference, continuity and change, and cause and consequence, are general processes which are clearly recognizable in history and geography.

Tables 5 and 6 show how two groups of teachers tried to illustrate these ideas in their approaches to various topics planned for children of 8 to 12.[9]

The approach through skills and ideas gives order and purpose to each selected topic. Better still, it provides a clear framework for a series of lessons without preventing a teacher from choosing material which is of local or current interest. Such a framework is needed if there is to be a reasonable degree of continuity and progression in this area of the curriculum. The unfortunate lack of such a framework is apparent in much topic work, so we return to this point in that context, in Chapter IX.

The need for continuity and progression applies to the transition from school to school as well as the transition from one class to another within a school. Recognizing how important continuity and progression are, teachers from almost every first, middle and secondary school in one LEA joined together to try to develop a common approach to social studies.

The most detailed example of their thinking has to do with mapping skills.

a Using the contents and index to seek information about the position of countries, towns, rivers, lakes, oceans, mountain ranges, deserts.

b Drawing simple sketch maps within a prepared outline to show the distributions in **a**.

c Understanding the use of colour to represent height and use of symbols to represent particular distributions, for instance, gas-fields in the North Sea.

d Learning the use of scale to measure distances by (i) comparing distances on the map with the divided line or rule, (ii) using the written statement, for example, 1 cm represents 20 km (the use of the ratio 1 : 2 000 000 would come much later).

e Drawing maps – either by tracing or by using a grid pattern drawn in the exercise book to match the grid pattern of the coordinates on the map.

f Extracting more detailed information about a country or region, e.g. its position, size, shape, relief and rivers, types of environment, population, towns, mineral resources, farming, fishing, industries, communications.

Table 5 Sequence A

	Term 1		Term 2		Term 3	
	Theme	*Key concepts*	*Theme*	*Key concepts*	*Theme*	*Key concepts*
8+	Children's games, songs and pastimes	Communication Similarity/Difference Continuity/Change	The family	Similarity/Difference Continuity/Change Values/Beliefs	A non-literate society – the Bushmen	Similarity/Difference Values/Beliefs
9+	The local community	Communication Continuity/Change	Going to school	Continuity/Change Values/Beliefs	Farming	Similarity/Difference Continuity/Change Conflict/Consensus
10+	Workers and local industry	Power Similarity/Difference Continuity/Change	Leisure	Conflict/Consensus Similarity/Difference Continuity/Change	Living in Towns	Power Conflict/Consensus Similarity/Difference
11+	Children 100 years ago	Continuity/Change Causes and Consequences	Money	Power Values/Beliefs Similarity/Difference	Rich and Poor	Power Conflict/Consensus Causes and Consequences
12+	The Second World War	Conflict/Consensus Causes and Consequences	S. America	Power Conflict/Consensus Values/Beliefs Causes and Consequences	Great Britain and Europe	Power Conflict/Consensus Continuity/Change Causes and Consequences

Table 6 Sequence B – substantive key concepts

	Communication	Power	Values/beliefs	Conflict/consensus	Methodological key concepts
8 +	Transport in a local setting. Local road patterns. Local transport services.	Preserving law and order. The Police Service past and present.	Rules: safety rules, highway code, rules in games. Belonging to groups with rules, Scouts, etc.	Simulation: setting up an Island Society	Similarity/Difference
9 +	National network of motorways. Railways. Airports. Why is the pattern as it is?	Simulation: The siting of a new airport. Who decides?	Families in different cultures. Comparison of roles of individuals in families.	Conflict over the use of domestic space, local space.	Continuity/Change
10 +	Barriers to communication and how these are overcome. Crossing rivers, estuaries. Tunnels, the Channel Tunnel.	Floods: living with the threat of floods.	Going to school. Ways in which the young are taught in different cultures.	Providing for leisure need – conflicts of interest. Tourist v. Conservationist.	
11 +	Communication through the media. Newspapers, radio, T.V.	Working in a factory. Trades Unions. Strikes.	Victorian life.	Life during the Second World War.	Causes and Consequences
12 +	Advertising. Can we believe all we are told?	The Oil Crisis. Who has the power?	Culture clash. The Aborigines of Australia.	Enclosures: Simulations.	

g Examining routes – extracting specific information about the landscape and local features on journeys which the children might undertake, for instance, from Morden to the Gower.

h Using population density and rainfall maps to extract more abstract generalizations about countries, for example, south-east England has a high density of population and the Welsh uplands a low one.

i Comparing relief and rainfall maps to reach the conclusion that one is closely related to the other.

j Understanding time zones.[10]

Other schools might profitably work out similarly detailed notes on other skills. They are likely, we think, to use a good deal of local material to develop the skills and ideas we have mentioned. Increasingly, as they grow older, children should have opportunities to use their skills and see how the key ideas apply in other countries and at other times.

Points to consider and discuss

1. What skills and understanding are you trying to develop in this area of the curriculum?
2. Have you prepared charts like those on pages 68–9 for two or three locations near your own school?
3. Can you explain how you would use some specific topic to practise some of the skills mentioned in the table on page 71?
4. How would you treat another specific topic to help children understand some of the key ideas mentioned on pages 72 and 74–5? Can you name appropriate topics to illustrate each of these key ideas?
5. What more needs to be done to ensure that the common approach to social studies mentioned on pages 73 and 76 does actually ensure continuity and progression?
6. Do the guidelines used in your school for studying people past and present serve to develop the skills and understandings mentioned on pages 70–75?

VII. Imagination, feeling and sensory expression

For young children, playing with sand and water, collecting pebbles, twigs or leaves, making shapes and patterns, and countless other activities are ways into talking and listening, grasping ideas of size, weight and number, and developing a feel for neighbourhood and nature. They are, too, a way of training eye, ear and touch, learning discrimination, developing manipulative skills, feeding the imagination and educating the right as well as the logical left hemisphere. Art and craft, drama and music, dance and physical education make a special contribution to developing this side of a child's abilities. Not the only contribution, since there is ample room and need for imagination, creativity, feeling and practical skills in science and mathematics, social studies and the use of words, and other aspects of the curriculum. Art and craft, drama and music, dance and physical education make a special contribution and that is why schools need to provide a balanced and progressive programme in these areas to match the rest of their curriculum. Furthermore, such a programme has other benefits. A programme which includes art and craft, history and geography, music and physical education may well contribute both to children's general educational progress and to their competence in language and number.[1]

These areas of art and craft, drama and music, dance and physical education are among the most difficult to plan, provide and assess. More than half the schools in HMI's first school survey had no guidelines. Many teachers seem not to bother a great deal about long-term planning in these areas, nor to make very much use of pupil assessments in their planning.[2] Primary schools often lack necessary resources: though schools sometimes have specialist teachers for music and physical education they often have no special rooms for art and craft, drama, music or physical education.[3]

This evidence is persuasive. We believe it points to a need for many schools to review their policies, planning and practice in these areas of the curriculum. Given clear objectives, the main requirements for success are resources to stimulate imagination, feeling and the senses, and media for the children to express themselves, in the four main modes of perception, visual, tactile, kinaesthetic and aural. Since people respond to different kinds of stimuli, the provision should be varied, and there should always be sufficient time for children to complete the work they have in hand. An uncompleted piece of work cannot be satisfying.

Art, craft and design

Sophisticated adults sometimes draw fine distinctions between the visual arts, craft, and design. For young children there are no such distinctions, only vast worlds of doing and making to explore. As their experience grows they begin to refine and control their actions, learning first some physical control over materials, objects and their own movements.[4]

Children need opportunities to explore natural objects and materials: pebbles, stones, shells, fossils, crystals, sand, snowflakes, insect webs, feathers, bones, horns, wool, cotton, thread, string, twine, grasses, straw, lichen, leaves, petals, bark, twigs and plants. What is their shape, size, colour, pattern and texture? What are they like to touch, to handle, to smell, or even to taste? After this first exploration comes the next stage of doing and making. Can you play with these objects, draw them, or make patterns and designs with them? Children should quickly begin to work in different media, including paints, crayon, ink, paper, cane, cloth and clay. They experiment with different techniques, brushwork, collage, printing, fabric, brass-rubbing and modelling. They may start work with other materials, wood, metal, stone and plastic.

These varied activities give children practice in different media, various techniques and diverse materials. They need help in developing control over their materials and acquiring higher levels of skill and coordination. It may not always be easy for class teachers to know what standards to expect from children of different ages. They should certainly be looking for technical skills; and for evidence in the visual arts of increasing sensitivity to pattern and colour, awareness of the way in which forms and mechanisms operate, and a growing capacity to express themselves in ways which combine personal meaning with the power to affect others.[5] Teachers need opportunities for seeing a wide range of work by younger and older children, as well as others of the same age or stage of development, since this is the easiest way for teachers to set their own standards. Displaying children's work in the school's circulation and common areas is also a great stimulus to the children themselves.

As in other areas of the curriculum teachers will certainly find it necessary to keep some record of the materials children have worked with, the activities they have engaged in and the progress they have made. The following checklist may provide some helpful ideas for teachers who are thinking about how to plan and record their pupils' work.

A. DEVELOPMENTAL STAGES

i *The human figure*
Draws a person as a circle with arms and legs
Adds eyes, mouth and ears in the right place
Gives right number of fingers
Adds a body
Indicates dress
Shows detail of dress
Draws figure in profile
Places figures behind one another
Makes figures smaller when they are further away.

ii *Pictorial composition*
Scribbles in a variety of ways
Appears to be making marks on paper with care and deliberation
Talks about the shapes he draws and gives them meaning
Draws symbols which are recognizable as houses, trees, figures, etc.
Relates symbols in picture, e.g. draws curtains at the window, people at the table, etc.
Uses base line
Draws what he knows, e.g. shows inside and outside of a house in the same drawing
Attempts to draw what he sees rather than symbols or what he knows to be there
Makes sky and earth join
Places things behind each other
Attempts to show a third dimension
Makes distant things smaller than those nearby.

B. SKILLS AND TECHNIQUES
Draws with pencil, felt pens, chalk
Uses mixed paint to draw lines and make shapes
Mixes own paint to make colours
Knows effect of combining colours
Controls paint well using a variety of brushes
Attempts to show texture in different media
Can draw a range of common objects from observation
Attempts to show shape and depth in different media
Can plan work by drawing and use the plans
Can relate lines and shapes to produce an effect by intention
Can use colours to produce an effect by intention.

C. USE OF MATERIALS
Has experimented with the material
Makes objects of his own choice
    without tools
    with simple tools
Use tools competently, safely and appropriately

Carries out processes
Plans and makes objects of his own choice
Uses materials in ways appropriate to
    nature of material
    purpose
Gives weight to aesthetic qualities
Can work to levels of accuracy appropriate to the material and the task
Achieves appropriate levels of finish.

D. KNOWLEDGE OF MATERIALS
Recognizes different types of material
Is aware of obvious characteristics of each
Knows their sources
    preparation
    possible uses
    common methods of manufacture
    properties
    common classifications
    the range of tools normally used with each
    their uses and limitations
    the language used to talk about the material.

E. VISUAL COMMUNICATION SKILLS
Uses diagrams and models to explain something
Recognizes common three-dimensional shapes such as the cube, when seen from new angles, or in a line drawing
Understands simple ground plans (such as the classroom)
Can interpret a map showing a known route
Can draw diagrams to explain something
Draws common three-dimensional shapes such as the cube from various angles, using a model
Draws simple ground plans
Draws simple route maps
Can use a street map
Can use an ordnance survey map
Recognizes and interprets symbols used on maps
Understands the idea of scale
Understands contours
Can use an atlas
Understands the use of symbols in visual communication
Is aware of the symbolic overtones of different shapes and colours
Is conscious of the way they are used in advertising
Knows and uses a wide range of communication symbols
Selects appropriate forms for a communication
    for the material of the communication

for the audience
for a given purpose
Can use diagrams to explain how something works
Can record visually for a variety of purposes.

F. INVENTIVENESS AND CAPACITY FOR DEALING WITH IDEAS
Has many ideas of his own
Can build on easily from a given stimulus
Often produces ideas which are different from those of others
Shows a capacity for seeing relationships and possibilities
Carries work through to a conclusion
Is self-critical
Has capacity for developing ideas.

G. DESIGN
Assesses the factors in a design problem including a consideration of
    function in relation to social context
    materials in relation to aesthetic considerations; suitability for function; manu-
    facture; cost
Generates ideas to meet a given need
Selects intelligently from these ideas
Carries through a chosen idea
Evaluates the results

H. AWARENESS AND SENSITIVITY
Is conscious of the visual world and comments on it spontaneously
Enjoys touching and handling things
Reflects movement and feeling in his own work
Is aware of the qualities of different materials
Enjoys colour
Can discriminate subtle difference in colour
Enjoys shape
    texture
Enjoys the work of others and comments intelligently on it
Is developing the ability to evaluate man-made objects in relation to
    use of materials
    functionality
    aesthetic qualities.[6]

There is a need, however, for more than a richly varied programme of activities and some simple means of judging relative standards. Teachers need a framework of aims and objectives to give meaning and coherence to their work. An excellent summary of objectives in the visual arts comes from *The Arts in Schools*.

In the visual arts, the curriculum from 5 to 11 should enable children to:

a experiment with different media – watercolour, crayon, paper, cloth, clay, etc.;

b explore different techniques, tools and modes of manipulation in each – modelling, brush-work, etc.;

c understand the basic ideas of, for example, tone, colour, texture and contrast, and, eventually, of more complicated ideas of, for example, balance, focus and proportion;

d begin to respond to a variety of styles and forms of visual art, including differences between cultural forms (e.g. Western, Oriental, African) and between historical periods (e.g. primitive, ancient, medieval, modern);

e develop an awareness of the use of visual symbols to convey ideas and feelings;

f develop an awareness of design – the relationships between materials, forms and functions of objects and constructions;

g develop powers of observation and description.[7]

Schools would almost certainly find it helpful to review their own programme of activities to see how each teacher's work fits into the programme, and how far the programme as a whole meets the criteria implied by this statement.

In the early stages there is no clear distinction between the visual arts and craft and design, but as children grow older schools need to provide for each of these aspects of children's visual, tactile and manipulative education. Both girls and boys need opportunities to handle and use resistant and pliable materials, to use tools and simple machines, to apply their minds and imagination to problems in design and construction. What children can achieve is splendidly illustrated in *Children's Growth through Creative Experience*.

The scope is enormous: moulding clay, working in balsa, ply, soft or hardwood, or with wire, foil, sheet, strip or tube metal. Soft iron is easily bent or cut to make patterns or pictures, and wire is easily worked to make frames for models, jewellery and other articles. Expanded polystyrene, PVC, sheets of acetate, resin and other plastics are easily worked. Sandstone, chalk, bricks and cement are readily available for carving. In this kind of three-dimensional work children need to learn the three basic processes, of subtraction by carving, chipping and so on, addition by sticking or fastening things together, and rearrangement of materials.[8]

Parents, governors and others in the local community may be able to help with offcuts of wood, scrap from packaging firms, builders, decorators, industrial firms, electrical and TV dealers, quarrymen and others. Scrap materials and discarded watches, clocks, typewriters, sewing and other machines may provide wonderful stimuli for the visual and applied arts. With scrap materials or, a little less imaginatively, construction kits, children will make houses, robots, cars and many other fascinating artefacts.

One 8-year-old makes a model car, another builds a house, some learn to weave, to knit and to crochet, a 12-year-old boy uses a sewing machine to work out a design, a 12-year-old girl brazes a piece of wire, a group of children make seals of clay and soap like the Chinese seals they have seen in a museum, others make simple gears with Meccano or use electric motors to drive their machines. In attempting tasks like these children will find they need to be able to design what they want to make, to visualize and plan a series of tasks, to apply various practical skills. As they grow older some will find that analysing a practical problem and preparing drawings and designs for solving the problem are satisfying in themselves.

Activities like these need space, time and materials. The sketch overleaf shows the kind of facilities provided at Forelands Middle School.[9] Falling rolls may offer opportunities to adapt spare accommodation to provide facilities on this scale.

Kinaesthetic education: drama, movement and dance, and physical education

Between the ages of 5 and 11 or 12 most children make great progress in physical coordination, muscular control and manipulative skill. The APU's recent report on physical development[10] lists five categories of motor skill which might be used for assessing physical development. They are

i Skills of manipulation
  e.g. cutting, holding, guiding, writing, drawing.
ii Skills of construction
  e.g. building, assembling, adjusting, arranging, lifting, carrying, placing.
iii Skills of projection
  e.g. throwing, catching, grasping, releasing, kicking, heading, striking.
iv Skills of agility
  e.g. extending, contracting, twisting, running, crawling, rolling, jumping, climbing, balancing, vaulting, swimming.
v Skills of communication
  e.g. non-verbal communication, voice production, holding, touching, gesture.

The report also suggests a way of classifying tasks requiring the use of these skills, either in isolation, in sequence or in combination with other skills, or in applying skills in unfamiliar circumstances. The report's illustrations of these different levels clearly show that motor skills are used and developed in almost every area of the curriculum.

i *Task demanding the use of skill in isolation*
The task is performed on its own, with no movement preceding or following. The movement is complete by itself, e.g. circle drawing with a pair of compasses, forward roll, riveting metal, single colour screen or lino-printing.

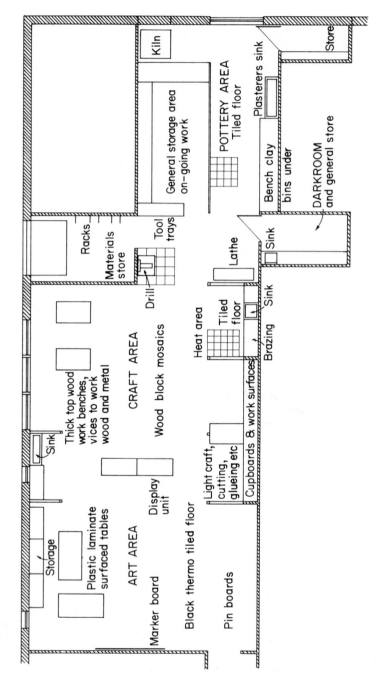

Figure 4 Art and Craft area of Forelands Middle School. Reproduced by courtesy of the Headmaster.

ii *Task demanding the use of skill in sequence or in combination with other skills*
The task concerned may involve preceding or following movements and/or a combination thereof as a simultaneous action, but the performer is still in control of all the variables, e.g. playing a musical instrument, doing a handstand-forward roll, ice-skating, using a foot-operated sewing machine for straightforward working, metal turning, throwing a pot, lifesaving in a swimming pool, roping up, climbing and belaying to a stance.

iii *Task demanding adaptability in the use of skills*
The task must take account of changing and/or unpredictable demands, and may be used in isolation, sequence or in a combination of both, e.g. playing a musical instrument with another person, working hot metals, sailing, using a foot-operated sewing machine with material offering differing degrees of resistance or thickness, running and dribbling a hockey ball in a game, lifesaving in the sea.

Choosing the most appropriate motor action for a task needs both a degree of physical control and motor skill, and the ability to appraise one's own and possibly other people's movements. Developing this ability to perceive and appraise movement is an important element in developing motor competence.

In assessing ability to perceive, teachers may find it helpful to use the different kinds of perception mentioned by the APU.

a *Perception as part of action*
i.e. inferred from actions:

    i children's estimates of spatial and temporal factors in catching, kicking or striking a ball;
    ii children's awareness of bodily movements in activities like gymnastics, dancing, trampolining and diving;
    iii children's awareness of the movements, abilities and limitations of others, as in team games, dancing, choral or orchestral work.

b *Perception independent of action*
i.e. detecting, recognizing and categorizing:

    i what children observe of a demonstration of skilled action or of a professional performance of dance or drama;
    ii what children hear of pitch, rhythm, loud and soft sound;
    iii what children taste and smell: flavour, smells indicative of danger, burning, etc.;
    iv what children touch and feel: size, shape, texture.

Through their increasing powers of perception and understanding children learn how to express themselves in movement. They can, of course, already express themselves through movement well before they come to school. All day long they express emotion and personality as they run and jump and climb, skip and play and dance. They make pretend, and more self-consciously begin to act and play different roles.

In all these ways they are already using movement as a vigorous form of self-expression. The task for schools is to relate these natural gifts to the development of motor skills and the associated perceptive powers. Their pupils need opportunities to practise these skills, and develop the ability to express themselves in movement, through well-planned programmes of drama, movement and dance, and physical education.

The drama programme in one infant school was based on the following approaches:

1. Listening to sounds and responding.
2. Using sound, music and movement to stretch imagination.
3. Individual dramatic activities followed by cooperative group work using group or class themes.
4. Emphasis on language situations in groups.
5. Situations involving more complex issues, perhaps fantasy or reality, more thinking and discovering for themselves.

For other children the approach through drama needs to take account of their own stage of development. Some of their characteristics are

1. A more conscious entering of the drama world and appreciation of its possibilities.
2. Greater awareness of relationships and role, yet perhaps not seeing 'shades of grey' in roles encountered.
3. Growing ability to sort out and organize ideas at their own level.
4. More careful appraisal of their individual and group work.
5. Deeper interest in teasing out issues and threads of argument.
6. A working basis of social, linguistic and movement skills.
7. Ability to concentrate and apply themselves to specific tasks.
8. Improved learning skills; finding, reading, selecting and coordinating relevant material.
9. Sensory awareness.[11]

As in other areas of the curriculum, teachers need to combine this kind of grasp of children's development with a knowledge of the levels of skill and understanding they hope their pupils will achieve, if they are to develop well-balanced and progressive schemes of kinaesthetic education.

Music

Most children are born with wonderfully acute hearing, a remarkable capacity to learn by listening, and an innate sense of rhythm. Schools have as much to build on in aural and musical education as in any area of the curriculum.

The ability to listen with discrimination and sensitivity plays an important part in several areas of the curriculum: in interpreting speech and other ways of using language such as poetry, drama and role play; in interpreting other audible and non-verbal forms of expression, most obviously perhaps in music, movement and dance; and also in interpreting audible signals about much of what is happening in physical education, social studies, field studies, and in laboratories and workshops. Like other aspects of primary education, aural education extends across the curriculum, and should concern every teacher, not just those teaching music.

There is indeed no longer any reason why all primary teachers should not include music in their repertoire. Most schools now have radios, cassette tape recorders, and a supply of simple percussion instruments. These and the materials developed by a Schools Council project on Music Education of Young Children provide all that teachers without any previous knowledge of music need to introduce their pupils to basic musical ideas and activities.

Children's aural and musical development follows much the same course as other kinds of development. At 3 they can make and imitate a wide range of sounds without necessarily understanding ideas like loudness, duration or pitch. A well-planned programme should introduce them to making their own improvised sounds and performing established music, the two aspects of creativity in music. By the time they are 9 many children are capable of reading simple melodies, and by the time they are 11 or 12 many contribute enthusiastically and expertly to many different kinds of music-making.

The youngest primary children need first to experiment with sounds, and explore what different instruments can do. One class of 6-year-olds found that 'the alto xylophone has thirteen notes. You can make low bumpy sounds on it. These bells make gentle silvery tinkling sounds. A pair of cymbals can make clashing crashing sounds.'[12]

Another class of 7-year-olds made many exciting discoveries:

We decided to experiment with the musical instruments and try to find out how they made sounds. We started with the cymbals, and found that if we touched them after we had struck them, we felt a tickle. We decided to do the same thing with the chime bars, and they tickled our fingers, too ...

Kevin said that it reminded him of 'pinging' a rubber band, and so we got some rubber bands to see if we could watch the vibrations. It worked quite well, and the rubber bands made an interesting sound ...

Gareth had another good idea and suggested that we could try striking the wooden sound box of the xylophone to see if it made a nice noise ... It did. I also found out that the different lengths and widths of the wood made different sounds.[13]

Experiments like these lead on to exploring rhythm. Clapping or foot-tapping in time with speech patterns, perhaps to the children's own names, or the names of towns or football teams, can lead to other simple experiments in stamping, finger-snapping, tapping and clapping. The children may be encouraged to imitate and then respond to rhythms clapped by their teacher or beaten on a drum, and then gradually begin to build short phrases and practise simple canons. While one claps with a flat hand, others may stamp, clap with hollow hands, or slap knees. This in turn leads to one maintaining an accompaniment while others add their own parts.

The next step might be to introduce the idea of pitch, with simple two-note phrases in G and E, adding A, D and then C as the children grow more expert. This pentatonic scale, C D E G A, is all that children need to improvise their own simple melodies, gradually adding a drone as accompaniment, and beginning to sing and play in canon.

As they grow more expert children can begin to make sound pictures. One class of 10-year-olds had written about wind and rain, and a line from each child's writing was used to make a poem.

> The wind, the wind whistles through the door,
> Trees are swaying briskly.
> Leaves are blown in all directions.
> Apples from the market are rolling with the wind.
> People are putting their collars up.
> Flowers heads are beaten from their stems.
> The wind cuts my face.
> It's like sharp icicles piercing my skin.
> A fierce wind, the March wind.
> Dustbin lids are lifted.
> They clatter down the street.
>
> The rubbish is spilt all over the road.
> People's hats are blown off.
> The hats roll down the street.
> A piece of paper is lifted.
> The wind comes galloping over the hills.
> Everything shudders, nothing is still.
> It pulls at the trees and tugs at the grass.
> It comes along wild and furious.
> It whips up waves on the brook
> As it gallops by.

The children were then encouraged to express the poem in musical sounds. This sometimes meant listening attentively to everyday sounds, like the sound of dustbin lids, to discover how to express them in music.[14]

Another group of 10-year-olds explored the idea of light and then decided to add descriptive music to the following poem.

Twinkling in the silent sky
Stars shed their shimmering, glimmering, glowing radiance.
Golden light twinkling down on the earth below.
The stars of heaven appear to lighten the pitch-black sky.
Silvery shadows everywhere.
Starlight is welcome,
How wonderful the light is.
The moon creeps out to help the stars,
Then drifting clouds float across the moon.
All is dark for a brief moment.
Brilliant was the eastern star
That moved on, giving precious light
For three kings to follow.
A heavenly beam pours over them.
As morning comes the starlight fades away.[15]

After a good deal of discussion and experiment, 'the poem was read by three children who paused at suitable places for the music to be given full expression, and in the final line, voices, instruments and choral speech all subsided in a gradual and most effective diminuendo'.[16]

Other teachers have linked music and art, encouraging their pupils to draw or paint or make collages reflecting pieces of music. One 12-year-old described his picture in this way:

The picture – this is my interpretation of a musical composition made by about eight people. I played the basic ostinato on a xylophone, which went from C to G to E to G over and over again. The lively theme was played on another xylophone, and additional harmony was provided by two glockenspiels and a metallophone, which played a chord. This formed a chorus, after which each instrument improvised upon the chorus in turn.

In the picture, the large, brown zig-zag line is my tune, the red wavy line is the theme and the other prominent lines travelling across the paper are the others' parts in the chorus. The spirals, flourishes, 'explosion' and the 'steps' depict the modifications and improvisations, and the same colours usually mean that one is the improvisation and one the chorus on the same instrument (e.g. the red line across the very top of the picture is the improvisation on the main theme). The background is the atmosphere.[17]

Experiences like these contribute to a coherent programme of musical education. A possible framework of such a programme has been helpfully summarized by the Gulbenkian Foundation's report on *The Arts in Schools*.

An overall aim of music in the curriculum from 5 to 11 is to enable children to use and to understand sound as a medium of expression and communication. This will include enabling them to:

a experiment with, and develop skills in, producing sounds with:
  the voice
  a variety of musical instruments
  other means of sound production
b work in a variety of groupings, large and small, using all of these
c discriminate and use timbre, pitch, intensity, rhythm and duration with increasing accuracy
d use conventional and accepted musical forms and styles as well as experimenting with others
e begin to respond to a variety of styles and forms of composition – Western and non-Western – and to appreciate their use and appropriateness in different situations
f develop individual interests and abilities in making and appreciating music.

In ways like these, and through the kinds of activities described in this section, schools can help their pupils to use and to make music a rewarding and progressive experience for all their pupils. Success need not depend on having an expert specialist on the staff, nor should it be confined to a minority of pupils.

Points to consider and discuss

1. What needs to be done to ensure that your school adapts and uses helpful guidelines in art, craft and design?
2. What more should be done to help teachers in your school to set standards in art, craft and design?
3. Do the teachers in your school work to an agreed set of guidelines for kinaesthetic education? What needs to be done to achieve this?
4. Is the music programme in your school based on well-thought-out guidelines? What needs to be done to enable the school to provide an appropriate programme for all its pupils?
5. Does your school's work in these areas reflect Britain's cultural diversity, or make special provision for the contribution of children from ethnic minorities?
6. Have you and your colleagues looked systematically at the scope for imagination, feeling and sensory expression in each area of the curriculum?

VIII. Personal and social development

Children spend more time at school than anywhere else except home. They follow the formal curriculum, take part in the extramural life, and are exposed to the ethos of the school. Schools cannot avoid, and no teacher would wish to avoid, a large measure of responsibility for their pupils' personal and social development.

The words 'personal and social education' encompass a vast area, hard to describe, and hard to map. The authors of the three sets of aims quoted on pages 16 and 17 have each grappled with the problem of finding words to express the elusive concepts of personal and social development. They seem to have identified four main aspects of this area of the curriculum, personal qualities, relationships with other people, religious education and moral education.

It may be helpful to draw together the phrases these authors used to describe what schools might aim for. The suggestions relating to personal qualities and relationships with other people come near to providing schools with usable checklists.

Personal qualities
1. qualities of mind, body, spirit, feeling and imagination
2. capacity for enjoyment
3. lively enquiring minds, the ability to question and argue rationally, and to apply themselves to tasks and physical skills
4. the will to use knowledge, skills and practical abilities
5. a reasoned set of attitudes, values and beliefs
6. habits of self-discipline and acceptable behaviour
7. a sense of self-respect, the capacity to live as independent, self-motivated adults
8. achieving as much independence as possible.

Relationships with other people
1. tolerance of other races, religions and ways of life
2. to understand the interdependence of individuals, groups and nations
3. an active participant in society and a responsible contributor to it

91

4. the ability to function as contributing members of cooperative groups
5. awareness of self and sensitivity to others.

Religious education
1. respect for religious and moral values.

Moral education
1. awareness of moral values
2. respect for religious and moral values
3. acquire a set of moral values and the confidence to make and hold to moral judgements.

To the extent that these summaries do describe satisfactorily a school's long-term aims, teachers need to consider next what they can and should do to help their pupils develop these abilities.

Personal qualities

In this area of education more than most teachers need a clear view of what they are trying to achieve and how to do it, because there is unlikely to be a separate slot in the timetable for developing personal qualities. Most of what schools can do will arise from the teaching of other parts of the curriculum, and from the school's organization and ethos. Many different strategies are needed. It may be helpful for example to tell children what behaviour is acceptable, and to teach them how to question and argue rationally. Teachers may need to work hard to provide opportunities for every child to succeed at some things, and to develop a sense of self-esteem. But developing lively enquiring minds is perhaps more a matter of encouraging and setting an example of lively enquiry. Young children, like other creatures, learn by imitating older members of the species and may depend heavily on their teachers as models of self-respect, self-discipline, application and enjoyment. The fact that teachers are so important to young children, as models, as surrogate parents for much of the waking day, as founts of advice and information, may make it particularly difficult for teachers to make opportunities for their pupils to practise independence.

Relationships with other people

The teacher's high authority makes it easy and natural for teachers to develop effective one-to-one relationships with pupils. It may be somewhat harder for teachers to help their pupils to develop effective working and social relationships with their peers, their juniors and their seniors. Children need practice as members of cooperating groups, contributing to group discussions, analysis and activities, taking the lead or accepting the leadership of others when appropriate, and, perhaps especially as leader, finding ways of accommodating the interests and preferences of other people. There are of course many such opportunities in the playground and the park, but children are not all equally active or successful in outdoor play. They all need similarly enlarging experiences in their normal work. Creating suitable conditions for this kind of experience is not easy. Sitting children in groups round small tables may look like group work but may turn out to be merely another way of arranging children doing individual work. Strenuous efforts are needed to ensure that groups of children do work collaboratively, and that each child has practice in making different contributions and playing different roles. Creating an environment in which specific skills like politeness, empathy, social competence and helpfulness can flourish is the key task.

Religious education

The 1944 Education Act gives religious education a unique place in English and Welsh schools. All county schools are required to provide religious education, and to do so in accordance with an Agreed Syllabus adopted by their local education authority. There are no similar requirements in any other area of the curriculum, and those for religious education now raise some difficulties because the assumptions which lay behind the 1944 Act can no longer be taken for granted. This is partly because active participation in the life and work of a Christian church is less common than it was forty years ago, and partly because many families of other faiths have now settled in Britain.

In these circumstances the rationale of religious education needs to be restated in convincing terms.

The introductory handbook produced by the Schools Council Religious Education in Primary Schools Project suggests that

religious education can build upon the desire to make sense of life. It tries to help pupils to enter imaginatively into the experience of a believer so that they can appreciate the importance to him of what he believes and does. It can provide a basis of understanding and appreciation upon which reasoned assessments and informed decisions can be made. In short, religious education is helping pupils to understand religion. However, such an understanding is not quickly acquired; for many it is a lifelong process. So, in the primary school, teachers are concerned with laying foundations, with the question of the extent to which we can equip children with the tools for understanding.[1]

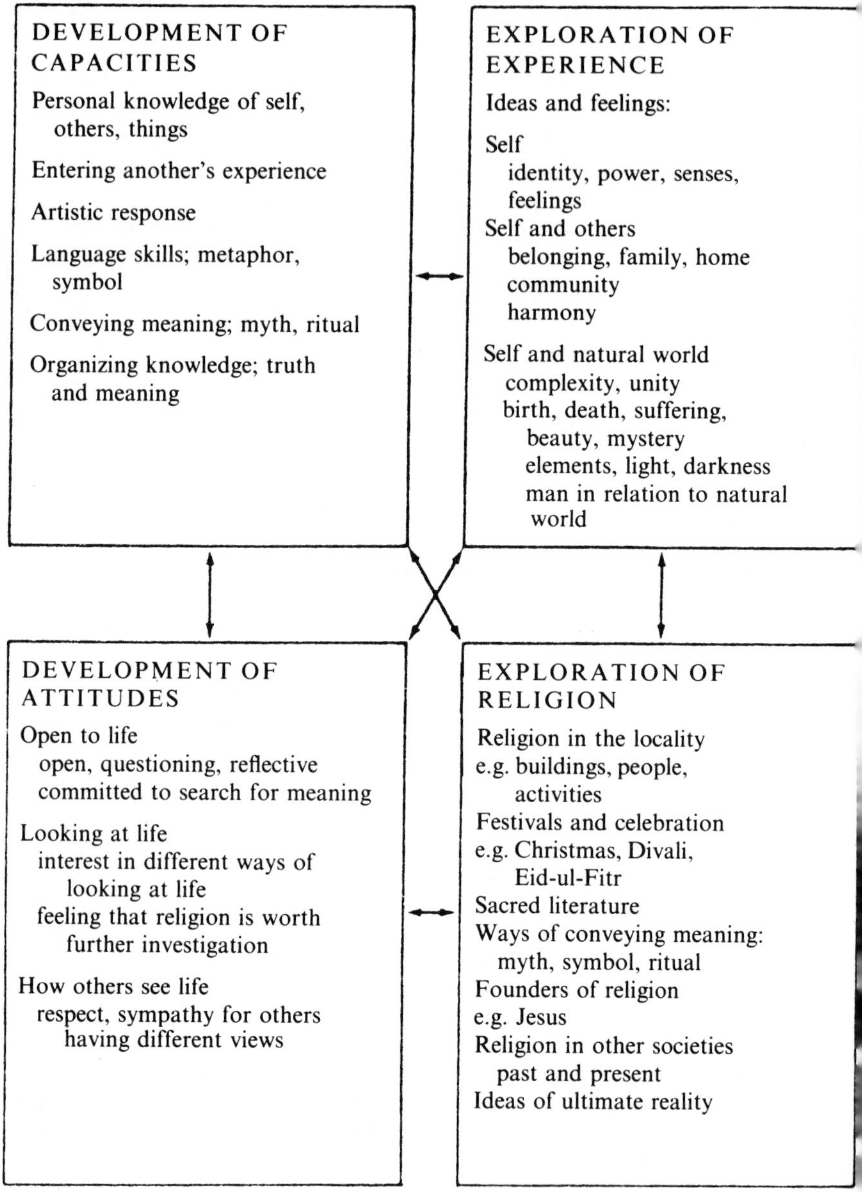

DEVELOPMENT OF CAPACITIES

Personal knowledge of self, others, things

Entering another's experience

Artistic response

Language skills; metaphor, symbol

Conveying meaning; myth, ritual

Organizing knowledge; truth and meaning

EXPLORATION OF EXPERIENCE

Ideas and feelings:

Self
identity, power, senses, feelings
Self and others
belonging, family, home community
harmony

Self and natural world
complexity, unity
birth, death, suffering, beauty, mystery
elements, light, darkness
man in relation to natural world

DEVELOPMENT OF ATTITUDES

Open to life
open, questioning, reflective
committed to search for meaning

Looking at life
interest in different ways of looking at life
feeling that religion is worth further investigation

How others see life
respect, sympathy for others having different views

EXPLORATION OF RELIGION

Religion in the locality
e.g. buildings, people, activities
Festivals and celebration
e.g. Christmas, Divali, Eid-ul-Fitr
Sacred literature
Ways of conveying meaning: myth, symbol, ritual
Founders of religion
e.g. Jesus
Religion in other societies past and present
Ideas of ultimate reality

Figure 5

It goes on to suggest four ways in which teachers can help. They can interest children in different ways of responding to and interpreting life, help children to develop capacities necessary to understand religion, encourage children to reflect on their experience, and help children to explore various aspects of religion. The handbook goes on to suggest more detailed objectives corresponding to each of these four strands in religious education. These objectives are set out in Figure 5.[2]

If primary schools can devise programmes of activities which contribute to these objectives they will have made a useful start in helping their pupils towards understanding religious ideas, feelings and activities.

That is, of course, the underlying aim of education in religion. As well as reassurance about how they can help, teachers may find it useful to consider exactly what religious education is, and what it is not. The following statement of principles from a recent Agreed Syllabus tackles this question, and may be a helpful starting point for others who wish to clear their own minds.

1. Religious education is the education of children in religion. It is not primarily social education or education in personal relationships. Nevertheless, as the aims show, there are opportunities for both within this area of the curriculum. Neither is religious education directly concerned with political and non-religious philosophies, except in so far as such philosophies relate to religion.

2. Religious education should not be confused with moral education. Morality is not necessarily dependent on particular religious beliefs, but can exist independently of them. Responsibility for moral education should run across the whole curriculum. The overlap of religious education with moral education occurs when children are exploring the ideas, feelings and actions involved in the ethical teaching of religious traditions and in the moral conflicts that may arise in the life of the believer.

3. Religious education is concerned with the spiritual growth of the individual, with those feelings and beliefs that arise out of experience and that influence the search for meaning and purpose to life. For some, such experience will be interpreted in religious terms. Spiritual growth is the concern of both the school and the faith community. The latter will encourage spiritual growth in accordance with its own tradition. The school's task in religious education is to enable pupils to become aware of a wide range of religious interpretations of personal experience and their importance to believers.

4. Religious education must include the study of Christianity. It is the example of religion most readily available in our society for study; and it is the religion that has most influenced our culture, giving rise to social institutions, moral codes and patterns of behaviour.

5. Religious education must also develop some understanding of the religious beliefs and practices that affect the attitudes and actions of people throughout the world. Many examples are to be found in the variety of beliefs and ways of life that are accepted and practised in Britain today.

Table 7

	1st Year	2nd Year	3rd Year	4th Year
A	*Belonging* home, school, club roles, rules.	*The world around* trees – life cycle, as a resource, use and misuse (Harvest)	*Food* dependence, interdependence, plenty, want; symbolism: care, unity, celebration. (Harvest)	*Creation myths* making sense of the world, myths compared, place of origin, motifs.
U T	*Guy Fawkes* colours, sounds, dark, light, fire, customs, rituals, symbols.	*Autumn* turn of year, Fall, patterns of death and renewal.	*Hallowe'en* ghosts, witches, spells, real and unreal experiences, dark, shadows, fears, good, evil, heaven, hell.	*Festivals* motif – light Celtic
U M N	*What is precious* favourite things, people who are important, what is precious?	*Background to life of Jesus* Synagogue school, Jewish Bible, Hebrew, types of writing, poetry, law, stories, Festivals, Passover in Jerusalem, pilgrim songs.	*Exploring myself* X-rays: inside, outside, doing, thinking, imagining, feeling; conscience.	Divali Hanukkah Advent
	Christmas (Santa Claus)	*Christmas* (exploring customs)	*Christmas* (meaning of celebration)	Christmas (light)

SPRING

	A	B	C	D
S / P	*Background to the life of Jesus* growing up in a Jewish home, family life, Passover meal, Synagogue, stories from Jewish Scriptures.	*North American Indians* patterns of community life, dependence on nature, customs, myths, stories, rituals.	*Life in a mining village* coalmining – methods and history, being a miner, underground, pit disaster, life in the village.	*Cortez and the Aztecs* Aztec society, way of life, festivals, rituals, myths, the coming of Cortez, clash of cultures.
R / I / N	*Spring* plants and animals, new life and growth.	*Night and day* light and growth, nocturnal animals, time and seasons, sun and moon, stories and myths, light and dark.	*How the Bible came to us* translation, transmission, William Tyndale, James Evans.	*Jesus* as others saw him (friends and enemies) at the end of his life.
G	→ *Easter*	→ *Easter*	→ *Easter* (customs).	→ *Easter*

SUMMER

	A	B	C	D
S / U / M	*Communication* (non-verbal) 'language' of music, dance, art, expressing ideas, feelings, Beethoven.	*Man and animals* pets: care, companionship, animals for food, work, clothing, animals for sport.	*Living with others* using *The Diddakoi* to explore: acceptance, rejection, homelessness, death of animal.	*Maccabeus* history, Greeks and Jews, Zealots, dying for beliefs.
M / E	*The world around* a local stream, water and life, dependence on water, pollution.	*Signs and symbols* road signs, flags, mathematical signs, codes, metaphors, symbols, cross, Star of David, crescent.	*Religion in the locality* the local churches – building, communities, leaders.	*Time and space* using *A Wrinkle in Time* to explore ideas of time, travel through space, overcoming evil.
R				*Growing up* looking back and forward, changes, going to secondary school.

6. Religious education, to be educationally acceptable, must be characterized by open enquiry and awareness of prejudice. It should help children to appreciate that religion offers a distinctive interpretation of life. It should also encourage them to think honestly for themselves about their own beliefs and values.
7. Religious education seeks not only to impart knowledge but also to develop understanding of religious experiences, feelings and attitudes. The use of the imagination is an essential tool for exploring religious beliefs and practices.

In so far as education is involved in the development of the whole person, religious education fosters the personal search for meaning and purpose to life in the wider context of the religious traditions of mankind. In so far as education is a preparation for life in a changing society, religious education clearly has a part to play by introducing pupils to society's religious traditions and to its present plurality. In so far as education is concerned with disciplines and areas of knowledge, religious education offers a distinctive area for study. It stands, therefore, in its own right within the curriculum of the school, making a unique contribution to the education of children.[3]

The lack of a detailed syllabus may seem strange to teachers who grew up with very prescriptive Agreed Syllabuses. The following example shows how one junior school in another local authority which had adopted a similar framework of aims and objectives used the framework to shape a detailed programme of work. The suggested objectives for children of 8 to 12 were as follows:

To enable pupils:

a to develop a sense of their own identity and worth
b to understand some features of human groups and communities
c to become aware of different forms of verbal communication
d to appreciate that symbols and artefacts can express human feelings and ideas
e to explore the natural world and various human responses to it
f to extend their awareness that people commit themselves to beliefs and causes.[4]

The teachers listed various activities and topics which might contribute to these objectives and then arranged these in a programme which was intended to cover the six main objectives and to match the developing capacities of the children. Table 7 shows the suggested programme for the first year. It was not intended as a blueprint for every subsequent year even in that school, but other schools may find it helpful in their own discussion of an RE programme.[5]

As in other areas of the curriculum teachers are quick to respond to circumstances in their own school and the community it serves.

The following example comes from a junior school with about 250 children. Built seventy years ago in a small county town, the school now serves an industrialized area with a canal, an airport and numerous factories. The area has attracted a good many West Indian and Asian families, and a third of the children are Asian, mainly Sikh but some Hindus and Muslims, and about 7 per cent West Indian. Most of them seem to have strong religious affiliations at home, but their parents are happy for them to join in every aspect of school life. 'The English children seem to have little or no contact with organized religion.'

Celebrating the school's seventieth anniversary created a new sense of excitement and purpose and a new sense of interest in the community. This, and the associated infant school's concern about religious education and the deputy head's attendance at a short course on world religions, led to a joint review of aims for religious education in those two schools. The teachers agreed on five objectives:

1. We wanted to introduce the children to the experience and ideas of community.
2. As the children explored what is of importance to various communities we would encourage them to respond as individuals and to reflect upon themselves as individuals.
3. Man's relationship with the natural world would be explored as a result of looking at patterns of interdependence.
4. The importance of attitudes, especially of tolerance and of interest in the idea of religion.
5. Developing skills appropriate to this and other areas of the curriculum, particularly sharing through words, art, music and movement what the children felt was important.

The teachers found it difficult to work out a detailed programme of work so they charted important areas of exploration to provide a balanced programme for each year. Their suggestions are set out in Table 8 overleaf.[6]

The chart does not bring out the extent to which this school took advantage of its multicultural make-up, though the programme is broad enough to allow the ethnic minorities to contribute their own experiences and insights. Teachers without that advantage may have to make a greater effort to introduce faiths other than Christianity to their programme of work.

Such a programme of religious education might involve close links with studies of the local environment, and work in language and art. Bringing out such connections will help children towards understanding, and may lead helpfully to some economy in time and effort. The power of these connections is revealed in the following account of how some children in a Roman Catholic school in Northern Ireland visited two local churches, one Roman Catholic and one Church of Ireland.

The same questionnaire was used for both visits which surprised the children as they had not realized how much the two buildings had in common. They looked at the shape and furnishing of the churches, learning the names of the various parts of

Table 8

The Infant Years	1st Year	2nd Year	3rd Year	4th Year
Favourite Things e.g. games, toys, stories, people, colours, sounds, smells, sensations (enjoyed through out senses).	*Things that make me feel happy, sad, etc.* e.g. time I will always remember	*Who am I?* beginning with a simple physiological study, e.g. the senses – looking at what marks an individual, his 'outside' or his 'inside'?	*Things that make other people feel happy, sad, etc.* explored through literature and the arts. An opportunity to look at the stories behind some religious festivals, e.g. Easter as a time of great happiness for Christians – why? – the origins of the festival.	*Important People* their motivation and how they have motivated other people – the children's own particular heroes and introducing others including Jesus as others saw him. Who is St Peter? (The name of the local church). Guru Gobind Singh (of great importance to the Sikh children).
Feelings e.g. happiness, sadness. excitement, fear, loneliness (explored mainly through movement and other creative activities).	*Celebration* looking at different kinds of celebration – weddings, christenings. festivals, for example. Drawing out ideas, e.g. the giving of gifts, special food and clothes.	*Homes* looking at the children's homes and countries of origin where appropriate, what's important there? customs, festivals, the stories that are told.	*A local study* patterns of interdependence in the neighbourhood, important places in the neighbourhood (e.g. sacred buildings) and important people (visiting speakers).	*Exploring a culture or community outside our own* e.g. Ancient Egyptian. What motivates them? How do they communicate their ideas? behaviour, celebrations, sacred writings, myths, rituals.
Happy Times e.g. birthdays, parties of different kinds (an opportunity for children to share their experiences).	*The Family of the School* e.g. doing things together, people who contribute to the school community.	*Night and Day* to be explored creatively, imaginatively, scientifically.	*Light and Dark* exploring the importance of these ideas especially for religious festivals, e.g. Christmas, Divali, Easter, etc.	*Change in the children's lives* looking forward, looking back, change and continuity, making decisions.
Homes and families ideas of home and family from the experience of some of the children, children's literature or through themes such as 'People who care for me' or 'People who help me', 'Babies'.	*Change and Pattern in Nature* e.g. life cycles, frog, butterfly, the patterns of flower petals and snow flakes.	*Animals and Plants* looking at animals and plants as a result of or in preparation for visits to the zoo and local botanical gardens.	*A changing world* looking at adaptation to the environment, taking examples from the natural world and various cultures, e.g. Eskimos, Vikings, Man's responsibility, pollution,	*Creation* to be explored creatively, imaginatively, scientifically, and mythically.
Pattern the turn of the seasons.	*Living Things* small animals, e.g. insects, large animals, e.g. dinosaurs.			
Living Things growing things and animals cared for in the classroom.				

the buildings and of the objects and their significance in the life of churches. The minister from the Church of Ireland church visited the school to answer questions. He had a gift for talking with children and the interview was a great success.

The patron saints of the churches were St John the Baptist and St John the Evangelist. The children used the Gospels and other books to find out about the lives of these two men.

At the same time they carried out a survey among their friends and relations and discovered both Catholics and Protestants among them. This realization contributed to a discussion of the idea of 'neighbours' when applied to people of different faiths living in the same community. They became very interested in peace movements and visited the Corrymeela community. They made a collage to convey their feelings about the divided community in which they live and showed great interest in the situation in Northern Ireland and the part religion played in it.

The teacher felt that visits to the two churches were important; they suggested a number of points for discussion. The children were interested in the idea of visiting an unfamiliar church. It was a new experience for many of them. They thoroughly enjoyed their talk with the Church of Ireland minister, and it was important to meet somebody associated with the church building they had visited.

Attitudes are difficult to evaluate, but the teacher has noticed that these children have shown a more positive attitude to 'the other side'. There was some realization that beliefs and practices, although different from one's own, are important and meaningful to those who hold them. Certainly, they learnt more both about their own church and the one down the road which previously had been just another building to them.[7]

This example illustrates how a teacher can organize experiences which contribute to the different strands of religious education mentioned on pages 95 and 98. The challenge for other teachers is to find similar examples in their own community.

Moral education

Like religious education, moral education is one of the most important aspects of personal and social development. They have much in common, but one important difference. As Charles Bailey put it in a contribution to *Personal and Social Education in Secondary Schools*: 'It cannot be the aim of a state school in a pluralist society that all its pupils necessarily become religious, but it should be its aim that all its pupils become moral.'[8]

It is necessary therefore to agree what being moral is, and see whether there are stages in becoming moral as there are in becoming a scientist, a musician or a gymnast, and see what schools might do to help children through some of these stages.

The first question is what we mean by a moral person, or what we mean by acting morally. It is not enough just to do things which are themselves right. If a burglar decides not to burgle a house because there happens to be a policeman outside, no one would regard his decision as a moral one. A decision is moral only if the intention behind it is a moral one, and only if the person performing the action is a free agent. If you are thrown from a window, fall on someone else and kill that person you are clearly not responsible for your actions. Concepts like 'telling the truth' and 'keeping a promise' involve more than just a set of words. They involve also ideas of intention, understanding and responsibility. You cannot tell a lie by mistake. It seems therefore that the ideas of intention and responsibility are both bound up in what we mean by a moral action.

To behave morally in the way we have outlined a person needs sympathy, to be able to identify with other people, and insight, to be able to understand other people's feelings as well as his or her own. To be moral a person needs to be able to understand the consequences of his or her actions, and on the basis of this insight and understanding to be rational enough to formulate a set of rules or principles to govern both relations with other people and personal conduct. Above all, of course, a moral person will live up to his or her principles, having both the ability and the will to translate rules and principles into action. A morally mature person seems to be one who is altruistic, rational and morally independent.

This attempt to describe what we mean by being moral may seem rather theoretical and remote from the classroom. But we hope teachers will use these ideas to shape their own thoughts about the long-term aim of moral education.

The next step is to relate this to what we know about children's development. As far as we know children are born without any moral awareness. Their first ideas of morality come from parents, teachers and other people. They become morally independent only over many years, and some may never reach that stage. Most observers and thinkers agree in recognizing about six stages altogether. In the first children behave in the approved way to avoid punishment, and in the second they learn to conform to obtain approval and rewards. These two essentially pre-moral stages lead on to two in which children begin to act independently. They learn to conform first in order to avoid the signs and marks of disapproval, and then to avoid their own feelings of guilt if and when they are censured by other people. Only after that do they reach the stage of understanding and adopting rules and principles of their own free will. First they make contracts with other people, and avoid violating the agreed rights of other people. Then at last they develop their own principles, to which they conform to avoid having to condemn themselves.

These stages of moral development should not cause teachers any great difficulty. They correspond to the stages we recognize in intellectual development. The problem teachers face is relating the ultimate aims of moral education to what they know of children's development, to shape an appropriate programme. In this task teachers need to bear in mind the three dimensions of moral education in schools, the formal curriculum, the informal extramural activities of the school, and its ethos and values, the hidden curriculum of assumptions, rules, procedures and practices. Even within the formal curriculum, as *The Practical Curriculum* said, 'Sometimes the mode or process of learning has its own lessons, more potent than the formal subject-matter of the lesson.'[9] If the aim is to help children to become responsible, rational, independent decision-makers, we have to ask whether it is enough to instruct them in these matters, or whether they need opportunities to practise these skills. As Ken David says in *Personal and Social Education in Secondary Schools*, young people come to know and live under many rules and principles emanating from parents, teachers and others. If, however, the young person is to be involved in these rules and principles from the point of view of moral education, rather than that of convenient social control, then he or she must be involved in them in an educative way. There may be some room for discussion about the age when children should be so involved, but some children will be able to make some responsible, rational and independent decisions when they are quite young.

Even, or perhaps especially, those who have not reached that stage need appropriate models of moral communities. A school's rules, regulations and expectations about behaviour 'must be shown to be part of a rationally justifiable structure, attached to the educational purpose of the school, rather than the arbitrary likes and dislikes of those in authority'.[10] Teachers may find that it is much more effective to help a child to think through some disapproved action and its consequences than to punish it. Toilet training, tidiness and good manners may be necessary if children are to develop the habits and standards which are needed for moral thinking. But long hair, jeans and jewellery may not prevent children from developing moral standards. Every school should examine its rules from time to time to see whether they still meet this test. Children may find it difficult to understand, for example, why infants are free to go straight to their rooms when they arrive at school in the morning, whereas juniors have to wait outside until ten to nine. They may see the point of rules about keeping to the left and walking in the corridors, but be puzzled why only some teachers insist on ruled margins and ruled headings. They may be puzzled about the equity of whole class punishments when they know only a few are responsible.

Schools are small societies, and like all other societies they develop conventional systems of behaviour and reward. It is important for children's confidence in these systems to be consistently maintained. It is important, too, that teachers themselves, quite possibly the children's most respected adult models outside the family, should appear as the mature adults described earlier.

What we have described is a counsel of perfection. We know that teachers need to know where and how to make a start. The ten points which follow may be a useful starting point for thinking about practical methods.

1. The pupil's need for a secure framework in terms of a group identity.
2. His or her need for a personal identity in terms of feeling confident, successful, useful, and wanted, particularly in the case of underprivileged children.
3. The importance of close personal contact with adults.
4. His or her ability to develop moral concepts, and to communicate linguistically.
5. The relevance of rule-governed activities and sticking to agreements.
6. The importance of parent-figures and of a firm and clearly defined authority, which is consistent.
7. The need to channel or institutionalize aggressive feeling.
8. The merits of cooperation and competition.
9. The need to enable the pupil to objectify his or her own feelings.
10. The importance of getting the pupil to participate, and to make the educational situation 'come alive'.[11]

If the whole staff can accept this as the starting point they may need a brainstorming session to find practical ways of moving ahead. The following questions may help to stimulate discussion about the context in which moral education takes place.

1. Is the concept of moral education properly understood, and the task undertaken responsibly?
2. Are the school's ground rules based on the appropriate sort of criteria?
3. Are the rules and the points of the rules clear to the pupils?
4. Do the pupils have any means of self-government, or involvement in making decisions?
5. Are there opportunities for the pupils to let off steam and channel aggression?
6. Do all the school's criteria of success allow everyone to succeed in something, and win some prestige and self-confidence?

The following questions refer to the content of the curriculum:

1. How can the teaching in other curriculum areas be designed to increase awareness of other people in the class, and in society?
2. Is sufficient opportunity made of music and drama to present moral issues in an objective way, and to give the pupils opportunities for

imaginative role play? Are music and the arts used in ways which allow children to express and objectify their emotions?

3. Do the pupils have opportunities of discussing moral questions, and learning to handle them precisely and calmly?
4. Do the pupils have opportunities to play games, to see the point of rules and procedures, to act out ideas of equality, honesty, duty and justice?
5. Do the pupils have opportunities of helping younger children, old people, the poor, or animals, so that they feel needed and develop powers of sympathy?
6. Do they take part in activities like swimming, and school journeys, to see the need for prompt and precise discipline in certain situations?

These questions illustrate the interdependence of moral education and the growth of personal qualities and interpersonal relationships.

Points to consider and discuss

1. What more can you do to ensure that what you teach and how you teach helps to promote each of the personal qualities your school is aiming at?
2. What more can you do to create opportunities for each of your pupils to have practice in different kinds of relationship, and in particular of different roles within a cooperative group?
3. Compare the statement of principle about religious education on pages 95 and 98 with the principles on which your own school's work is based. Does your practice satisfactorily reflect the principles?
4. What use do you make in religious education of material and examples drawn from other faiths? Could you be doing more?
5. Have you set aside sufficient time for the whole staff to consider the questions about moral education on pages 104 and 105?
6. Have you described how the treatment of each area of the curriculum can contribute to achieving your aims in personal and social education?

IX. Cohesion through topic work

The examples mentioned in the chapters on mathematics and the study of people show how much a good topic can contribute, in the lines of interest it opens up and the varied skills it demands. A well-conceived topic comes near to matching the depth and range of everyday experience and helps to counter the divisiveness of subject boundaries. It can help to bring home the unity of knowledge, and can both demonstrate and cause cohesion between the different curricular elements.

To organize one topic well is a triumph. Two examples show the thought and planning required.

Miss Jones's class has been watching the York Mystery Plays. The teacher decides to give over two half-days a week for half a term to class production of Orton School Mystery Play. The pupils are divided into groups, each with a specific task. One group writes the script, another will act, yet another prepares and paints the props and scenery. At the end of term the whole school watches the final performance, in which everyone in Miss Jones's class has become involved, sharing jobs such as curtain-raisers, prompter and scene shifters amongst those who do not actually take part in the performance.

In another primary school

there is a 'mathematics week'. The aim of the topic is to make all pupils more aware of numbers in their daily lives. Each morning in assembly the head sets the whole school a problem, the teachers later use class time to help children work according to age and ability on possible solutions. Some time is given over at each assembly to reviewing the previous day's puzzle. The school hall and the corridors are filled with displays, children's work and equipment which reinforce the theme. Emphasis is firmly on fun, and on the usefulness of thinking mathematically; and the display is brightly coloured and composed with an emphasis on 'things to do'.[1]

In the first example Miss Jones would certainly need to know what each different group would learn from its activity, and how the activities contribute to developing different skills. Sometimes the logic of a topic is clear only to the originator. Material from the Bible may be introduced, to add a religious dimension to a project: so that a topic on flight has included the flight into Egypt, or one on buildings, houses in Palestine.[2]

If to plan one topic well is difficult, to organize a programme of topics successfully is almost a miracle.

The conclusion of a survey of schools in one L E A was that 'few schools or teachers seem to have an overall plan for thematic studies'. Only 30 per cent of teachers interviewed in the autumn term could give the themes they planned to develop during the rest of the school year.[3] To some extent, of course, teachers are right to take topics of immediate interest and build on these, and programmes should be flexible enough to accommodate some unforeseen possibilities. How flexible, is the question teachers need to ask.

Teachers probably need a fairly clear programme for at least a term or two ahead because the complexity of most topics requires particularly careful planning. This might be based on half a dozen key questions. Clear answers would remove the anxieties sometimes expressed about continuity, coherence and progression in topic work, and about assessing and recording the work done.

1. What is the subject matter of the project?
2. What resources are available and what will the children be doing?
3. What are its aims, and what knowledge, skills (intellectual, social and physical), concepts and values will it require and develop?
4. How does it relate to other parts of the curriculum, past, present and future?
5. How will each pupil's contribution be noticed, assessed and recorded?
6. What will the teacher's role be while the children are working on the project?

It may well be very helpful to tell parents and other friends about what is planned, because they may be able to help a great deal, as the New Tredegar project (see pages 68–70 above) showed so splendidly.

The ability of the local public library to help, at the right time, should also be established well in advance.

Teachers will almost certainly need to commit their plan to paper. One possibility is a form covering the questions suggested above. Another possibility is a statement of aims and objectives like the one used by a teacher of 6- and 7-year-olds who had chosen the topic 'Ourselves'.

AIMS

To enable the children to gain a general knowledge of geographical, historical and social aspects of their local environment leading to an understanding of the world beyond.

To give the children the opportunity to paint and experiment with various media in art and craft.

To enable the children to acquire knowledge about people and their environment past and present.

To help the children develop the ability to make reasoned judgements concerning choice of relevant information and a critical attitude towards their own experience and that of others.

OBJECTIVES
To give the children the opportunity to acquire knowledge and information from verbal material (i.e. stories told to them by grandparents).
To add to the children's general knowledge of other times.
To stimulate the children's imaginative and creative techniques (through adventure story).
To give the children the means of expressing their thoughts and viewpoints through painting and collage in art and craft.

RELATIONSHIP TO OTHER SCHEMES OF WORK
Although the theme of 'Ourselves' will serve as an introductory topic, it will run throughout the entire period to the extent that in the basic mathematics topic of 'measuring', improvised units will be provided by the children themselves using hand-spans, feet, etc.
The theme will also recur in some art and craft work, as we will be exploring techniques involved in the making of garments, e.g. printing, weaving, embroidery and appliqué.
The following topic of 'Water' will also continue the theme of 'Ourselves' to some extent, as it will be introduced as something we need in order to live, in addition to food, clothes, etc.[4]

This statement is a useful start, but other readers may wonder whether it ought to say precisely what the children will do, and how the teacher will find out whether they have learned what they were expected to learn.

Other teachers have found a flow diagram most helpful in planning and managing a topic (see Figure 6).[5]

Once a topic is under way teachers need to monitor and assess their children's work and progress. In one survey only half the teachers kept any kind of record of the work done, and only some of their records referred also to how the children were progressing or what they had learned.

One reason for this alarming state of affairs may be the lack of any convenient way of recording progress. Teachers may find it helpful to think of each topic in terms of its main objectives and four kinds of desired learning, factual knowledge, appropriate language, skills and basic ideas.

Planning and recording topic work

The following extended description shows how one topic might be planned, how it could relate to several different areas of the curriculum, and how the

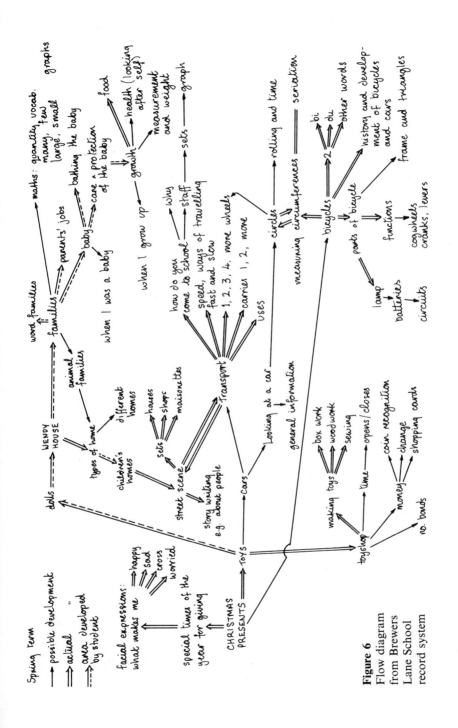

Figure 6
Flow diagram
from Brewers
Lane School
record system

detailed plans might be the basis for recording each child's work and achievements.

Consider the cross-curricular learning which you want to establish.
The development of study skills and personal and social learning needs consideration and plans for teaching and practice, normally as part of other work.

Consider your objectives in training children to work in the organization you have in mind.
If you can state these objectives, it will help you to clarify what you are attempting.

SHORT-TERM PLANNING
The planning we have been looking at so far is planning done at the beginning of the school year. You also need to plan week by week and day by day and to see as you go along how what you are doing relates to your long-term thinking. The steps for doing this are much the same as those for your long-term plans. You need to consider the objectives you hope to achieve in terms of knowledge, language, skill and basic ideas and the way you plan to achieve them, looking at the experiences children will need and thinking how you will provide them.

It may be helpful at this stage to take a particular piece of work and look at what might be involved. The way this actually works out depends on the particular children you teach and their age and stage of development, but there would actually be something in this particular study which would fit almost any primary-school age group.

The topic I am using is the Parish Church. This is a very common topic in schools and many teachers will be familiar with the sorts of possibilities it offers.

Start planning by jotting down any ideas you have and linking them by lines and arrows. It is sensible to visit the church before doing this, because many good ideas will come out of looking round and perhaps talking with someone who knows its history. Even a fairly modern church has lots of possibilities.

When you have put down all the ideas you can, look to see if you can break them up into the evidence you will use, factual knowledge, language, skills (activities) and basic ideas. Some of your items will come into all the groups and you may find that you need to re-word some of the things you have written.

Figure 7 below suggests using shapes to differentiate, using rectangles for evidence, triangles for factual knowledge which is here linked with language, diamond shapes for activities and the related skills, and circles for basic ideas. You will see from this that you may need some slight changes in the classifications when you do this, which will vary according to the topic. This doesn't matter providing you keep your analysis clear in your own mind and include elements likely to lead to the ends you want in the long term.

The example given could be extended much further. I have deliberately limited the outline to keep it simple.

I have then taken the chart and set it out in Table 9 under the headings, knowledge, language, skills, basic ideas, and creative work, and at the same time

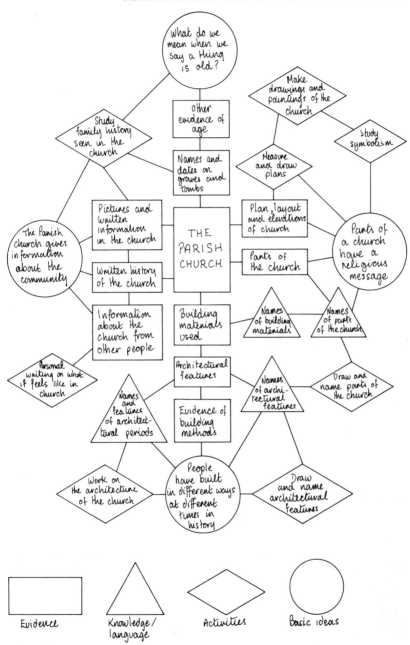

The Parish Church

What do we mean when we say a thing is old?

Other evidence of age

Make drawings and paintings of the church

Study family history seen in the church

Study symbolism

Names and dates on graves and tombs

Pictures and written information in the church

Measure and draw plans

Plan, layout and elevations of church

Parts of a church have a religious message

The Parish church gives information about the community

THE PARISH CHURCH

Parts of the church

Written history of the church

Information about the church from other people

Building materials used

Names of building materials

Names of parts of the church

Personal writing on what it feels like in church

Architectural features

Names of architectural features

Draw and name parts of the church

Names and features of architectural periods

Evidence of building methods

Work on the architecture of the church

People have built in different ways at different times in history

Draw and name architectural features

Evidence □

Knowledge/language △

Activities ◇

Basic ideas ○

Figure 7

Table 9 Project on Parish Church

	Knowledge	Language	Skills	Basic ideas	Creative work
Preparation	Outline history of church as background to visit. Consideration of likely building materials. Features of a church, e.g. font, etc.	Parts of a church. Architectural terms. Building materials.	Estimating and measuring. Drawing plans. Drawing architecture.	What we mean by 'old'. People build differently at different times. The church once represented the community. People symbolize ideas.	Discussion on possible approaches to personal response, e.g. What does the church make you feel like? Possibilities of drawing, etc., writing poetry or stories, etc.
During the visit	Estimate and measure church. Note building materials. Note architecture. Note features, e.g. font, lectern, etc.	Look for and label parts of church, architecture, etc. Note language on tombstones, etc.	Draw sketch plans and elevations.	Look for evidence of: Age. Past communities. The role of the church. Symbolism.	Draw, write poems and stories, etc.

After the visit	Discuss findings: architecture, parts of church, special features, building materials and methods, and find ways of recording	Discuss and record new words Discuss language used on tombstones, etc.	Make more detailed drawings of plans and elevations using a scale	Discuss evidence of: Age Past communities The role of the church Use of symbols	Continue and complete creative work already started Make model of church
Further extension	Extend knowledge of architecture by looking at other buildings Extend work on building and building materials	Add to language of architecture, etc. Consider differences in language at different times in the past and language for different purposes	Further work on plans and elevations and drawing to scale	Consider other examples of signs of age, church and community symbolism	Draw, paint, write, make models, etc., on related topics

This study also provides opportunities for consolidating work in mathematics (estimation and measurement, drawing to scale), language work (writing letters to make arrangements for visit, recording of visit, writing of stories, poems, etc., discussion and planning, etc.) art, craft (drawing, painting, model-making), religious education (parts of church, religious symbols, church and community).

have charted what could be done at the planning and preparation stage with the children, work for the visit, follow-up and possible extension of the work. This table only gives a few of the many possibilities, and you may like to think what else you would like to add in each cell.

The amount of time you spend on each part of this work depends on what is available and the extent to which children are interested. You also need to look at your long-term objectives and see whether there are more which might be met if you added to the topic in some way.

A project of this kind could also benefit from the use of drama to give the work a point of view. Some possible ideas might include the following:

1. Children look at the church as stonemasons from a given period in history, with the idea that they need information about how to build a similar church in their own town or village. Preliminary work would then involve studying the way stone was worked and the tools used at that period; consideration of ways of measuring and looking at construction; drawing plans and the information you need to do this, etc.
2. Children look at the church as people of a given historical period, who have not learned to read and therefore need to consider what they can learn from the artefacts and things about the church and discuss the meaning of these. Preliminary preparation might involve work on symbolism and the idea that in a church everything is placed with certain ideas behind it, rather than by arbitrary decision. Such objects as the font and the altar can be seen as symbolizing particular ideas which can be discussed with the children, with a certain amount of speculating rather than telling in the first instance.
3. The church could be viewed as if the children were of a different faith such as Muslims or Jews or Hindus. This would require work on the beliefs and customs of the religion the children were adopting and thought about the furnishings of mosques, synagogues or temples so that they could then look at where the ideas which are evident in a Christian church could be compared with the view from another religion. This could be particularly interesting where there are children of other faiths in the class, although parents might need to be consulted or perhaps involved.

It is not difficult to see ways in which many pieces of project work could involve this kind of opportunity to consider the topic from a somewhat different point of view. Ideally work in school should involve a good deal of activity which deals with actual problems, situations or people. For example, a letter which is written to a particular person with a purpose which involves the children is more likely to be well written and appropriate for its purpose than a letter written as an exercise. There are not enough opportunities to experience the discipline of the real situation in school as often as might be desirable; however, the drama work of this kind can make a contribution.[6]

Well-organized topic work provides a good opportunity to make special arrangements for markedly gifted or low-attaining children. A flow diagram might include special loops for the gifted or those with special interests to explore, as well as a critical path of knowledge or skills for the low attainers to practise. If special programmes, visits, displays, clubs, contests or other topics are organized to enrich the curriculum of some or all the children, they should be planned and the children's performance assessed and recorded in the same way as other work is planned and assessed.

Trying to record what each pupil has done and to assess what each has learned in a single topic is far from easy. Trying to ensure that there is some evident progression from one topic to the next, and coherence with the rest of the curriculum, is even harder.

Points to consider and discuss

1. Use the six questions on page 107 as a checklist to review and assess one topic your class has recently undertaken. What changes would you make in asking another class to tackle the same project?
2. List the topics your class has tackled in the current school year. Is there any evidence that the topics as planned would require and develop progressively greater knowledge, skills, concepts and values?
3. Use the parish church project described on pages 110 to 114 as a model, to prepare plans for another major topic.
4. How do you record what each child does, and assess what each has learned, (1) in an individual topic and (2) in a group topic? Do the records meet your needs satisfactorily?

X. Assessment and records: progression and continuity

Each area of the curriculum has its own logic and structure, its own inner coherence. We have tried to describe some of these structures in Chapters III to VIII, to show how they determine what standards a school should aim at, and to suggest how they influence a school's programme of work. The structure of the subject matter is one of the most important influences on the work schools do. But as every teacher knows, it would be pointless to follow that structure without regard to the pupils' understanding and ability to respond. The pupils' stages of development and their individual capacities and difficulties are the most important element in a school's work. To be able to assess this development, and to present each child with work of the right level of difficulty, are two of a teacher's most valuable skills.

How are a child's knowledge, achievements and capabilities to be assessed and used? How are work and assessments to be recorded, and how used to achieve progression and continuity?

Assessment

We know that children differ greatly by the time they arrive at a reception class. They differ in physique, general ability, achievement and personality. To some extent their differences are clearly hereditary: pigmentation and sex are genetically determined, and physique largely so. To some extent their differences are environmental: differences in interests and verbal abilities are probably attributable to family influence.

Teachers need to be aware of these differences, and the reasons for them, because they are of such importance in shaping strategies for teaching. Teachers may sometimes find it helpful to draw on research findings, to enrich their understanding. But they should do so with caution. Some research studies are based on quite small samples and their conclusions are necessarily tentative. Above all, they tend to generalize about whole groups of people, whereas teachers need strategies for helping the twenty, thirty or forty individuals in their class. In most studies the differences between individuals within a group are far greater than the average difference between that group and other groups. Subject to those provisos teachers may find it helpful to know of some tentative findings about differences between girls and boys.

By the time they reach school girls and boys display statistically significant differences in achievement and personality. Girls tend to have greater verbal and less visuo-spatial ability than boys; they seem to be more sedentary, have longer attention spans and greater persistence than boys; boys are more vigorous, and more aggressive. To some extent these differences may be innate.[1]

Whatever the differences at birth, early experiences differ in many important ways. Mothers touch, handle and talk to their girl babies much more than their boys. Girls are given different kinds of toys from boys, who are encouraged in any natural tendency they have to be active, to explore, to be independent and to be aggressive.

It is not surprising that girls take so readily to reading, which requires exactly the qualities they bring, not surprising that boys are told they might do better if they tried harder. Boys may get used to this message and become indifferent to failure, whereas girls are perhaps more discouraged by a single failure. From their first entry to school, boys are more demanding and less patient, tend to take more of their teacher's time, and to win more frequent praise and blame than girls. Teachers tend to respond more vigorously to disruptive behaviour by boys, thus confirming its effectiveness for those seeking attention. In short, it seems as though schools may unknowingly reinforce the differences which have begun to emerge by the time children come to school.[2]

This may leave some latent skills undeveloped and reinforce some unwelcome behaviour. Perhaps schools should do more to redress the balance. Education Survey 21[3] stressed the need to provide more opportunities for girls to practise spatial and mechanical skills, and boys to develop language skills. Both in these aspects of the formal curriculum, and in matters of personal development, it seems clear that teachers need to treat early assessments of ability, achievement and personality with caution, and to look for ways of helping children to develop their individual abilities.

And in the informal and the hidden curricula, as well as the formal, it may be necessary to consider the case for compensatory practices. Would it be a good idea, for example, to encourage girls to play more large-scale outdoor competitive games, and boys to work cooperatively in small groups? Is sufficient done in the everyday life of the school to help both girls and boys to develop every side of their personality? In preparing for an uncertain future, ought we to have in mind the possibility that sexual demarcation may be less rigid than in the past? 'For all our futures it will be just as important to have men who can be sensitive and caring as to have women who can be independent, confident and competent.'[4]

If girls and boys are already much influenced by their environments by the time they reach school, how much more are the children of different ethnic groups shaped by their background. For some of them English is a second or even a third language; some speak a dialect which may convey a false impression of their ability. The language models available at home are only one of the factors schools need to take into account. Intellectual interests and activities, academic guidance, the drive to explore, ambition to achieve and the emphasis on work habits are all powerful factors, at their strongest among some of the ethnic minorities. Even more important perhaps are relationships within the family and the group and their social, moral and religious codes. Children from some ethnic and other minority groups may come to school with very different values and habits from the majority. Teachers need knowledge and great insight to respond to the achievements and needs of children from unfamiliar cultures.

They need, too, to be alert to social factors. The National Child Development Study[5] has shown that some environmental factors tend to be associated with poor performance in reading. Overcrowding at home, lack of domestic amenities, and family size and position in the family are associated with differences in reading attainment. More recently the Assessment of Performance Unit has shown that performance in reading, writing and science tends to be lower where the take-up of free meals is high.[6] Schools need to find ways of compensating for the kind of under-performance attributable to social factors.

There are other differences too. For certain purposes it is convenient to group people by sex, ethnic group or class, and to draw on general studies of these groups. But we all know that individual differences between members of the same group, and similarities between members of different groups, make it absurd as well as dangerous to draw conclusions based mainly on a person's sex, ethnic group or class. By the time they are 5 children have learned a great deal; each has unique abilities and unique difficulties. To teach effectively reception teachers need to be able to find out what each new arrival's starting point is.

The process of assessing these young children is likely to extend over a lengthy period as the teacher creates varied opportunities for the child to play, to talk and to work, and uses systematic observation of these activities to decide when the child is ready to move on to the next stage. The teacher's skill lies in matching professional knowledge of the developmental stages through which children pass, knowledge of the difficulty of various classroom activities, and an informed assessment of each child's performance, abilities and readiness to proceed. This is the essence of professional expertise in teaching. It need not, should not, be in any way a threatening or testing matter. As the Bullock Report said, 'Let a child be put in situations which stimulate him, with materials that fascinate him, and there is no need to fret about the right mental age to start reading. It becomes almost an irrelevance'.[7] How right this is. One boy with a consuming wish to make model aeroplanes was seen teaching himself to read from quite technical and badly translated instructions on assembling foreign models. In that case the challenge met a lively and successful response. Teachers need the ability to devise and provide a progressive sequence of such challenges. 'In some parts of the curriculum, such as arithmetic, it is relatively easy to organize a series of targets for the pupils according to a logical sequence of difficulty. In others . . . it may not be possible to be so precise,'[8] though it is no less desirable. They need, too, the judgement to know when it is likely to be helpful to intervene to help a child through some difficulty.

Assessment is then a necessary part of matching work to a child's development and readiness to proceed. In reading and mathematics, where assessment is most used, teachers are generally more successful in providing suitable work than they are in other parts of the curriculum.[9] Assessment is needed, too, in diagnosing difficulties and identifying children who need special help. As a simple test of children's grasp of numbers one teacher put three collections of objects on the floor, thirteen bricks well spaced out, twelve marbles close together, and fourteen cylinders in a medium-sized space. The children were asked which collection contained the most objects. Some thought the spaced out bricks, others the dense group of marbles and some the in-between cylinders. Only some saw the need to count or match one to one.[10]

This kind of evidence of lack of understanding or poor performance should lead to remedial action, as it did in one school where all the pupils did the Leicester number test at the beginning of their last year, and those who did badly were given extra help in a withdrawal group.

Teachers often need also to identify the particular reasons for a child's poor performance. One disruptive and low-attaining boy was found only in his last year at junior school to have a severe hearing loss in both ears. He had to be addressed very clearly, perhaps helped with lip reading, and teachers had to check that he had not missed important information. His performance in mathematics was particularly poor and as he was interested in cars, soldiers, guns and strip cartoons, ways were found of presenting mathematical ideas in that context. Much earlier diagnosis might have saved that boy and his teachers much difficulty.

The early diagnosis of learning difficulties is of immense importance. Teachers are uniquely placed to notice low performers and to make some preliminary observations about the nature of a child's difficulties and the reasons for them. They may find it helpful to use standardized tests of intellectual function, attainment and social competence, diagnostic assessments of specific skills, and criteria-based assessments of behaviour. The information provided by any such formal assessment needs to be supplemented by and interpreted in the light of careful observation by experienced teachers.[11] Informed observation of children's classroom responses is perhaps most valuable in assessing the needs of children with moderate rather than severe difficulties. In some areas teams of advisers, educational psychologists, and sometimes medical officers, have helped teachers to develop skills in observation and early diagnosis.

In certain cases the assessment of individual pupils is part of the formal procedure for deciding how to meet their special educational needs. This procedure is described in *The Education (Special Education Needs) Regulations 1983*, and the accompanying DES Circular 1/83, *Assessments and Statements of Special Education Needs*. The resources and arrangements for formal diagnosis and assessment vary greatly from one area to another, but whatever the facilities and arrangements outside the school, within the local authority and the health service, classteachers have great responsibilities. They are in a unique position to know what a child's learning difficulties are and whether they themselves or the school as a whole can meet the child's needs. In accordance with the new regulations local authorities are asked to let schools in their area know of the arrangements for identifying, assessing and meeting special educational needs. Classteachers should not hesitate to inform their headteacher if they have any hint that a child needs more help.

Apart from its contribution to matching, diagnosis and placing, assessment might also contribute to planning the next stage of work. Unhappily, in their survey of first schools HM Inspectors found little evidence that this was happening. 'Frequently no adjustments were made to the previously planned programme or assignment; there were instances where individual differences revealed by assessment were disregarded and teachers mainly used a class-teaching approach irrespective of what was being taught.'[12]

Finally, of course, assessment of what the pupils have learned is among the possible measures of the effectiveness of the teaching. Assessment by external test is unlikely to be very helpful in this context unless it can be shown that the test measures exactly what school and teacher were hoping to achieve. But assessments devised by teachers to match their schools' aims and objectives can form part of the teaching process and would contribute most helpfully to the school's own processes of self-evaluation.

Most primary schools already use some kind of formal system for assessing reading. Ninety-three per cent of the schools surveyed for the Bullock Report used a published reading test, and the 80 per cent of the classes of 9- and 11-year-olds included in HMI's primary survey used standardized reading tests. Their use in mathematics is less common, and their use outside reading and mathematics is rare. This may be because few standardized tests are available in other areas, though the Schools Council has made a modest attempt to fill this gap by funding the development of methods of assessing pupils' social knowledge and awareness.[13]

In the absence of standardized tests teachers must rely on their own observation and subjective impressions. These are often expert, relevant and helpful, though in the areas where it is possible teachers often like to check their own assessments by occasional use of a standardized test.

One teacher of 11-year-olds introduced a game of snakes and ladders adding the scores of two dice labelled 1 to 6. From this he was able to assess:

> whether pupils could match one to one;
> their facility with simple addition bonds;
> the quality of their eye-hand coordination;
> their ability to work cooperatively and resolve difficulties;
> any flair or creativity in extending the game and developing new rules;
> social maturity, for example in being the loser; and
> when they cheated, how subtle it was!

In a rural middle school, a group of teachers asked their new first-year class to write a story to illustrate the multiplication sum 9 × 3. From this, considerable information was quickly obtained about language skills and interests as well as each pupil's understanding of the meaning of multiplication.[14]

Informal assessments may be wide of the mark. There is evidence for example of failure to identify gifted children. At one primary school where the teachers said there were no gifted children, tests revealed fourteen children with a reading quotient of 130 or more, six of whom had a quotient of 150 or more.[15]

In this instance the use of standardized tests helped to identify certain high achievers. These standardized norm-referenced tests, criteria-referenced and teacher-made tests can all be helpful in identifying some kinds of academic ability and aptitude. Some kinds of ability are not as readily tested in this way. They include creative or productive thinking, technical capability, psychomotor ability, ability in the visual and perform-ing arts, and interpersonal abilities. In identifying special abilities in these fields, teachers may find it helpful to seek information from colleagues, parents, the children themselves, or an outside expert. They are likely to find, however, that they have to rely very largely on their own observations. Some kind of checklist may be helpful in deciding what to look for. Teachers who wish to prepare their own checklist may like to compare their own thoughts with the two examples below. The first was compiled by a group of Essex primary teachers, and the second is from the USA.

Possesses extensive general knowledge
Has quick mastery and recall of information
Has exceptional curiosity
Shows good insight into cause–effect relationship
Asks many provocative, searching questions
Easily grasps underlying principles and needs the minimum of explanation
Quickly makes generalizations
Often seeks unusual, rather than conventional relationships
Listens only to part of the explanation
Jumps stages in learning
Leaps from the concrete to the abstract
Is a keen and alert observer
Sees greater significance in a story or film, etc.
When interested becomes absorbed for periods
Is persistent in seeking task completion
Is more than usually interested in 'adult' problems such as religion, politics, etc.
Displays intellectual playfulness: fantasizes, imagines, manipulates ideas
Is concerned to adapt and improve institutions, objects, systems
Has a keen sense of humour; sees humour in the unusual
Appreciates verbal puns, cartoons, jokes, etc.
Criticizes constructively
Is unwilling to accept authoritarian pronouncements without critical examination
Mental speed faster than physical capabilities
Prefers to talk rather than write
Daydreams
Reluctant to practise skills already mastered
Reads rapidly and retains what is read
Has advanced understanding and use of language
Shows sensitivity
Shows empathy towards others
Sees the problem quickly and takes the initiative.[16]

*

1. Learns easily
2. Original, imaginative, creative
3. Widely informed
4. Persistent, resourceful, self-directed
5. Common sense
6. Inquisitive, sceptical
7. Informed in unusual areas
8. Artistic
9. Outstanding vocabulary, verbally fluent
10. Musical

11. Independent work, shows initiative
12. Good judgement, logical
13. Flexible, open
14. Versatile, many interests
15. Shows unusual insights
16. Shows high level of sensitivity, empathy
17. Has excellent sense of humour.[17]

The value of checklists like these is twofold. They help to identify highly gifted children. They may also be helpful in identifying the special abilities of other children who would not usually be described as gifted. Picking out the strengths of ordinary children and building on them is a particularly difficult but necessary task. Such checklists may also help more generally in deciding what tasks children are ready for, so that the work they are given is relevant and effective.

The use of checklists and tests may also be helpful in other contexts. There is evidence for example that some teachers may find it difficult to judge pupils' ability. One teacher estimated a reading age of 11 years 6 months for a girl of 8 whose actual reading age was 8. Another 8-year-old boy who was thought to have a reading age of 8 years 6 months proved to have a reading age of 11 years 2 months. These examples are unusually wide of the mark, though they come from a survey of teachers of 1638 first- and second-year juniors in which only 36 per cent of estimates were correct to within three months and 64 per cent within six months. There was a tendency for teachers to underestimate the proficiency of first-year pupils, but overestimate that of the second year, to underestimate for boys and overestimate for girls.[18] We wonder whether more systematic observation, based on checklists of reading skills, might have helped these teachers.

There is a particularly interesting and informative chapter on assessment methods in *Record Keeping in Primary Schools*. This includes useful sections on teacher-made tests and observation techniques which we have reproduced in full in Appendix C together with a note on what to look for in standardized tests.

Records

Much of the information teachers have about their pupils arises from assessments of one kind or another, the outcome of standardized tests, teacher-made tests or observations. Other information comes from parents, colleagues or the children themselves, or is a simple matter of fact: that Shirley is absent again, Naomi is the board monitor, Hussein and Lee are playing football, and Kevin has completed a task. Teachers store a vast amount of this information in their own memories, where it may be readily accessible when it is needed. It may not. A classteacher can hardly be expected to remember exactly what each of twenty-five or thirty or more children has attempted and achieved in such a way as to be able to use it in planning the next work; and is most unlikely to be in a position to pass that information on to other teachers or other schools.

Each teacher needs a simple aide memoire for personal use to help him or her teach each child appropriately. Each school needs a more elaborate recording system, to keep a record over time of each girl's and boy's progress and difficulty. Several teachers will contribute to and have access to these systems and they will be used for transferring information to other schools.

Most local authorities have standard school record cards but their returns to enquiries by the Department of Education and Science in 1977[19] showed that the cards varied greatly in the terms used, the scope and degree of detail for which they provided, and the way in which information was requested. Fewer than half the authorities gave any guidance on completing the forms.

Most of the forms had space for recording performance in literacy and numeracy, and about 40 per cent for performance in other areas. Most provided also for the results of standardized tests or public examinations, notes on pupil behaviour and family background, and medical and other information.

The returns to this enquiry make it difficult to judge whether existing record cards are used in a way which provides helpful information to other schools, particularly to schools in other authorities which may use different systems. It seems not. One junior school received from an infant school records which described most pupils as having 'done: addition, multiplication, subtraction, division, tens and units, measurement of lengths, capacity and weight'. There was, however, no indication as to the level at which these had been studied, the way the pupils had been taught, what functions and written activities had been undertaken, or the level of proficiency reached.[20] Another junior school was more successful.

The teachers filled in a section of a record sheet for each section of the popular standard textbook when it was finished. This record listed the pages which had been successfully completed and noted any difficulties which pupils had experienced. Notes were also made in a different column on the same sheet about any other related work which the pupil had done, from another textbook, from a worksheet made by the teacher, or as part of a general topic, developed across the curriculum. In addition, a folder was kept for each child, containing examples of work in different aspects of the curriculum.

The feeder infant school used the infant level of the same textbook series and the junior school staff saw this as a distinct advantage. As well as receiving records of achievement the lower junior teachers visited the infant school. Consequently they felt they had a good idea of their pupils' infant school experiences.

The head of the mathematics department in the comprehensive school to which virtually all the pupils transferred, visited the older junior pupils on several occasions and did some mathematics with them. This gave him a fair idea of the range of attainment of his first-year pupils.[21]

Among the areas for which records might be kept are

1. reading
2. oral language development
3. written language development
4. mathematics (1) topics
           (2) concept
5. social and personal development
6. scientific development
7. study skills development
8. physical development
9. aesthetic development

Some schools are already using records in these areas. A survey of some 200 schools which were said by their local authorities to keep very good records provided a wealth of information.[22] A full report of the survey's findings about records of study skills and aesthetic development is included in Appendix D.

It is tempting to suggest that these findings should be used as the basis of a system of record-keeping which would fit all primary schools. Whatever gleams such an idea might bring to a bureaucrat's eye, it seems unlikely to help very much in practice. This is because the systems which were being used thoroughly, even enthusiastically, were usually the recent product of a collaborative exercise by the teachers as a whole. If the records are intended to communicate information to teachers at the next stage, they too should contribute. Though it may be impracticable to think of all schools using the same record-keeping system, it might be helpful if schools had some general guidelines on design and content.

The following criteria might serve as a starting point:

Design
Record should have:

1. a clear layout;
2. clear, stable printing that will not fade;
3. clear section headings;

4. the pupil's name in a prominent position (official forms generally use the top right-hand corner of a sheet);
5. sufficient space provided for comments;
6. a prominently placed key (or a user's handbook) to explain the use of abbreviations, symbols and criteria for the assessment of pupils.

Content

Record content should:

1. be relevant to the purpose of the record;
2. be clearly sequenced;
3. include for each child books, materials and approaches used, and with what success;
4. given direct indications rather than implications for future teaching;
5. give a clear distinction between entries concerned with pupils' school experiences and those which are assessments of attainment;
6. clearly present assessment information, stating:
   a the derivation of norms used when grading or rating,
   b the criteria used when deciding on pupils' competence,
   c details of standardized tests used as a basis for grading or rating,
   d details of other testing techniques used,
   e teacher-made test marks in a standardized form, possibly as standardized scores to indicate the range and distribution of scores. (This is particularly necessary where sets of marks from different sources have to be compared.)[23]

We see record-keeping as an integral and necessary part of the process of teaching. It needs to be done well, but that is bound to take a great deal of time. Some teachers have been able to help themselves by enlisting their pupils' help. The children do some of their own record-keeping, sometimes keeping a private note of work done which they can discuss with their teacher from time to time, and sometimes noting the work done on a chart in the classroom. One school had an electronic scoreboard with flashing lights, which was a great stimulus to a group of slow learners, as it acknowledged their success.

Making use of the children's help in record-keeping has the added educational advantage of engaging them personally and winning their commitment. Even with help like this much remains for the teachers themselves. If record-keeping is to be well done, it will take a good deal of time. This investment could contribute a great deal to teaching, and merits more time than other activities which contribute less to a school's main purpose. With well-developed systems of assessment and record-keeping schools would be well on the way to cracking the problems of progression and continuity.

Progression and continuity

'We did weather last year, Miss.' The refrain is not uncommon. Of course, they 'did' weather, or penicillin, or Queen Elizabeth, or decimals, or symmetry, at a different level which was supposed to match their abilities and interests then. They are expected to dig more deeply into the subject now, to extend their knowledge, acquire new skills and develop greater understanding of a wider range of issues. That is what we mean by progression. To assess the difficulty of a piece of work and match it to the children's developing abilities is among the most important skills a teacher has.

It is equally important in all areas of the curriculum. In areas where there is an obvious hierarchy of skills to be mastered, some children succeed more quickly than others, and then practise those skills again and again, at the same level of difficulty, while the rest of the class catch up. There is no evident progression in doing another page of examples, or another piece of craft work, and gifted children will quickly see these exercises as time-fillers.

A different sort of difficulty arises in other areas of the curriculum. It would be quite possible to go into some topics at many different levels, of knowledge, skill, imagination and expression. Some of us have suffered from doing North America, or parts of the Old Testament or *Macbeth* in exactly that way, at what our teachers doubtless believed were ever-increasing levels of complexity and sophistication. Such a spiral curriculum may match the children's developing abilities, but runs the risk of losing their interest. Choice of subject matter should be progressive too, to match and extend the children's interests.

A somewhat different kind of difficulty arises in planning the work of low attainers. For them the problem may be that now and again the whole class marches forward to a new topic without their having mastered the previous stage. What seems like steady progression for most of the class may look like an increasingly difficult steeplechase for others. In such a race those the teacher has identified as low attainers may be less at risk than children who have been away for a few weeks, or have come from other schools with different schemes of work.

In striving to ensure that all their pupils have a reasonably progressive course teachers may find it helpful to use some sort of checklist for choosing materials or topics. The following checklist is a guide to choosing materials for low attainers in mathematics. We wonder whether teachers might use this example to draw up such checklists for other areas of the curriculum or more able children.

1. Have all the teachers who are to use the written materials been involved in the choice?

2. Does the material incorporate, or is it compatible with, the balance between practical activities, discussion, mental work and recorded work which is considered appropriate for the pupils?
3. Does the text match the reading ability of the pupils?
4. Is there a reasonable balance between different aspects of mathematics, i.e. number, space, measurement, etc.? Are connections made between these areas?
5. Does it match, or is it compatible with, the preferred balance between individual work, group work and class work?
6. What materials or apparatus does the text recommend? Are these considered suitable and are they available?
7. To what extent are the explanations clear to the pupils? Is there likely to be a need for so much extra support from the teacher in understanding the text that it would be simpler to abandon parts of it entirely?
8. Is the rate at which ideas are introduced too fast for the majority of low attainers?
9. Is there any flexibility in the scheme to allow pupils with different needs to follow different paths through it?
10. Are the activities likely to motivate the pupils? Is there variety in the types of activity? Do they present the pupil with sufficient challenge, even at a simple level?
11. Is the mathematical language which is used at about the right level? Does the text match the teacher's preferences in priorities of introducing mathematical terms?
12. Are pupils generally only expected to repeat a procedure shown in a worked example, or is there a genuine attempt to encourage pupils to think out their own methods? Are the exercises stereotyped or is there a reasonable variety in the questions in each exercise to allow an idea to be approached from different angles?
13. Are the illustrations likely to motivate the pupils? Are they culturally acceptable? Are they at the right level of maturity/sophistication?
14. Is the format likely to motivate the pupils? Is it clearly set out and is the size of print, amount of writing on each page, etc., appropriate?
15. Is there a comprehensive teacher's guide?
16. If the scheme is separate from that used with the majority of pupils, is it compatible with it so that pupils can easily transfer from one set of materials to another?[24]

Continuity

Going up to the big school is an awesome prospect, no less feared at 11 than at 5. Even the move from Mr Hamid's to Mrs Williams's class is a step into the unknown. What can be done to ensure that at best the transition is an exciting and enlarging experience, and that at worst it marks no sharp discontinuity in a child's education?

In their replies to Circular 14/77[25] few local authorities saw any serious problems in the transition from nursery to infant schools, or infant to junior schools. Contacts between schools, especially those on the same site, were said to be frequent, with a consequent awareness of each other's curricular objectives, and often the same schemes of work. There can certainly be no doubt that frequent contact, shared objectives and common schemes of work are necessary for children to move smoothly from one school to another. The local authorities were more concerned about the transition to secondary schools. Their concern seems to be justified, judging by reports that 30 per cent of the children in one sample study fell back in English, reading and mathematics in their first year at secondary school.[26] Where a limited number of primary schools feed a single secondary school, the primary schools can agree a basic minimum body of experience, knowledge and skills in all areas of the curriculum, and discuss these with teachers from the secondary schools. This is harder than it sounds. One small group of teachers wrote about continuity in English between primary and secondary schools. They described five sorts of liaison in practice: indifference, studied insolence, problems of size, small beginnings and talking about our children; they defined the stages in a developing relationship between schools as discussion, visits, doing something together, looking at the children and the record system, looking at the curriculum and reviewing achievement; and offered this advice: make the effort, be tactful, be patient, make sound relationships, be specific, start with the children, aim for a two-way exchange, and persevere.[27]

Authorities and their schools have adopted many ways of promoting continuity, publishing curriculum guidelines, organizing in-service courses, giving advisers a pastoral responsibility for a group of primary and secondary schools, expecting secondary schools to appoint a liaison teacher, encouraging visits and exchanges between teachers in linked schools.[28]

Where infant and junior schools share a site, they sometimes organize joint activities, including assemblies, plays and outings, or share common working and quiet areas. The teachers in the junior school can more easily visit the children who are soon to come to them, and the infant teachers can keep in touch with their former pupils. In these ways the tension of going up to the big school is much reduced.

To promote continuity of teaching is more difficult. The two schools need a thorough knowledge of each other's aims and methods, and a shared philosophy. There are examples of an infant school using one mathematics or reading scheme, or one style of handwriting, and its junior partner rejecting it entirely, doubtless causing great difficulty to children who were not ready for a move at 7.

Similar discontinuities sometimes occur within schools. Differences in the approach to reading or mathematics can puzzle or confuse a child.

Whether children learn any art or history or science sometimes seems to depend more on who their teachers are now than on any school policy. There may be, but is not always, a discernible thread linking the topics covered in history or geography. The teachers may have one or several approaches to handwriting. At one school 2a consisted of children from 1a and children from 1b. The 2a teacher found that 1a had been taught subtraction by decomposition, wrote rough versions of all their work, and wrote italic script in ink. 1b had been taught subtraction by equal addition, wrote straight into their exercise books, and printed in pencil. What was he to do?[29]

Many schools are working to overcome these difficulties. In one case teachers from seven primary schools and one secondary school met weekly for a year to agree a programme of scientific activities and investigations for children from 5 to 11. A second group from nine primary and two secondary schools also tried to involve other teachers from the primary schools. Developing a common programme in this way and involving other teachers would help to promote continuity of experience within each primary school and between all the primary schools and the secondary schools.

In another area a group of seven or eight teachers from one authority's remedial service began to develop a language development scheme for children of average and below-average ability in infant and junior schools. It was thought that the scheme might serve as a model for schools to accept or reject, or become the central spine of a school's language curriculum. Local schools have taken an unexpected interest in the scheme and about forty or fifty schools are now testing the materials.

In a third area two groups of teachers are developing schemes for music. One group consists of teachers from first, middle and secondary schools, the other of six classteachers from a first school. Each group is trying to develop and test a detailed programme of skill and concept learning in music. The teachers from the first school are also testing the ideas of the other group and have clearly gone a long way to creating a music curriculum for their school. Their work will help to ensure that their pupils benefit from teaching which is both progressive and continuous.

Points to consider and discuss

1. How do you set about assessing your pupil's educational development? To what extent do you rely on tests, whether standardized or teacher-made, checklists, and observations?
2. How do you ascertain whether pupils have learning difficulties? Are the instruments available for diagnosing their difficulties satisfactory?

3. Do you discuss the records of individual pupils with the teachers who take the class which feeds yours, or the teachers of the classes your own feeds? Have you identified and agreed on any changes in the format or the detail of these records?

4. Does your own system for noting the work and performance of each pupil enable you to plan their work and help them with their difficulties?

5. Could you and your colleagues prepare guidelines like those on pages 127–8 on match and progression for other areas of the curriculum?

6. Do you and your colleagues know whether there are any discontinuities in teaching method or syllabus in your school, and have you decided whether any which do exist are acceptable?

XI. Organization: making the most of finite resources

We turn now to organizational issues. They may seem more mundane than principles or people, but are none the less important. Efficient organization matters because it is about schools making the most of finite resources to serve their pupils. Organization matters, but it is not the be all and end all of a school's life. Few headteachers could go all the way with Alexander Pope's dictum that 'whate'er is best administered is best', because they know that the choice of one form of organization or another may raise important principles.

This is particularly true of decisions about how the children are to be organized. Decisions about grouping within a class may lie with class-teachers. The implications of grouping by admission date, measured ability, friendship, attainment, readiness for new teaching, or even sometimes by sex, need to be most carefully weighed. The organization of classroom activities and the organization of staff may also raise important principles. The organization of staff in small schools, or the lack of staff in small schools, may be a particular problem.

Questions about the age when children are to be admitted to school are usually decided by local authorities. Decisions about whether to have a single starting day for new entrants, or a system of phased admissions, and whether to have an initiation period of half rather than full days, may lie with individual schools. In making these decisions schools should consider the problem of receiving a full class of newcomers at once, or absorbing a fairly large group in a vertically grouped class. They and their local authorities should also consider whether it is wise to delay admitting one group until the summer term, since those who spend only four terms in infants' schools seem to become relatively low achievers.

Small schools with too few pupils to form separate classes for each age group may have no alternative to some vertical grouping with children from more than one age group in a class. Larger schools sometimes choose vertical grouping deliberately and schools with falling numbers may be forced into it.

Mixed age groups mean there is an even greater spread of developmental age and levels of performance among the pupils in each class than in year-grouped classes. The change may sometimes be so great as to impose on the remaining teachers a need to reconsider their classroom organization and teaching methods. Help may well be needed from in-service courses, discussion with other schools with similar problems, the local authority's advisers or its teachers' centres.

Since the change may mean so much to some of the teachers we were surprised to learn from one survey that the staff had been consulted in only 70 per cent of infant and somewhat less than 60 per cent of junior schools which had made this change. One in five of the infant heads and one in six of the junior heads made the decision alone. It seems that these heads may have underestimated the consequences of the organizational change for classroom management and teaching methods.

Schools which group their pupils by age may have to make a conscious decision whether to have streamed or mixed-ability classes. *Education*'s digest on primary schools said categorically 'What is beyond doubt is that streaming, in its classic form, has to all intents and purposes been abandoned',[1] but many middle and some of the larger junior schools tend to stream their older pupils. Some schools make special provision within the class for high or low attainers by setting, or withdrawal groups. Setting is likely to be part of the normal structure throughout the school year, whereas withdrawal groups or special classes may involve either intensive bursts of special teaching, or regular withdrawal perhaps for a few lessons each week. Sometimes these arrangements work well. In an 8–12 middle school where third- and fourth-year pupils were set for mathematics, the deputy head, who was also responsible for mathematics throughout the school, took the third-year lowest set. This teacher was enthusiastic, and very interested in mathematics. Her room was attractively decorated. There was a pleasant atmosphere, the pupils seemed highly motivated, responsive and interested in their work and there was no evidence of a 'bottom-set mentality'.[2]

We cannot suggest a 'best buy' among these various forms of organization. Each has drawbacks as well as merits. There is a very useful discussion of mixed-ability groups, streaming, setting and team teaching in *Low Attainers in Mathematics*. A few examples illustrate some of the advantages and disadvantages of these and other forms of organization and may provide a useful stimulus for schools to reconsider their own arrangements.

In an open-plan infant school children were taught in five vertically grouped classes. Nearly all of the pupils had previously attended the nursery class; consequently the headmistress was able to allocate children so that each class had a fairly even distribution of pupils who were likely to have learning difficulties or behaviour problems.

The headmistress was committed to open-plan education and teachers had come to share this view. They saw several advantages:

a As each of the classes covered the full age and ability range, each teacher had responsibility for a similar group of pupils. Thus many problems were common, and they were shared and discussed.

b The sharing of problems was also facilitated by the open-plan classroom which allowed teachers to observe each other and encouraged honesty between teachers. They could admit not knowing how to tackle a difficulty and discuss it with others without fear of ridicule.

c On the whole teachers wanted to teach mathematics on an individual basis, especially with the low attainers, because they felt that children were more likely to respond in a one-to-one situation and also that this method made it easier to present work at an appropriate level for each child. The openness of the building facilitated this: children who were not the focus of their own teacher's attentions could be seen by several other teachers and this inhibited anti-social behaviour.

d Because of the organization and the individual approach, the low attainers in mathematics were not labelled as a group who were different from other pupils. In fact, although the teachers clearly knew which pupils had difficulty with mathematics, this was one of the few schools visited where project team members could not quickly identify which pupils the school considered to be low attainers in mathematics.

In another infant school, 'rising fives' were admitted in September, but those with birthdays in the second half of the year attended mornings only for one term. It was pointed out to the project team that in the middle infant classes many of the children who had most difficulty with language work, reading and mathematics were these younger pupils with birthdays between March and August. They had a double handicap: not only were they younger and less mature, but their slightly older peers had benefited from having more schooling in the first year and from the additional advantage of being in a very small class in the afternoons.

There were three classes in each of the three years. Every class had pupils from the full ability range and age range for that year. Each class was a little larger than it would have been if all the staff had responsibility for a class; one full-time teacher, one part-time teacher and the headmistress each taught children in small extraction groups. These groups were not specifically for less able or more able pupils, but so that all children, at some time, would have the opportunity for more individual attention in many aspects of the curriculum, including language, reading, writing mathematics, art, craft, environmental subjects and music. Sometimes more than one group at a time was withdrawn from a class, leaving the teacher herself with only a small group. The teacher with responsibility for mathematics, who also had a particular interest in the low-attaining pupils, often took groups of pupils who were having difficulty with mathematics. Because of her particular interest and expertise she was able to offer these pupils stimulating work at an appropriate level. Since many other groups were also withdrawn from their class at different levels and for a variety of subjects, these pupils did not feel particularly singled out or labelled as different from other children ...

From the observations made in primary and middle schools, it seemed that when pupils were streamed or placed in a 'remedial class' the selection was almost invariably made on reading skill and this led, almost inevitably, to many pupils receiving inappropriate teaching in mathematics.

The headmistress of a first school (5–9 years) in which there were many children from ethnic minorities, some of whom spoke no English, had been at the school for four years. When she first came she had felt that morale in the school was low. Teachers had been attempting to do individualized work in mixed-ability classes but she felt that this was not successful. In mathematics, for example, children simply worked through a textbook scheme and teachers spent their time chiefly in marking and administration so that there was little time for teaching.

An attempt to overcome these problems was made by setting pupils for English and mathematics in the third and fourth years (7- to 9-year-olds). After a trial period of one year the situation was reconsidered. It was decided to continue setting for mathematics but to stop the setting for English chiefly because it was felt that:

> it made the timetable too rigid;
> it precluded the development of ideas across the curriculum; and
> it was not an ideal long-term solution: additional support staff used flexibly as float teachers in the classroom would be much better.

The head felt that setting had been a useful step in improving the teaching of mathematics in the school in general, but that she would like to abandon it in the future and use the extra teacher made available by larger class sizes to offer both a withdrawal system and additional help in the classroom.

In an 8–12 middle school, staff used information from the one feeder first school to allocate pupils to classes so that the range of abilities and the number of children with behaviour problems was approximately the same in each class. In the first year (8- to 9-year-olds) and the fourth year (11- to 12-year-olds) each class covered the full ability range but there was a 'remedial class' in each of the second and third years.

Children were selected for the remedial classes primarily because they were poor readers, and these classes were considerably smaller than the mainstream classes. There was no remedial class in the fourth year because it was felt that pupils should get used to being in a larger class before moving on to the upper school. In the first year there was no remedial class because staff had thought that the number of pupils needing extra help would not justify it.

In the first two years pupils were taught mathematics mainly by their own classteacher. Some pupils in these two years had extra help in extraction groups: from a language specialist in reading and language, and from a compensatory teacher in a variety of subjects, including mathematics. The headmaster spoke of his concern about the widespread use of extraction groups. He felt it was important to arrange that only one or two teachers have responsibility for emotionally insecure pupils, because of the difficulty such pupils have in responding positively to a greater number of teachers.

In the third and fourth years pupils were set for mathematics; the lower the set the smaller was the pupil : teacher ratio. The mathematics specialist wrote tests for third- and fourth-year pupils which were administered at the beginning of the year. The tests were divided into number work and topic work, and the results were used to allocate pupils to sets. Subsequent movement between sets took place at the first half-term when the teachers had had time to judge if any pupil was wrongly setted. After that there was little movement between sets for the rest of the year because this would have led to a lack of continuity for pupils who were moved.[3]

In some schools decisions on certain issues, such as whether to introduce team teaching, may be greatly influenced by the shape of the building. Many open-plan schools were clearly designed to make team teaching possible, but in some schools the shape of the building precludes team teaching. It is not an option. In other schools it is a rejected option. But however strongly schools are committed to a system of class teaching, many do assign specific responsibilities to some of their teachers. This may serve one of two purposes. Some teachers concentrate on areas of the curriculum like science, art, music and physical education, and relieve some of their colleagues of all responsibility for these areas of work. Others become curricular leaders, in areas like mathematics, language or multicultural education, with a responsibility for helping all their colleagues and developing consistent policies, progression and continuity throughout the school.

Asking a teacher to concentrate on one area does need careful planning. 'The teacher responsible for the class may be the best placed to coordinate the whole programme of the class. Care needs to be taken to ensure that the programme of the specialist's own class is not too fragmented, and is arranged to utilize the complementary strengths of other teachers.'[4]

And the need to programme one teacher's day may lead a school to timetable in a way which leaves little flexibility for teachers and pupils to explore fully all the opportunities offered by topic work in other areas of the curriculum. Collaborative work among pupils may be particularly at risk if the days consist entirely of lessons of a fixed length. The evidence so far is that collaborative work hardly exists.[5] In this as in other matters schools need to ask whether what they are doing, and how they have organized their work, helps or hinders the achievement of their aims.

Many graded posts are intended not so much to fill gaps in the class-teachers' repertoire as to provide leadership in major areas of the curriculum. Somewhat ironically, if a school has no teacher with obvious qualifications to do this in a major area it may be all the more important to persuade someone who is without any existing expertise to make themselves more expert and take on the responsibility.

Such posts are a relatively recent innovation in English primary schools, and may perhaps seem threatening to the classroom teacher's traditional autonomy. Their responsibilities need therefore to be agreed through consultations between the head and assistant teachers, and the holders need to carry conviction through their expertise, enthusiasm and tact. Keeping up to date on developments in their specialism and finding ways to inspire the quality of teaching in their area are among the most important functions of specialist post-holders. They should take the lead, in consultation with their colleagues, in developing aims, teaching guidelines and assessment procedures. They may also have a special responsibility for liaison with other schools. From time to time they should initiate a systematic evaluation of what their school is achieving within their area of the curriculum. The ultimate test of their success is of course the pupil's performance. It is somewhat surprising, and disturbing, that in science at least, there is little association between the levels of performance and the existence of posts of responsibility for science.[6] If that is equally true of other posts of responsibility there is a most serious need to review and improve the way these posts are used. One wonders what help their heads and colleagues should offer to enable them to make more impact. They and other post-holders may find the following checklist helpful in evaluating their own contribution.

QUESTIONS FOR SCALE POST-HOLDERS

1. Has the area of my responsibility been clearly defined by the headteacher to me and to my colleagues?
2. Have schemes of work or guidelines for my aspect of the curriculum been drawn up, circulated to, and discussed with all members of staff? If so, when were they drawn up and by whom?
3. What opportunities have there been to review or revise the schemes in the light of any courses I or other member of staff have attended?
4. What have I done in the last twelve months to enable teachers to understand and make full use of these guidelines?
5. How successfully are the schemes being implemented in each class in the school? What criteria should I use in measuring success?
6. In assessing a child's progress in my area of responsibility what are the most important points for teachers (i) to observe and (ii) to record?
7. To what extent are the records currently made by teachers successful in assembling information that is relevant for:
   i retaining by the headteacher?
   ii discussing with parents?
   iii indicating what another teacher needs to know?

    iv transferring a pupil's record to another school?
8. Are all the resources (equipment, books, etc.) for which I am responsible:
    i safely stored yet made readily accessible to colleagues?
    ii regularly checked against a stock record, and, if necessary, serviced?
9. How do we provide for the most and least able children? Is this provision adequate?
10. Am I doing enough to make my colleagues aware of the equipment and materials available in the school for them to use?
11. What suggestions could I make for improving the use and range of the school's resources next year and in the long term?
12. Am I developing my appreciation of my responsibilities as a post-holder by:.........?[7]

How small schools manage

Whatever the effectiveness of existing post-holders, in larger schools the number of teachers and scale posts does make possible both a degree of specialism, and some spread of responsibility. In small schools these possibilities do not exist. Somewhat surprisingly, there is evidence that some small schools do succeed in offering as wide a curriculum as large schools.[8] Sometimes they meet the challenge through cooperation between schools. In one area fourteen teachers from three small schools joined together to produce a joint curriculum in language. In another, teachers from one village college and its seven contributory primary schools joined together to produce guidelines on mathematics, language and science for pupils of 5 to 16. They are now going on to produce guidelines in physical education and health education. Other areas have held half-day and Saturday conferences for teachers from many schools. In ways like these the teachers in small schools can and do compensate for their relative professional isolation.

    Such schools rely heavily, too, on outside specialist help. One authority appointed an area support teacher to encourage and help the development of science teaching in five rural schools. The support teacher developed materials and worked alongside teachers in the five schools.[9] Another authority has begun employing support teachers to help in the smaller schools. These are not necessarily specialists, but are appointed for their breadth of experience and a personality that is likely to fit into a number of schools. These are Scale 2 appointments in order to encourage experienced staff to apply and it is hoped that they will not only bring their expertise into the school but act as a catalyst or adviser in the school. They spend half a day or more in a group of six or eight schools and have been used for topic and science work. The first two to be employed (another three posts are being advertised) found planning their work and achieving continuity in the schools difficult. Being in six or eight schools in a week means it is difficult to feel fully involved in the schools. They found storage a problem with no 'home' base to keep the equipment.

One head was hopeful of overcoming this problem in his school by the use of two spare rooms in the school house. These rooms had a supply of water and a door into the school garden and he was hoping to get the support teacher to set up an environmental centre for all the six schools.

Other schools are not so fortunate in having to hand so simple a remedy for the lack of specialist accommodation. The lack of space for a library, or an area equipped for science, or separate clean and dirty crafts, is a serious handicap. Some small schools have established useful links with larger primary or secondary schools, and have been able to use their laboratories and workshops. In one area three small schools have agreed that each should develop a specialism which it can offer to children from the other schools. One offered environmental studies, another science and health education, and the third pottery and craft. The three schools have contributed jointly to buying equipment. Children from the three schools meet for an hour each Wednesday for a shared lesson in one of the specialisms.[10]

In one part of Cornwall three small parish schools serve a rural area where the larger settlements have about 150, 70 and 100 people respectively. The schools are not situated in these settlements, so almost all their pupils come by bus, though the schools are only ten minutes apart by car. They have a total of 115 children, six full- and two part-time teachers. The three heads decided to pool their resources in music, science and environmental studies, in the hope that this would broaden the curriculum of the three schools, and bring some economy of effort. The scheme involved each of the heads visiting each of the other schools once a week to give the same lesson in his specialism. Although they had to prepare only one lesson, they found that they spent more time and care in preparing to teach the children they knew less well in the other schools. Preliminary visits to discuss and plan the whole venture, travelling at break time to teach at the other schools, and the need to maintain weekly meetings to share ideas also took a good deal of time. Though the children undoubtedly benefited from a wider curriculum, meeting other adults, and other contacts which grew up, the scheme proved very demanding for the teachers. One particular difficulty was matching work to the different abilities of children in those mixed age and ability classes which the three exchange teachers did not know well.

The Northamptonshire rural schools project is one which has attracted great interest since its start in 1972. The authority first assessed the advantages and disadvantages of being educated in a small rural school, and concluded that many of the disadvantages could be offset because they arose from the limited resources at the school's disposal. The authority decided to take remedial action. Small schools in each of three areas were offered additional equipment to bring their provision up to the standard of a newly opened school: their establishments of teaching and ancillary staff were reviewed, and slightly improved. More important, the cluster of schools in each area was given some shared resources – a very senior advisory teacher, a peripatetic class music teacher, free use of a minibus, a kiln, and improved office, reprographic and audiovisual equipment. These measures have been most successful, and the authority has gradually extended them to include forty of the ninety schools it has with fewer than 100 children on the roll.

Another cooperative venture involving four local authorities and the Schools Council's Committee for Wales[11] has sought to find ways of enriching the curriculum in small rural primary school. Groups of schools in each LEA have taken part in many cooperative activities. They have included workshops in art and craft, science and physical education, curriculum policy statements, the production of science and mathematics materials, a joint music festival, a group magazine of children's writing, a joint educational visit and a group directory of local resources. One of the groups helpfully identified five main areas for investigation: the use of space; the selection, use and development of materials; the scope for using LEA resources such as a centre for educational technology, resource library, public library, teachers' centre and advisory service; the scope for sharing human resources; and the scope for joint curriculum guidelines and developments. They might perhaps have added a sixth area, the scope for joint pupil activities.

The evidence is that small schools can do a great deal to compensate for their size and very limited resources, particularly when they have the active support of their local authority.

Resources

Knowing what is there, and knowing how to use it to achieve the school's aims: those are the first priorities in planning a school's use of resources. Knowing what might be useful, and knowing how to get it, are also important; but only if the getting does not involve disproportionate expenditure of time, energy or cash.

Noting what resources are available, inside and outside the school, may be a useful first step. Some will contribute directly to the teaching, and others indirectly. It may be useful to think about resources in the way outlined in Table 10.

Table 10

Kind of resource	Available INSIDE SCHOOL		Available OUTSIDE SCHOOL	
	Used directly in teaching	*Used indirectly*	*Direct*	*Indirect*
People				
Services				
Physical environment:				
1. Buildings				
2. Furnishings				
Equipment and materials:				
1. Non-book: Machines				
Materials				
2. Book				
Money				

People are mentioned in various other parts of this booklet. Tnis section is concerned with the other kinds of resource. The resources available to schools are so numerous and so varied that we could not possibly attempt a guide to resources for schools. All we can do is to highlight a few of the issues teachers may need to consider.

The first need is for the school as an entity and the individual teachers in it to be familiar with the equipment and materials already available in the school, and locally. Accessible information about what is already available is the only rational basis for judging whether a school is reasonably well equipped to achieve its aims, where it has gaps, and how these might be filled. This information is also the starting point for teachers planning their lessons. Newly appointed teachers may need a good deal of help in dis-covering what equipment and materials the school has. Finding out what is available outside the school is even harder. Some local authorities or their teachers' centres have tried to meet this need, and have prepared useful guides to the services offered locally by teachers' centres, colleges, the LEA itself, libraries, art galleries, museums, field centres, local radio and so on. Teachers also need to know about other services used by some of their pupils, including particularly cultural centres and supplementary schools serving some minority groups. Useful information is also available from many national bodies, some of whose addresses are given on pp. 222–3.

Some teachers tend to see the school building as a constraint in achieving their educational aims. Some schools lack important facilities, particularly for science and other practical work and very often for storage. Others lack proper accommodation for their library, and this may make it difficult to initiate children into the system of classifying and arranging books. It may be possible to visit a public library to give children some idea of how to use a larger library, but schools will certainly need to help children to use the school's resources of books and materials, to develop skills in finding and retrieving information and other aspects of independent study. If the school's resources are very scattered teachers may need great ingenuity to develop a progressive scheme for training pupils in their use.

Similar imagination in rethinking the arrangement of furniture within a classroom, and conceiving the whole room, its furniture and equipment, and any associated areas, as a total environment for learning might sometimes be profitable. It might then be possible to plan, in a way for which few schools are designed or furnished, for the full integration of audiovisual aids in the normal classroom. Even without elaborate rearrangement,

> The school itself is a visual resource worth exploring. It contains forms which are coloured, patterned, textured, solid, transparent, reflecting soft, hard, warm, cold, noisy or quiet. Its people wear different clothes, have different shapes and different hair styles. They move, play games and make funny faces. There are hundreds of exciting and interesting views in, from, through, around and of a school. Its children need help in focusing onto one aspect at a time and scrutinizing it in visual terms. As well as the display set to catch and hold the eye, there are the pets, the aviary, the aquarium, the climbing frame, and many views down corridors, out of windows, into windows and into the boiler house or kitchen. There is the gas meter or electricity cupboard, the view under the tables, the caretaker's store, and PE cupboard, the head's room, the staff room, the delivery van at the door, parked cars and the refuse lorry.
>
> The large schools with their specialist areas offer a wealth of additional stimuli in their music rooms and domestic studies area, greenhouses and workshops. All these are there to be focused on, to be better known and to be understood. They are a rich source of stimuli too valuable to neglect.[12]

The Schools Council Art Committee has suggested what these environmental resources might offer for visual education:[13]

A worthwhile task for staff would be to get together and compile their own list of environmental resources. In itself it would be an invaluable school resource. Obviously, the list would be peculiar to the school and reflect the way its teachers thought and felt. Here is one school's list:

Place	Elements	Visual Opportunities
Wild patch at end of Water Lane	Ash tree, elderberry, hawthorne, broken walls, bushes, flowers, plants, lichens, mosses, spiders, snails, etc.	Investigation of small things through lenses, microscopes – 'a fly's view of a spider'. Contrast and textures and colours in the wall. Tree study through the seasons – a good cure for lollipop trees. Investigate subtlety of lichen colours on stone. Notice specular reflections on fruit or snails, put weed seeds between slide glasses and into projector.
Joe's garage	Mechanics – Joe will do some welding if asked. The forecourt lettering, old cars round the back. Workshop machinery, engines, scrap. Joe will let groups go into pit under car.	Good for dynamic figures, contrast between straight and curved lines, the rich colours of old paint and rust, corrosion, spectra on oil and a chance to really investigate 'black' colours. Don't miss opportunity to make display of scrap and also machine parts. Try displaying shiny steel parts under different coloured lights – what colour are the parts? Shine a light through a bottle of new oil or anti-freeze, cast silhouettes of machine parts. Good chance for detailed line drawing.
Power station	Good view from end of street.	Investigate what happens to shadows through the day, contrast of forms, e.g. linear geometric against vapour or smoke. Scrutinize atmospheric dilution of colour with distance compare with nearby objects included in the picture view.
The back of shops	Dustbins, peeling paintwork, scattered rubbish, broken fences, graffiti, dogs, children	What does use plus weathering do to man-made surfaces? Investigate contrasts of colour and texture. What colour is the glass in a window? Or a hole in that glass?

Place	Elements	Visual opportunities
	playing, good viewpoints available. A good place for regular patterns and shadow effects.	How can you show that something is behind or far behind something else?
Gable-ends and Corporation Street	Chimneys, mid-air fireplaces, patterns, textures, faded posters, wooden shoring and aerial plant life.	Contrast strong shapes with mellowed textures, powerful linear elements with softer arabesques, lettering with surrounding surfaces. What do the torn and worn pieces do to the poster images?
Mr Jackson's pigeon loft	Birds, interesting textures, soft colours plus black and white, pigeon feathers, Mr Jackson himself.	Bird portraits, a study of Mr Jackson (plus flat cap), a grand opportunity for interesting viewpoints, e.g. a bird very close up with others far off, etc. Borrow a bird for really close up detailed observation; back in class put a tiny feather into a slide and project. Do flying birds always look like a letter m?
School car-park	Reflections in bonnets, bumpers and wheel hubs. Under the bonnet details. Front side elevations of cars.	Excellent opportunity for detailed scrutiny of reflections or study of engine parts. How do motor tyres vary in tread pattern? What happens when a wing mirror occupies half the picture?

A teacher in Gravesend found the local river a rich resource for a class of 8-year-olds:

It was through discussion with a group of children, who were examining some clay pipes which were found in the river mud, that it became clear that many of them had no real concept of the river, and certainly no clear understanding that it flowed to the sea. Sadly I realized that very rarely did the children go to the river, nor were they particularly aware of its existence. Several children thought it was just a large pond. These were average-ability children and in no way were they being silly or difficult or lacking in interest. Apart from shattering a few illusions about what one can take for granted when considering what children might know and understand about their environment, this prompted the thought that visits to the River Thames at Gravesend would be valuable.

The river was visited with small groups of about eight children, at a place close to St Andrew's Mission Church. Here there is an extensive beach at low tide which leads to a disused Victorian pier. This gives an interesting aspect of the river looking across to Tilbury.

During the visits made to the beach the activities varied. A fundamental activity, however, was the conversation which took place and the clearing away of misconceptions which existed about the nature of the river. 'Is the water deep?', 'When the tide goes out this side does the water get deeper on the other side at Tilbury?', 'How can such big ships float?', 'How far is it to the other side?', 'How old is the pier?' The children were interested to see what they could find on the beach. Some children collected a number of different shells, others found pieces of coloured glass. A number of glass bottle stoppers, some round musket shot, an old pair of glasses and a metal float were discovered. One of the most interesting finds was a fragment of bottle naming the old brewery at the local 'Three Daws' pub which stands on the waterfront and was famous in the past as an escape from the press gangs because of its many doors. Seaweed, water samples and insect life were collected and became part of a small display in the classroom, which also included books about rivers and a map of the course of the Thames.

Many drawings were made of the buildings, some particularly fine work being derived from the 'Three Daws' public house, the church, and Tilbury power station. The ships on the river gave rise to talk about travel and ideas of drawings and research about shipping. In the classroom a number of children further developed their drawings made on site, some adding watercolour. Others made mono prints and silk-screen prints of the power station and the church, while one boy produced a detailed lino cut derived from his drawing of the old pier.

On a final visit to the river, we decided to take the ferry across the river to Tilbury and walk along the river bank to visit Tilbury Fort. Part of the Essex Marshes can be seen and a number of horses and cows graze by the river. The journey across the river is always exciting and the children never cease to be amazed at the scale of everything. The river is deep and wide, the houses so small, the ships so very large at close quarters.[14]

The local environment can also contribute many of the things a school might like to have in its own resource bank:

rocks, stones, fossils
stuffed animals, birds, skins and parts of animals, such as bones, owl
    pellets, horns, claws, wings, feathers, mounted butterflies, moths
dried objects such as twigs, tree roots, pressed flowers, leaves, everlast-
    ing flowers, seed boxes
objects of the sea: coral, shells, sand, crab cases and claws, starfish, sea
    urchins, lobster pots, fish nets, cork floats, driftwood
dolls, dolls' clothing, old or new
old or modern machine parts: ball bearings, cogs, wheels, nuts, bolts,
    screws, tools
scrap metal bits and pieces
old hats and shoes.[15]

A collection like this provides stimuli for visual education, drama, language and number. It need cost very little.

The school grounds may also prove a rich resource. A few schools are lucky enough to have grounds in which they can create small nature trails, or patches of ground which can be left wild. One city school with such a patch found that its trees and bushes and its proximity to a large reservoir meant it had an extraordinarily varied bird life. Others have called on the help of their authority's parks or recreation staff to plant their grounds so that they become a valued resource for studying plants and living creatures.

All the children, whatever their ability, will use the sorts of resource we have mentioned in previous paragraphs. Schools may find it more difficult to provide enough material to extend their more gifted pupils. *Mathematics for Gifted Pupils* has an invaluable guide to resources for enriching the curriculum for mathematically gifted pupils. It lists many different kinds of resource:

> Magazines/periodicals for pupils
> Material for a puzzle corner
> Competitions/contests
> Lectures/courses for pupils
> Correspondence courses
> Radio and television programmes
> Video-cassette programmes
> Films
> Film strips
> Slide packs
> Cassette tapes or slide/tape packs
> Posters
> Calculator and microcomputer material
> Commercially produced games and puzzles
> Games/puzzles/recreational books for teachers or pupils
> Classroom material for pupils
> 'Ideas' books for teachers
> Background reading books for teachers or pupils
> University courses
> Miscellaneous catalogues[16]

and provides useful ideas for teachers of pupils who are gifted in other areas than mathematics. Similar help for teachers of low attainers is to be found in *Low Attainers in Mathematics*, which has many suggestions of value in other areas than mathematics.

This kind of guide to resources to enrich and extend the curriculum of gifted children is immensely useful, if only because it saves each teacher from having to compile a personal aide memoire of these resources. But such guides save teachers from only a small part of their responsibility for judging which materials are suitable for their pupils. The ability to assess materials is among the most important skills a teacher has.

The first questions most teachers seem to ask are whether the content of the materials they are assessing is relevant, what ideas are presented, what skills and attitudes fostered. Some materials have implications for teaching and learning styles, and may depend on individualized learning or small-group work rather than whole-class teaching. Some require extensive supporting resources or a good deal of advance planning. All these questions need careful consideration. So, too, does one further question, perhaps the most important of all, that of the level of difficulty of the language used in any written or spoken materials. There is much evidence that children in primary[17] as well as secondary schools[18] are often presented with reading matter so difficult that they are unable to master the content. Six primary schools in one area have taken part in a systematic examination of the materials they use to see how far this is a serious problem. There are various objective measures of readability, such as standard word lists and various readability formulae usually based on the number of words in a sentence and the number of syllables in a word. The schools in our sample used the Powers–Sumner–Kearch formula, Fry's Graph, and the Forecast formula for materials not in sentence form.[19]

Teachers may also find it helpful to cooperate with teachers from other schools in evaluating the hidden messages of many books. Children recognize that a narrative is 'only a story' but they are inclined to accept the author's judgement and attitudes, and it is these which leave 'a residue in the child's mind'.[20] Equally, of course, to critical and perceptive readers, other books, of history, biography, geography and other fields often carry hidden as well as open messages. It is worth asking whether, taken as a whole, the books children have access to have a consistent tendency to portray certain groups of people in one way, and one way only. Are characters, whether fictional or real, from certain parts of Britain almost always described as bluff and hearty, near to the point of meanness, lively and sharp-witted, slow and lumbering, comical or whatever is held to be typical of an area? Are members of certain occupations almost always assumed to be dedicated, well turned out, brave, popular, fawning or dishonest? Is there reliable evidence that historical personages had the characteristics habitually ascribed to them?

It is worth asking, too, whether taken as a whole the books available present a reasonably balanced picture of society. Is there a tendency for the fictional characters to represent only a limited number of occupations, few parts of the country, few family structures, and few social, cultural or religious groups? Is there a tendency for the non-fiction to give a similarly skewed picture of events or places?

What we are suggesting is, in effect, that the book stock as a whole should present a reasonably balanced and unprejudiced view of events, places and people. Individual books should be scrutinized to ensure that they do not discriminate offensively against any group of people, whether on grounds of sex, race or creed, occupation or age.

The following list of criteria for a school's book stock has been prepared with education for a multicultural society in mind.

A balanced view of the world, seen from many different perspectives.

Books which relate experiences common to children of all ethnic groups and in which they can all share, for example, the wobbling of that first baby tooth in *Berron's Tooth* by Joan Solomon (Hamish Hamilton, 1978).

Books among which children from the variety of ethnic groups represented in Britain today can find characters which will confirm their own sense of self and enhance their self-esteem; in which ethnic minority characters have important social roles; where adults are seen to be supportive in family relationships and to hold positions of responsibility, doctors as well as orderlies; where ethnic minority children are seen to make their own decisions (see, for example, *Save Our School* by Gillian Cross (Methuen, 1980)).

Books which communicate vividly and perceptively how it feels to be a member of another ethnic or cultural group.

Books in which ethnic minority characters do not have to justify their blackness to the white characters (or readers) by being unbelievably good, or brave, or strong.

Books in which illustrations of ethnic minority characters are accurate and avoid caricature by using sensitive artists or photographs of real individuals.

Books which accurately reflect the population of Britain – so that those with an urban setting show not just a 'token black' (prevalent in publications of the 1970s), but represent cities and towns as truly multicultural – for example, Methuen's Terraced House series or *Mother Goose Comes to Cable Street* by Rosemary Stones and Andrew Mann (Kestrel, 1978).

Books in which language does not evoke stereotypes (avoid books in which 'savages' 'jabber and shriek' or the 'brown boy's eyes roll'); in which dialect is used appropriately – to extend expression and contribute to children's respect for one another's speech – as in James Berry's or Linton Kwese Johnson's poems, Charles Keeping's *Cockney Ding-dong* (Kestrel, 1975), C. Everard Palmer's *Baba and Mr Big* (Collins, 1976).[21]

Schools might usefully try to prepare similar criteria to help promote equality between the sexes, or regard for people from religious, cultural or social minorities.

People outside the school: community and parents

Even the largest primary schools serve a relatively small population, at most only a few thousand people. This is because even with today's depressed birth rates 5000 people are likely to have enough children to fill a two-form-entry school. If that population is scattered over a fairly large area, the need to save young children from having long journeys to school usually persuades the authorities to have smaller schools.

The consequence is that primary schools usually serve a fairly compact community. Whether the schools themselves are voluntary or county schools, community and school usually identify closely with each other. That is why there is usually strong support for a school threatened with closure.

Even in less stressful times school and community can benefit mutually from a close understanding. As we suggested in Chapter III, a good deal of the curriculum can and should be based on knowledge and experience acquired within the local community. And as several of our examples show, many people in the community are able and very willing to put their own knowledge at the school's service.

The experience of the Schools Council's Industry Project in preparing secondary pupils for the world of work shows that involving adults other than teachers can be of great benefit to pupils and adults alike. Most primary schools will find in their local community a good many people who are ready to explain things about their work, or special interests of their own, in ways that can be fitted into a school's programme. In one area for example farmers have clubbed together to make it possible for local schools to arrange farm visits for their children. In another the husband of the caretaker of a school now used as a day field centre for city children is a quarryman who devotes many hours to showing children round his quarry and explaining his craft.

The main difficulty may be that people with much of value to offer may be unnecessarily nervous about their ability or about the welcome they will receive. Schools may have to work quite hard to overcome this kind of reserve. At any time of course schools may reasonably hope for special help from the parents of children at the school. For the time being at least they have a special interest and a special commitment to the school.

More important still they and the school's teachers share responsibilities and aims. At its most formal level parents have a statutory duty, as have local education authorities, to ensure that children are properly educated. The local authorities' duties, and the corresponding rights of parents, have recently been extended. Parents have a right now to receive information about local schools, to exercise some choice of school, and to take a greater part in assessing any special educational need their children may have. Some, however, may find it hard to take advantage of these opportunities because they are apprehensive about working with experienced professionals.

It is not only in formal assessment, but more generally, that parents and teachers can usefully share their expertise. Parent and teacher each know something of the child, and each has something special to offer the child. They have an interest in listening to each other, and pooling their insights, so that what they do is complementary.

Many schools and authorities have tried to build understanding and shared commitment with their pupils' parents. Sometimes they start with toy libraries or drop-in centres where parents join trained staff in playing with toddlers. Some schools have parents' rooms, where parents can meet to make and repair articles or audiovisual aids and other equipment, or help the school in other ways. Where there are libraries parents can help children to choose books, and help to service the library itself. Above all, to have the opportunity of meeting and exchanging views is itself beneficial.

Parents and teachers might find it helpful to get together to discuss the suggestions in a booklet like *How to Help a Child at Home*.[22] This booklet is written for parents, but such a joint discussion would do much to help parents and teachers understand each other and be mutually supportive in what they do.

At one infant school with twenty-one nationalities among its 170 pupils, parents are invited to read school library books in their home language to groups of children as a normal part of the school's language work. Parents have an open invitation to stay for school assembly, and the school has a mothers' choir with a multi-ethnic repertoire. Mothers and children join in demonstrating clothes and cookery from their home cultures.

Sometimes multicultural schools may need interpreters on hand to help in discussion with parents. In one school Greek and Turkish volunteer parents hold classes for children one afternoon each week; these classes are mainly for teaching spoken language but include topics related to the Greek or Turkish culture.[23]

In these schools teachers and parents develop understanding through shared aims and shared activity. Shared activity for a wider purpose can prove wonderfully rewarding in other ways too. The staff at one nursery school[24] conceived the idea of making a garden and playground to stimulate purposeful and imaginative play. Three dads helped to make a tree house and slide, a builder gave some concrete drainpipes, community service workers helped to make a stockade and picnic area, and secondary-school pupils designed and built a paddling pool. Parents helped with a mural, an outdoor play area and a covered play area. Following this venture, when the neighbouring caretaker's house was vacant and condemned, parents who had helped with the play area were encouraged to think of creating a parents' centre. The centre will include a mother and toddler area, an art and craft room, a toy library, a book library including books in Urdu, Punjabi and Cantonese, and other rooms for teachers from the adult literacy unit and a tutor working with Asian mothers. This scheme is very similar to four centres in Toxteth. These have grown from a Parent Support Programme, and include English language classes, family health, knitting, sewing, keep fit and outings to museums and galleries as well as hospitals, churches and shops. 'Culture Swap' activities have included explanations of Easter and Ramadan, an African hair plaiting demonstration and Chinese New Year celebrations. In these schools parents, friends, and staff have shared an enterprise which enriches the whole neighbourhood including the school.

Other schools have been more concerned to enrol the parents as partners in their children's formal education. A team from one teachers' centre with this aim prepared a guide for parents on *Helping your Child with Reading*. It has useful chapters on Reading; Listening, Talking and Writing; Reading for Information; Children with Reading Difficulties; Do's and Don'ts; Books, Books, Books; Sources of Interest; and Games.[25] These teachers are trying to make parents' natural interest and concern in their children's reading support what the school is doing.

In another area seven primary schools took part in a project whose aim is to 'enhance the effectiveness of individual teachers through establishing and extending home–school links in the teaching of language – spoken, written and reading'. The team believed that if parents became more aware of patterns of learning and child development their children would progress faster. Children took their reading books, flash cards, spelling test cards and other books home, and parents were asked to hear them read or mark their reading cards. The experiment led to greater parental understanding and interest, and some evidence of greater trust between parents and teachers. There was, too, a greater exchange of knowledge and experience between schools, and between teachers in the same school. Many of the children seemed to enjoy their reading more, and some of the parents claimed that their own reading had improved.[26] These successes seem to owe much to the school's success in supporting and guiding parents' natural interest and motivation.[27]

In other schools parental interest is stimulated by open evenings and invitations to assemblies, carol services, concerts and exhibitions. All these activities help to promote understanding and support.

Once contact and mutual confidence has been established teachers may be able to enlist parents' help with home assignments. The following examples of home assignments with children of 8 to 11 have been successful.

Looking for patterns on wrappings, wallpaper and curtains in connection with some mathematical work on tessellations.

Identifying and classifying different materials in the home to study their properties in a subsequent science lesson.

Recording the cost of certain grocery items to compare the cost per unit weight.

Measuring the perimeters of rooms in the house following work on linear measurement.

Collecting examples of trade marks in connection with a class project on 'Heraldry'.

Locating different road signs for subsequent art work on symmetry in our environment.

Finding labels and containers marked in imperial and metric measures for adding to the class conversion graph.

Monitoring the family's intake of food for a day, arising from a television programme about health and diet.

Finding the location of local police stations, hospitals and fire stations for subsequent location on a map of the area.

Interviewing the father about his job after a discussion about the life of a newspaper reporter.

Tracing the family tree in relation to work on 'Heredity'.

Measuring the heights and weights of everyone in the house for incorporation into class family histograms.

Collecting, identifying and pressing some leaves as part of some project work on 'Trees'.

Finding out where all known relatives live and where they were born to help the class examine how family members spread geographically.

Writing an identikit description of a parent to use in group work concerned with the differences between people.

Locating unusual notices and plaques in the environs – 'Things we see but never see.'

Making papier mâché masks or objects using a balloon as a base following a preliminary effort at school.

Collecting different types of lettering from magazines and newspapers to help develop various formats for some illuminated lettering work.

Logging details of a family outing or journey for the subsequent construction of travelgraphs, and speed calculations.

Writing a percussion accompaniment to a tune composed at school and written out by the teacher.[28]

Some schools go further, and use parental help directly. Many have parents helping with a wide range of non-teaching tasks similar to those undertaken by paid ancillaries.[29] Despite their attraction such schemes can pose problems. Two deserve a special mention. One is that the interests of ancillary staff and the views of their trade unions should be considered before a scheme is introduced. Second and more difficult is that not all the parents who offer enthusiastic help will be equally competent. Some offers may even have to be refused, with possible embarrassment and anger. Despite these dangers, such schemes can be valuable. One school has involved parents in activities or hobbies afternoons. Groups of children were taught pottery, Chinese painting, tie-dyeing, macramé, crochet, model-making, chess, sewing, pop-mobility (dancing), cooking and knitting. Each group worked with a parent, with a teacher overseeing the work and discipline of a small cluster of groups.

A good many schools also have formally constituted associations of parents or friends, sometimes meeting to discuss educational, social or health topics but more often engaged in raising funds.[30]

What kinds of links between home and school are possible clearly depends on local circumstances. What is not in doubt is that its pupils' parents constitute for every school one of its richest resources.

Apart from its immediate community and the current generation of parents, a school can also call on other adults who represent the services described in the previous section on resources. The value of these services can be multiplied many times if a school can engage the personal interest and support of their members of staff.

Sometimes formal arrangements may help. Liaison groups in early education were recently established in eleven areas. They included teachers, educational social workers, social workers from the social service departments, health visitors and educational advisers, though they did not include the community or home beat police officer. The groups' regular meetings have succeeded in identifying fruitful areas of cooperation, and establishing the habit of consultation and cooperation.

Such groups may be based on a single school, or perhaps two neighbouring infant schools. In some areas somewhat similar groups with a more extensive membership, including clergy, voluntary and community workers, exist to serve one secondary school and its contributory primary schools.

Groups like these sometimes include also representatives of the school psychological and school health services, whose advice on general as well as individual problems may prove valuable. They may have a particular contribution to make to discussions of assessment and diagnosis, as well as social and personal development. They are, however, more likely to be involved in more detailed discussion about the development of individual children. It is here, too, that parents are most likely to contribute, though some of the liaison groups valued the contribution of their parent members.

We have been able in this chapter to touch on only a few aspects of organization in schools. Our greatest concern is that schools should identify and make the most of the many resources they can have for the asking.

Points to consider and discuss

1. How are the pupils organized in your school, or in each class? Do the considerations which led to the adoption of these forms of organization still apply with equal force?
2. What more could head and assistants do in your school to help those holding special responsibilities to be more effective?
3. Does your school suffer from any of the disadvantages of a small school? What has been done, could be done, by the school to compensate for these disadvantages?
4. Is information about the resources available in the school, and in the community, readily accessible to new teachers? Have you prepared a list of environmental resources in the immediate vicinity of the school? Are there special lists of resources for gifted pupils and slow learners?
5. Have you and your colleagues assessed the difficulty of the teaching and learning materials you use, and established their suitability for the use you make of them? Have you and your colleagues checked that your bookstock does present a reasonably balanced and comprehensive view of events, places and people?
6. What contribution do people outside the school make to its life and work? In what ways and to what extent could this contribution be extended?

XII. Could we be doing better?

'Could we be doing better?' is the simple question which lies behind fundamental ideas like staff development and self-evaluation. The question suggests both a sense of professional responsibility and a very human itch to explore new worlds. It implies too the existence of criteria for assessing what is being done, and readiness to change if current practice falls short of a reasonable standard. Self-assessment is in our blood along with a slight feeling of professional inadequacy, and a belief that that inadequacy could be remedied by reading, learning, discussion, observation, experience or training.

The habits of self-assessment and self-evaluation preceded formal programmes of staff development or school self-evaluation by many generations. This habit led many thousands of teachers to devote a great deal of time and energy to their own professional development. Much of this work may be said to move from practice to aims, unlike formal, top-down programmes of staff development which tend to start with aims and move to practice.

This chapter brings together first a good many examples of self-starting staff development before going on to describe more formal approaches to school evaluation. They in turn should help to identify weaknesses which might be remedied by further programmes of staff development. The process is cyclical and has no end.

Staff development

A great deal of this booklet is about staff development. We are concerned not so much about the scope for staff development outside school, important though that is, but about how schools can initiate their own programmes of staff development. That may mean making use of the facilities offered by teachers' centres, local authorities, colleges, universities, Her Majesty's Inspectorate and others. If they mean attending courses or study away from school, the most important question is how the whole school can benefit. But there is great scope for staff development inside even the smallest schools.

Teachers who are thinking hard about aims and objectives or about describing the curriculum, teachers who are working on systems of assessment or records, teachers who are making careful surveys of resources, all these and others whose innovative work is mentioned in these pages are making themselves better teachers.

This staff development is of two kinds. Sometimes it is about individual development. Sometimes it is about groups of teachers working more effectively together. Often the two go hand in hand as some of the following examples show. In some the initiative seems to have come from one person, in others from a group of teachers. In some the schools seem to be self-sufficient, in others the help of a college or an LEA is evident. In each case, the central question for those involved in the development, and for others who want to profit from their experience, is whether a different approach might have brought better results. Would it have been helpful, for example, to have adopted a whole-staff approach, or to have won active support from outside the school?

Introduction of new teaching approaches
In one first school which was open-plan, the headmistress, a member of the Association of Teachers of Mathematics, took a great interest in mathematics and wished to promote a particular way of working in which practical work and discussion were given a high priority. She felt that many of the difficulties pupils have with the subject stem from too much formal arithmetic, written down with little understanding, and a lack of practical work and discussion, particularly in the early stages. In order to implement her ideas she spent time working with pupils alongside their teachers. This led the staff to develop new teaching techniques: in particular there was much more discussion and questioning of pupils and informal recording of work by pupils. Changes were supported by the school's close contact with a lecturer in a local college of education. Student teachers visited and worked in the school; together with teachers they organized projects, including a study of 'the seashore'.

Keeping current practice under review
In an infant school, the staff met regularly over lunch once each week to discuss educational matters, such as policy about parts of the curriculum, concern about a child's or group of children's learning or how and when to teach a particular point. Visitors were invited to staff meetings from time to time; once an LEA mathematics adviser came and after a brief introductory talk from him they discussed problems related to the teaching of mathematics in their school. This encouraged further discussion, stimulated interest and led to changes in teaching.

Helping individual teachers to develop their skills
In another infant school there was a teacher with a post of responsibility for mathematics and one with responsibility for reading and language development, both of whom had attended L E A courses on 'slow learners' and had a particular interest in children's learning difficulties. The headmistress took occasional classes so that the teachers with special responsibility could go into the probationary teacher's classroom and work with her for a while, taking in some of the material which they had used and found successful. The head also took the probationer's class so that she could visit other rooms and see how teachers organized their classes, used materials and taught particular aspects of the curriculum. The headmistress hoped to extend this practice to involve the whole staff.[1]

The whole staff work on a recognized problem
At one inner-city school with about 100 pupils, of whom half have a mother tongue other than English, the teachers met regularly to find more effective ways of meeting their pupils' language needs, encouraging their interest in books, and developing the school's reading policies.[2]

Some teachers monitor the effects of change
When another infant school introduced a new mathematical scheme, four teachers agreed to monitor the change. They have studied the sequence in which children acquire knowledge and skills, and the link between their grasp of mathematical ideas and their use of language, particularly words like 'less' and 'more'. The teachers also devised a home mathematics pack for parents and are holding an open evening on mathematics. Two of the teachers have written detailed papers about their work.[3]

Two schools work together
The same teachers have also collaborated with, and provided mutual reinforcement for, a team of two teachers in another school. This second team were concerned with problems of understanding in the reception class. They say: 'by recording events as they happened and reflecting on them afterwards, by reading transcripts and discussing outcomes together, we were able to see patterns emerging, and the progression which had seemed to be imperceptible was made explicit'.[4]

A group of schools tackle a problem together
Collaboration between teachers in different schools sometimes occurs on a wider scale. In one area teachers from nine schools with a high proportion of children with English as a second language set out to discuss and seek solutions to the language problems they were finding. The teachers began

to produce materials. Through discussion of what they have produced they developed higher standards and have learned to accept criticism of their own work. The teachers have produced seventeen work packs ranging from a nursery starter pack to secondary mathematics, and have been able to provide materials for twelve other schools with only a few recent immigrants.[5]

Another group of teachers came into existence when one teacher asked whether a college could put her in touch with other infant teachers who would be interested in studying how children learn to write. The outcome was the creation of a group of six teachers, a retired headteacher and two college staff. They found little published work on the subject so decided that each teacher should make a special study of two boys and two girls in their existing class.[6]

Other similar groups depend on a local authority rather than a college connection. In one authority a group of twelve primary teachers contributed to the production of materials for local studies, and then began a systematic examination of the effects of using the materials. As part of their work the group has

i identified schools where the materials produced have been used by a variety of classes and age groups, and with teachers of varying interests;

ii devised instruments (e.g. a schedule) which have helped classroom observation of the ways in which interaction between teacher and child has been modified;

iii mounted an exhibition of pupils' work to demonstrate ways in which attitudes and skills have been changed by following a local studies work pack programme;

iv devised an instrument to help self-evaluation and assessment of the materials by the teacher, and also assessment of the relative merits of the various teaching styles in social and environmental studies teaching.[7]

Sharing the benefits of an outside course
Outside courses are among the most obvious form of staff development, but the longer they are, the more risk there is of the benefits being limited to those who attended the course. One large school tackled this problem by arranging a series of after-school workshops led by a teacher who had attended an outside course in science. The school also created four pairs of teachers who were to collaborate in turn, while they had some additional help from an extra part-time teacher in working on a small science project. When the trial materials were used, some of the lessons were taped so that the whole staff could discuss the transcript.[8]

Finding a critical friend – inside the school
At several other schools pairs of teachers have entered into a working partnership in which each takes it in turn to act as teacher and as observer. The teacher partner decides what is to be observed, and the observer then gathers evidence. The partners interpret the evidence together, and decide what response to make.[9] Headteachers and senior staff have a particular responsibility to offer this kind of help to their colleagues.

– and outside the school
In much the same way, other teachers have gone into partnership with an outsider, an LEA adviser, a university or college lecturer, or a teacher adviser, who collects evidence on a problem specified by the teacher. A teacher might ask an observer to note any recurring elements in the teacher's conduct, what style the teacher usually adopts, whether the teacher concentrates on a few children, whether the teacher uses praise much or little and whether there is any tendency to bias or discrimination. The two then interpret the evidence together.[10]

Recording and analysing your own activities
The use of a friendly observer, like the use of a tape, is based on the assumption that analysis of a careful record of what happened in a class will help to develop teachers' awareness. One way of doing this is to ask teachers to record their own behaviour as accurately as possible, and then reflect on it. They may be able to tape a lesson, or parts of a lesson, to listen critically to what they say or to record features of their behaviour. For example, a few infant teachers were asked to keep a systematic note of when they were in the habit of touching children, and then to touch children no less but only when they wanted to praise the children. This led to noticeable changes in the children's behaviour.

Assessing the children's response
The scope for young children to contribute to a teacher's self-evaluation is very limited. They find it hard enough to say whether they have enjoyed a particular lesson, and even harder to explain why. But one teacher persisted in his efforts to use his class of second-year juniors in his own self-evaluation. He used a cassette recorder to take his discussions with one group whom he hoped to engage in conversation and discussion. The technique helped the teacher to check whether his teaching points were clearly made, and whether his questions stimulated discussion. In that way the children's recorded response became part of the process of self-evaluation for one teacher. On a wider scale, assessing the children's

performance provides important evidence about the validity of a school's aims, and its success in achieving those aims.

Another teacher was concerned about whether the quiet and unobtrusive children in his class were making reasonable progress. He chose to watch two 7-year-olds who seemed to cope quite well, but who contributed little. He began by using a notebook to record their activities in class for a whole day, and then decided to tape-record group discussions in which these two children were involved. With experience he found that he and his fellow teachers were able to try different approaches to involve these two children in group and class activities, and that after a few weeks the children had become more confident. It is difficult for teachers to organize their classes so that they can bear a particular child in mind for a period, and difficult to justify the apparent unfairness of concentrating on one or two children. But this teacher found that he had developed his appreciation of different teaching methods and his awareness of individual pupils.[11]

Visits and exchanges
Another means of developing keener awareness is for teachers to visit other schools, or even to exchange posts with teachers in other schools. Their knowledge of the subtle differences between schools should help to make them more aware, and more self-critical. Some comparable benefit may come from a change in the same school, as one deputy head observed:

> After years in the upper end of the junior school, suddenly being confronted with a group of lower juniors proved an invigorating challenge for me. No longer could I use well-worn lessons; no longer could certain assumptions be made; abilities could not be taken for granted. Changes of age range and of classroom can involve different emphases, and often mean communicating and working with teachers with whom one would not normally become closely involved.

Sometimes secondary schools and their contributory primary schools arrange exchanges like this. One secondary school with one major contributory primary school arranged for teachers freed in the summer from fifth-year classes to visit the junior school and teach mathematics to the children who were to transfer later that year. This released some of the primary teachers to visit the secondary school to get a flavour of the mathematics their pupils would be doing.[12]

Art teachers at the same secondary school decided to visit the junior school instead of enjoying their annual moan about the low standard of work in the first year. To their surprise they were enthralled by the variety and quality of art in the junior school, and the quality of display. Instead of criticizing the junior teachers they found they had to ask why their first-year art was so dull. They decided their expectations, particularly of skills in drawing and painting, had been too high. For their part the junior teachers agreed that they had probably sacrificed skills for width of experience. Out of their exchange visits came mutual understanding, and commitment to developing a joint approach to the top junior and first-year secondary course.[13] Similarly teachers may learn much if they can arrange to visit special schools or special units, particularly those serving the same community as their own schools.

These examples could be multiplied many times. They show how many teachers are actively engaged in programmes of self-development, arising often from their immediate problems and concerns, and how many different approaches there are. They show, too, that much can be done, even in small schools, and how much is achieved in collaboration with other teachers in the same or other schools.

Many of the teachers in our examples made a point of emphasizing the benefits of working in partnership. This seems to us to highlight the need for all schools to have regular meetings of teachers to identify problems that can be tackled collaboratively. One head led her colleagues in a series of discussions to identify their own development needs. They began in an unthreatening way by reviewing their existing structure.

For example, the early discussions in my school were concerned with compiling a staff file from various papers issued during recent years. This included curriculum guidelines, useful information, notes on school organization and the use of programmed materials.

The next step was to devise an exercise. This consisted of a workshop in which play materials (e.g. House play, bricks, sand, water, paint, etc.), the teachers' strategies and the learning skills which could be expected to develop, were related. This was a useful activity and resulted in renewed awareness of the thought and careful planning necessary for the development of activities that could be regarded as therapeutic or occupational. This activity was extended to relate learning skills to each teacher's specialist curriculum area. In particular teachers described an activity plan, its aims, its relation to learning skills and evaluation. These discussions were interspersed with the dissemination of material from three courses attended by different members of staff.

To some extent these early discussions were extensions of long-established practice. It became apparent that to plan a programme of in-service work an appraisal of the school was necessary. An analysis of the school's stage of development in relation to teachers' ideas, parents' ideas, the authority's ideas and society's idea of what a school ought to be, is less threatening than beginning with the needs of individual teachers.[14]

They found it helpful to display much of this information under four main headings: outside influences, the curriculum, staff development, and in-service training. The notes on in-service training included details of the sources and methods of in-service training, and consideration of its purpose and how the school could make best use of the opportunities available. Whatever the outcome in formal in-service training the process described was itself an important exercise in collaborative staff development, and of great value for its own sake.

Evaluation and self-evaluation

A fairly systematic review of the existing structures may prove to be a useful starting point for some more extensive process of self-evaluation. At a time when there is a great and growing commitment to self-evaluation, we believe it is important to be clear about why schools should undertake so difficult and complex a task, and how they can benefit most from self-evaluation.

The interest in school self-evaluation is undeniable. About thirty local authorities have published booklets on school self-evaluation and another fifty have a somewhat less substantial document on the subject. Some of these documents seem to be based on the belief that schools and their teachers need some help in carrying out a responsibility which all accept, that of checking whether their work is as effective as they would wish it, or as it might be. These documents emphasize professional responsibility. Some of the others seem to start from the feeling that those who fund the schools have a right to know how the schools are doing, and might insist on some external evaluation if the schools did not evaluate themselves. These documents emphasize public accountability.

The problem now is not whether, but how, schools should embark on self-evaluation. There is of course a related need for individual teachers to evaluate their personal performance, but we are concerned here with how the school sets about evaluating itself.

The task is formidable. Gordon Elliot has published an extensive bibliography of publications relating to self-evaluation generally, and specifically in physical education and recreation, languages and mathematics.[15] The detailed schemes recommended by some local authorities run to 120 separate questions, or more. The categories for evaluation outlined in one such document are:

A. The curriculum

1. Aims and Objectives
2. Curriculum Design and Planning
   Language and Literacy
   Mathematics
   Religious and Moral Education
   Aesthetic Education

Social, Health and Safety Education
3. Curriculum Evaluation, Revision and Modification
4. Teaching Styles and Classroom Organization.

B. Staff development

1. School-focused In-service Education
2. Personal/Professional Development of Teaching Staff
3. Teachers with Special Responsibilities
4. Evaluation of Teachers within the School.

C. The school and the community

1. Information to Parents
2. Involvement of Parents in the Daily Organization of the School
3. Information to Governing Bodies
4. The School's Involvement in the Local Community.

D. Record-keeping and pupil profiles

1. County Procedures for Individual Pupil Profiles
2. Classroom Records
3. School Records.

E. Resources

1. Organization of Resources
2. Budgetary Policies
3. Maintenance and Care of the Environment, Plant and Equipment.[16]

Local authorities are naturally anxious that schools should consider reviewing all aspects of their being and activity. On the other hand, the kinds of checklist suggested by some local authorities involve a great deal of work in collecting information and evidence about a school. The only justification for such an expenditure of time, intelligence and effort is that the process of review and evaluation should provide teachers with signposts for action. Formal checklists might tend to concentrate on things which can be easily measured, and to skate over more difficult questions about what the pupils actually learned, whether it was worthwhile, and how the teachers might improve their own teaching and the pupils' performance. Those most intimately involved in the life of a school, and above all its teachers, will be particularly concerned with questions of quality like these.

In our view the schedules H M I used for their primary survey[17] provide the best basis for a wide-ranging curricular review and evaluation, and we have therefore reproduced them in Appendix E. In using even those schedules, schools need to be careful, since the authors of any scheme of review and evaluation have their own ideas about what is important. Before adopting this or any other scheme devised by people outside the school, teachers will need to assure themselves that the terms of the review and their own aims are compatible.

In using an outside checklist, teachers may also wish to consider whether it is worth answering all the questions at once. If their review is intended to lead to action, they may feel it is wiser to concentrate first on one area of the school's life and work which is causing particular concern. Collecting what is agreed to be appropriate information and evidence about one such problem area, deciding whether the evidence shows room for improvement, agreeing how to effect improvements, and taking action, is likely to consume a great deal of time and energy.

Another factor to take into account when considering the form and extent of any review is the climate of the school, and its readiness for such an exercise. Most primary schools have a relatively informal organization which encourages experiments and innovation, and provides opportunities to respond to children's individual differences and needs.

In some schools, however, this informality may make it difficult to embark on any very systematic discussion. In their recent first school survey H M I found, for example, that fewer than half the schools had staff meetings.[18] It is difficult to imagine how these schools could set about evaluating their aims, processes and achievement.

In other schools, the style of leadership may create somewhat different problems. Staff commitment is necessary for success, but the staff are unlikely to feel much commitment if they feel that the head has imposed institutional self-evaluation on them, or that the purpose of the review is to assess their own performance.

A fairly open style of leadership and group discussion and decision-making seem to be the best basis for self-evaluation. Success seems to depend on teachers showing some of the qualities of empathy, tolerance and mutual respect generated by a good programme of personal and social development.

It seems important that all the staff of a school should take part in any self-evaluation exercise and that they should all have an equal opportunity to contribute. Some teachers may not have sufficient confidence to do this, at first, so schools may need to make a cautious start by preparing a neutral statement of the existing position of the school.[19]

The first stage, in which schools may wish to involve governors, parents, pupils and possibly the community at large, should provide evidence on which teachers can decide which aspects of the school need to be changed.

They are then in a position to prepare a development programme. This should not be too ambitious. The development programme should above all be feasible in terms of available resources. Frustration and bitterness may follow if the time spent on evaluation does not lead to change and improvement. It may well be practicable only if the LEA's advisers also contribute their knowledge of the authority's resources and plans for curriculum development.

To summarize, we would suggest five checkpoints for schools contemplating a programme of review, evaluation and development.

1. Gain the commitment of staff to conducting the programme;
2. Decide the strategy and timing of the review and evaluation; in particular secure explicit agreement on the purposes of the evaluation;
3. Agree which members of staff are to be responsible for collecting, collating and analysing evidence;
4. After deciding which aspects of the school's work are to be developed, apply great care to planning what is to be done;
5. Ensure that all staff are kept informed of progress in the evaluation and development phases.

One group of twelve primary schools are taking part in a joint programme of self-evaluation.[20] They emphasized that procedures for self-evaluation should:

a be based upon clearly specified aims or objectives;
b be adaptable to the differing requirements of individual schools;
c provide information based on evidence whereby either
    i change can be justified, or
    ii the need for more evidence can be identified;
d be capable of involving all members of staff within the school;
e be operable within realistic time and resource parameters;
f lend itself to obtaining the support and involvement of governors and the authority; and
g lead to clearly identifiable pupil benefits.

These teachers clearly have their feet on the ground. For them self evaluation is not an airy fairy abstraction, but a practical matter of improving their pupils' education. This is illustrated in the experience of one of the schools whose teachers identified eight ways of responding to the principles they had agreed on. Their principles were as follows:

1. Each child is unique, and chronological age is but a rough guide to the state of a child's physical, emotional and intellectual development.
2. Children need to be active in their own learning.

3. Almost all (some might say all) children can become motivated. 'Naughty' and 'lazy' children are those we have failed to motivate.
4. It is important that children learn to discriminate and to help them they must be offered constant opportunities to make decisions.
5. Personal relationships between everyone in the school are extremely important.
6. There is a need to involve parents in the life of the school.

Their ways of putting these principles into effect were set out in the following terms:

1. To reduce the scale of relationships for the child and to encourage meaningful discussions between staff, the school is divided into three Houses which are fairly autonomous and which may be regarded as mini-schools within the whole school.
2. We believe that vertical grouping is a way to take account of individual development rates.
3. As far as possible each child should have individual programmes in the basic subjects.
4. Groups should be formed whenever appropriate but their composition must remain fluid.
5. The belief in activity is reflected in both the internal arrangement of teaching space and in the materials and time provided.
6. Each week teachers will take part in both a House lunch discussion and a full staff meeting.
7. The school is designated a Community School which results in the involvement of the school in the village and the village in the school.
8. Generally speaking each teacher is responsible for the basic subject work for the children in her group although the pairing of teachers does allow for cooperative teaching at all levels. Teachers wishing to go beyond this into team teaching arrangements do so only after careful thought and consultation.

Not all readers will necessarily agree with the principles these teachers adopted, or that they found the right means of putting their principles into effect. For the teachers in that school the most important aspect of their work is that it led on to a statement of more detailed objectives, and the whole document provides a splendid base for later review and evaluation.

Another junior and infant school[21] adopted the more formal approach suggested by the GRIDS project. The school is in two buildings one and a half miles apart and has had to share some of its temporary accommodation with another school. The local authority's chief adviser explained this approach to self-evaluation to the whole staff, each of whom then completed an initial survey intended to establish which area of the school's work should be reviewed first. The head collated these replies and decided that science should be the first, because she thought some of the other suggestions, like continuity, liaison with secondary schools, and subject integration, were too hard. The staff then agreed which teachers were to take part in the review, and the head agreed to make time for the review by taking some of their lessons. The review team met for half an hour once a week for one term with some help from an LEA adviser and two college lecturers, and came up with recommendations for a new science scheme from 5 to 11. The local authority provided funds for some necessary equipment and materials, and the lecturers gave demonstration lessons using the new scheme.

This specific review has been so successful that the staff have already adopted the same approach to reviewing the school's schemes of testing and assessment, and its mathematics programme. The process of review, energetically supported by LEA and college has been a great stimulus to an otherwise rather depressed community.

As in our comments on staff development, we have tended to emphasize in these notes on self-evaluation the extent to which schools can help themselves. But the last example shows how important external initiatives and support can be. In this instance, external support played a major part in creating staff unity and commitment to review, evaluation, and change.

That seems to us to be among the most valuable and creative contribution external agencies can make.

Conclusion

Throughout these chapters one theme recurs: how much the staff of a school can achieve, how much enhance their own effectiveness, if they can work collegially. That sort of unity and mutual understanding is born of shared experience. One possibility, not often mentioned, is that teachers should read and discuss some of the same professional books. Indeed, in preparing *The Practical Curriculum* we had in mind its use in that sort of way. We think every school staffroom ought to have a small collection of professional books, updated regularly, with each new acquisition the subject of systematic consideration by a group of teachers. On pages 220–21 we list the titles of twenty-six books costing only £100 in all, which might form the nucleus of such a collection in every primary school. We hope this *Primary Practice* will be among the most thumbed volumes in that collection.

Points to consider and discuss

Could you be doing better? What has to be done for you to do better?

Appendices

Appendix A Objectives for children learning science: guidelines to keep in mind

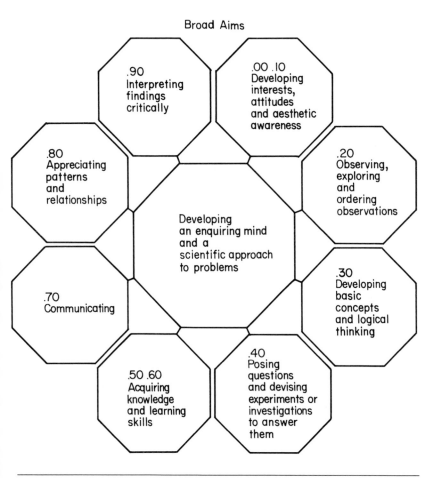

Broad Aims

.90 Interpreting findings critically

.00 .10 Developing interests, attitudes and aesthetic awareness

.80 Appreciating patterns and relationships

.20 Observing, exploring and ordering observations

Developing an enquiring mind and a scientific approach to problems

.70 Communicating

.30 Developing basic concepts and logical thinking

.50 .60 Acquiring knowledge and learning skills

.40 Posing questions and devising experiments or investigations to answer them

This appendix is reproduced from Schools Council Science 5/13 Project, *With Objectives in Mind*, Macdonald Educational for the Schools Council, 1972, pp. 60–65.

What we mean by Stage 1, Stage 2 and Stage 3

Stage 1
Transition from intuition to concrete operations. Infants generally.

The characteristics of thought among infant children differ in important respects from those of children over the age of about 7 years. Infant thought has been described as 'intuitive' by Piaget; it is closely associated with physical action and is dominated by immediate observation. Generally the infant is not able to think about or imagine the consequences of an action unless he has actually carried it out, nor is he yet likely to draw logical conclusions from his experiences. At this early stage the objectives are those concerned with active exploration of the immediate environment and the development of ability to discuss and communicate effectively: they relate to the kind of activities that are appropriate to these very young children, and which form an introduction to ways of exploring and of ordering observations.

Concrete operations. Early stage.

In this Stage, children are developing the ability to manipulate things mentally. At first this ability is limited to objects and materials that can be manipulated concretely, and even then only in a restricted way. The objectives here are concerned with developing these mental operations through exploration of concrete objects and materials – that is to say, objects and materials which, as physical things, have meaning for the child. Since older children, and even adults, prefer an introduction to new ideas and problems through concrete example and physical exploration, these objectives are suitable for all children, whatever their age, who are being introduced to certain science activities for the first time.

Stage 2
Concrete operations. Later stage.

In this Stage, a continuation of what Piaget calls the stage of concrete operations, the mental manipulations are becoming more varied and powerful. The developing ability to handle variables – for example, in dealing with multiple classification – means that problems can be solved in more ordered and quantitative ways than was previously possible. The objectives begin to be more specific to the exploration of the scientific aspects of the environment rather than to general experience as previously. These objectives are developments of those of Stage 1 and depend on them for a foundation. They are those thought of as being appropriate for all children who have progressed from Stage 1 and not merely for 9- to 11-year-olds.

Stage 3
Transition to stage of abstract thinking.

This is the Stage in which, for some children, the ability to think about abstractions is developing. When this development is complete their thought is capable of dealing with the possible and hypothetical, and is not tied to the concrete and to the here and now. It may take place between 11 and 13 for some able children, for some children it may happen later, and for others it may never occur. The objectives of this stage are ones which involve development of ability to use hypothetical reasoning and to separate and combine variables in a systematic way. They are appropriate to those who have achieved most of the Stage 2 objectives and who now show signs of ability to manipulate mentally ideas and propositions.

Attitudes, interests and aesthetic awareness
.00/.10

1.01 Willingness to ask questions.
1.02 Willingness to handle both living and non-living material.
1.03 Sensitivity to the need for giving proper care to living things.
1.04 Enjoyment in using all the senses for exploring and discriminating.
1.05 Willingness to collect material for observation or investigation.

1.06 Desire to find out things for oneself.
1.07 Willing participation in group work.
1.08 Willing compliance with safety regulations in handling tools and equipment.
1.09 Appreciation of the need to learn the meaning of new words and to use them correctly.

2.01 Willingness to cooperate with others in science activities.
2.02 Willingness to observe objectively.
2.03 Appreciation of the reasons for safety regulations.
2.04 Enjoyment in examining ambiguity in the use of words.
2.05 Interest in choosing suitable means of expressing results and observations.
2.06 Willingness to assume responsibility for the proper care of living things.
2.07 Willingness to examine critically the results of their own and others' work.
2.08 Preference for putting ideas to test before accepting or rejecting them.
2.09 Appreciation that approximate methods of comparison may be more appropriate than careful measurements.

3.01 Acceptance of responsibility for their own and others' safety in experiments.
3.02 Preference for using words correctly.
3.03 Commitment to the idea of physical cause and effect.
3.04 Recognition of the need to standardize measurements.
3.05 Willingness to examine evidence critically.
3.06 Willingness to consider beforehand the usefulness of the results from a possible experiment.
3.07 Preference for choosing the most appropriate means of expressing results or observations.
3.08 Recognition of the need to acquire new skills.
3.09 Willingness to consider the role of science in everyday life.

Attitudes, interests and aesthetic awareness
.00/.10

Stage 1
Transition from
intuition to
concrete
operations.
Infants
generally.

Concrete operations. Early stage.	*1.11*	Awareness that there are various ways of testing out ideas and making observations.
	1.12	Interest in comparing and classifying living or non-living things.
	1.13	Enjoyment in comparing measurements with estimates.
	1.14	Awareness that there are various ways of expressing results and observations.
	1.15	Willingness to wait and to keep records in order to observe change in things.
	1.16	Enjoyment in exploring the variety of living things in the environment.
	1.17	Interest in discussing and comparing the aesthetic qualities of materials.

Stage 2 Concrete operations. Later stage.	*2.11*	Enjoyment in developing methods for solving problems or testing ideas.
	2.12	Appreciation of the part that aesthetic qualities of materials play in determining their use.
	2.13	Interest in the way discoveries were made in the past.

Stage 3 Transition to stage of abstract thinking.	*3.11*	Appreciation of the main principles in the care of living things.
	3.12	Willingness to extend methods used in science activities to other fields of experience.

Observing, exploring and ordering observations
.20

1.21 Appreciation of the variety of living things and materials in the environment.
1.22 Awareness of changes which take place as time passes.
1.23 Recognition of common shapes – square, circle, triangle.
1.24 Recognition of regularity in patterns.
1.25 Ability to group things consistently according to chosen or given criteria.

1.26 Awareness of the structure and form of living things.
1.27 Awareness of change of living things and non-living materials.
1.28 Recognition of the action of force.
1.29 Ability to group living and non-living things by observable attributes.
1.29a Ability to distinguish regularity in events and motion.

2.21 Awareness of internal structure in living and non-living things.
2.22 Ability to construct and use keys for identification.
2.23 Recognition of similar and congruent shapes.
2.24 Awareness of symmetry in shapes and structures.
2.25 Ability to classify living things and non-living materials in different ways.
2.26 Ability to visualize objects from different angles and the shape of cross-sections.

3.21 Appreciation that classification criteria are arbitrary.
3.22 Ability to distinguish observations which are relevant to the solution of a problem from those which are not.
3.23 Ability to estimate the order of magnitude of physical quantities.

Developing basic concepts and logical thinking
.30

Stage 1 Transition from intuition to concrete operations. Infants generally.	*1.31* Awareness of the meaning of words which describe various types of quantity. *1.32* Appreciation that things which are different may have features in common.

Concrete operations. Early stage.	*1.33* Ability to predict the effect of certain changes through observation of similar changes. *1.34* Formation of the notions of the horizontal and the vertical. *1.35* Development of concepts of conservation of length and substance. *1.36* Awareness of the meaning of speed and of its relation to distance covered.

Stage 2 Concrete operations. Later stage.	*2.31* Appreciation of measurement as division into regular parts and repeated comparison with a unit. *2.32* Appreciation that comparisons can be made indirectly by use of an intermediary. *2.33* Development of concepts of conservation of weight, area and volume. *2.34* Appreciation of weight as a downward force. *2.35* Understanding of the speed, time, distance relation.

Stage 3 Transition to stage of abstract thinking.	*3.31* Familiarity with relationships involving velocity, distance, time, acceleration. *3.32* Ability to separate, exclude or combine variables in approaching problems. *3.33* Ability to formulate hypotheses not dependent upon direct observation. *3.34* Ability to extend reasoning beyond the actual to the possible. *3.35* Ability to distinguish a logically sound proof from others less sound.

Posing questions and devising experiments or investigations to answer them

.40

1.41 Ability to find answers to simple problems by investigation.
1.42 Ability to make comparisons in terms of one property or variable.

1.43 Appreciation of the need for measurement.
1.44 Awareness that more than one variable may be involved in a particular change.

2.41 Ability to frame questions likely to be answered through investigations.
2.42 Ability to investigate variables and to discover effective ones.
2.43 Appreciation of the need to control variables and use controls in investigations.
2.44 Ability to choose and use either arbitrary or standard units of measurement as appropriate.
2.45 Ability to select a suitable degree of approximation and work to it.
2.46 Ability to use representational models for investigating problems or relationships.

3.41 Attempting to identify the essential steps in approaching a problem scientifically.
3.42 Ability to design experiments with effective controls for testing hypotheses.
3.43 Ability to visualize a hypothetical situation as a useful simplification of actual observations.
3.44 Ability to construct scale models for investigation and to appreciate implications of changing the scale.

Acquiring knowledge and learning skills
.50/.60

Stage 1 Transition from intuition to concrete operations. Infants generally.	*1.51* Ability to discriminate between different materials. *1.52* Awareness of the characteristics of living things. *1.53* Awareness of properties which materials can have. *1.54* Ability to use displayed reference material for identifying living and non-living things.
Concrete operations. Early stage.	*1.55* Familiarity with sources of sound. *1.56* Awareness of sources of heat, light and electricity. *1.57* Knowledge that change can be produced in common substances. *1.58* Appreciation that ability to move or cause movement requires energy. *1.59* Knowledge of differences in properties between and within common groups of materials.
Stage 2 Concrete operations Later stage.	*2.51* Knowledge of conditions which promote changes in living things and non-living materials. *2.52* Familiarity with a wide range of forces and of ways in which they can be changed. *2.53* Knowledge of sources and simple properties of common forms of energy. *2.54* Knowledge of the origins of common materials. *2.55* Awareness of some discoveries and inventions by famous scientists. *2.56* Knowledge of ways to investigate and measure properties of living things and non-living materials. *2.57* Awareness of changes in the design of measuring instruments and tools during man's history. *2.58* Skill in devising and constructing simple apparatus. *2.59* Ability to select relevant information from books or other reference material.
Stage 3 Transition to stage of abstract thinking.	*3.51* Knowledge that chemical change results from interaction. *3.52* Knowledge that energy can be stored and converted in various ways. *3.53* Awareness of the universal nature of gravity. *3.54* Knowledge of the main constituents and variations in the composition of soil and of the earth. *3.55* Knowledge that properties of matter can be explained by reference to its particulate nature. *3.56* Knowledge of certain properties of heat, light, sound, electrical, mechanical and chemical energy. *3.57* Knowledge of a wide range of living organisms. *3.58* Development of the concept of an internal environment. *3.59* Knowledge of the nature and variations in basic life processes.

Acquiring knowledge and learning skills
.50/.60

1.61 Appreciation of man's use of other living things and their products.
1.62 Awareness that man's way of life has changed through the ages.
1.63 Skill in manipulating tools and materials.
1.64 Development of techniques for handling living things correctly.
1.65 Ability to use books for supplementing ideas or information.

3.61 Appreciation of levels of organization in living things.
3.62 Appreciation of the significance of the work and ideas of some famous scientists.
3.63 Ability to apply relevant knowledge without help of contextual cues.
3.64 Ability to use scientific equipment and instruments for extending the range of human senses.

Communicating

.70

Stage 1
Transition from
intuition to
concrete
operations.
Infants
generally.

1.71 Ability to use new words appropriately.
1.72 Ability to record events in their sequences.
1.73 Ability to discuss and record impressions of living and non-living things in the environment.
1.74 Ability to use representational symbols for recording information on charts or block graphs.

- -

Concrete
operations.
Early stage.

1.75 Ability to tabulate information and use tables.
1.76 Familiarity with names of living things and non-living materials.
1.77 Ability to record impressions by making models, painting or drawing.

Stage 2
Concrete
operations.
Later stage.

2.71 Ability to use non-representational symbols in plans, charts, etc.
2.72 Ability to interpret observations in terms of trends and rates of change.
2.73 Ability to use histograms and other simple graphical forms for communicating data.
2.74 Ability to construct models as a means of recording observations.

Stage 3
Transition to
stage of
abstract
thinking.

3.71 Ability to select the graphical form most appropriate to the information being recorded.
3.72 Ability to use three-dimensional models or graphs for recording results.
3.73 Ability to deduce information from graphs: from gradient, area, intercept.
3.74 Ability to use analogies to explain scientific ideas and theories.

Appreciating patterns and relationships
.80

1.81 Awareness of cause–effect relationships.

1.82 Development of a concept of environment.
1.83 Formation of a broad idea of variation in living things.
1.84 Awareness of seasonal changes in living things.
1.85 Awareness of differences in physical conditions between different parts of the Earth.

2.81 Awareness of sequences of change in natural phenomena.
2.82 Awareness of structure–function relationship in parts of living things.
2.83 Appreciation of interdependence among living things.
2.84 Awareness of the impact of man's activities on other living things.
2.85 Awareness of the changes in the physical environment brought about by man's activity.
2.86 Appreciation of the relationships of parts and wholes.

3.81 Recognition that the ratio of volume to surface area is significant.
3.82 Appreciation of the scale of the universe.
3.83 Understanding of the nature and significance of changes in living and non-living things.
3.84 Recognition that energy has many forms and is conserved when it is changed from one form to another.
3.85 Recognition of man's impact on living things – conservation, change, control.
3.86 Appreciation of the social implications of man's changing use of materials, historical and contemporary.
3.87 Appreciation of the social implications of research in science.
3.88 Appreciation of the role of science in the changing pattern of provision for human needs.

Interpreting findings critically
.90

Stage 1 Transition from intuition to concrete operations. Infants generally.	*1.91*	Awareness that the apparent size, shape and relationships of things depend on the position of the observer.

Concrete operations. Early stage.	*1.92*	Appreciation that properties of materials influence their use.

Stage 2 Concrete operations. Later stage.	*2.91* *2.92* *2.93* *2.94*	Appreciation of adaptation to environment. Appreciation of how the form and structure of materials relate to their function and properties. Awareness that many factors need to be considered when choosing a material for a particular use. Recognition of the role of chance in making measurements and experiments.

Stage 3 Transition to stage of abstract thinking.	*3.91* *3.92* *3.93* *3.94* *3.95* *3.96*	Ability to draw from observations conclusions that are unbiased by preconception. Willingness to accept factual evidence despite perceptual contradictions. Awareness that the degree of accuracy of measurements has to be taken into account when results are interpreted. Awareness that unstated assumptions can affect conclusions drawn from argument or experimental results. Appreciation of the need to integrate findings into a simplifying generalization. Willingness to check that conclusions are consistent with further evidence.

These Stages we have chosen conform to modern ideas about children's learning. They conveniently describe for us the mental development of children between the ages of 5 and 13 years, but it must be remembered that ALTHOUGH CHILDREN GO THROUGH THESE STAGES IN THE SAME ORDER THEY DO NOT GO THROUGH THEM AT THE SAME RATES.
SOME children achieve the later Stages at an early age.
SOME loiter in the early Stages for quite a time.
SOME never have the mental ability to develop to the later Stages.
ALL appear to be ragged in their movement from one Stage to another.
Our Stages, then, are not tied to chronological age, so in any one class of children there will be, almost certainly, some children at differing Stages of mental development.

Appendix B The curriculum in primary schools

By the time children enter primary schools at about 5 years of age most have learnt to behave in a reasonably social way, though they may be unaccustomed to being members of such a large community as a school. They are likely to have acquired the basic structures of their mother tongue, not always English, and be aware of and interested in the shapes, sizes, colours and quantities of things about them.

INDIVIDUAL DIFFERENCES AND COMMON NEEDS

Each individual brings a different set of experiences to bear on his schooling. These differences arise from variety in the surroundings in which children are brought up, from the degree of support and encouragement they have had from adults, and from differences in what their powers of imagination and intellect have allowed them to make of their experiences. At 5, a few have a vocabulary that is barely sufficient for their daily needs, while at the other extreme a small minority have a wide vocabulary, can detect fine shades of meaning and have begun to recognize written words; and a few have started to write.

At one level of generality, all children in primary schools need to be occupied in a programme that will enable them:

> to engage with other children and with adults in a variety of working and social relationships;
> to increase their range and understanding of English, and particularly to develop their ability and inclination to read and write for information and imaginative stimulation;
> to acquire better physical control when they are writing, or exercising utilitarian skills and engaging in imaginative expression in art, craft, music, drama or movement generally.

Furthermore, if they are to extend their powers of language, children must be brought into contact with new experiences and ideas or look afresh at old experiences through discussion with teachers and through the use of books, role playing and audio-visual material. Studies of the beliefs and ways of life of historical characters and of people and communities who live today in other parts of the world, or indeed elsewhere in Britain, provide opportunities for language develop-

Reproduced by permission of the Controller, HM Stationery Office, from Department of Education and Science, *A View of the Curriculum* (HMI Matters for Discussion Series), HMSO, 1980, pp. 7–12.

ment through discussion, reading and writing. Moreover, these studies are valuable in their own right. This is especially so in a country that is multi-cultural. Learning about the nature of materials and about the needs and life cycles of plants and animals provides further opportunities for the extension and application of language and of mathematical skills and ideas. It also helps children to appreciate the world around them and provides an early introduction to the industrial and scientific age in which they live.

SOME NECESSARY DIFFERENCES OF PROGRAMME

When described in these general terms, the curricula of primary schools show close conformity. Differences that occur from class to class, and even from pupil to pupil within a class, are in the particular topics chosen for study, the methods of study employed, the weight given to each part of the curriculum and the level of difficulty to which each part is taken. There are good reasons why, to some extent, this should be so.

The first arises from differences between children, such as those described earlier. For example, a child entering school who has already begun to read soon requires books covering a wide range of topics and stories and may well be able to progress quickly with only a modest amount of supervision. Another child, before he is ready to begin to read, will need to acquire a surer grasp of spoken language, skill in noticing relatively small differences in sounds and shapes, and the habit of looking at printed material in an orderly way. Even then much patient help and encouragement may be needed if the second child is to gain in skill and confidence. To treat both children the same is to do an injustice to one.

As children make progress their interests diversify and what is a stimulus to one may be a barrier to another. If the necessary skill or the underlying idea can be presented as well in one way as another then it may create unnecessary difficulties to use the same way with all children.

Teachers as well as children differ in their abilities and enthusiasms. Schools differ in the resources available to them both because of the purchasing policies of present and past incumbents and because of the accidents of locality. A school in Lincoln is better placed to develop historical studies based on Lincoln cathedral than is one in St Albans.

The development and use of local opportunities, the special skills of teachers and the enthusiasms of children should be used to enhance the quality of work beyond what might come from a simple uniformity of practice; though such uniformity may have the advantage that the work to be covered becomes very familiar to teachers, what is done may be only a loose fit to local circumstances and soon become threadbare. When teachers make good use of their particular interests and strengths they can take children much further than is now common.

CONDITIONS REQUIRED FOR THE INCLUSION OF A MODERN LANGUAGE

The presence of a teacher with strength in a subject does not necessarily justify the inclusion of the subject in the curriculum, even if the children are capable of studying it. In the short term, French can be taught successfully in a primary school where there are sufficient teachers who speak the language well enough, who know how to teach the subject to young children, and who have the resources necessary for the work. However, these conditions are only the first that must be satisfied if the time and effort spent is to be worthwhile in the long term. Additionally, there should be a reasonable expectation that the teaching will be continued even if the teachers now responsible for the work leave. It should also be possible to continue the teaching in the secondary school in such a way as to profit from what has already been done. This may be difficult and even impossible if children in other primary schools in the area have had no opportunity or substantially different opportunities for learning the language. Unless conditions are favourable in all these respects for including the subject, it is best excluded from the primary school curriculum. Plainly, there is need for agreement between schools in a neighbourhood and the LEA on whether and how the teaching of a foreign language is conducted in primary schools.

LEVELS OF DIFFICULTY IN THE WORK

In other parts of the primary school curriculum the decisions to be taken more usually concern the range of what should be done, the choice of priorities within the range and the level of difficulty of the work. In each of these, local circumstances and the differences between individual children and individual teachers have to be taken into account, but some common requirements remain.

SKILLS

All children should learn to use English better as they grow older, and to read and write English with a growing sureness. Some children come to school with little or no English. It is essential for them to become fluent in English but, whatever is done to achieve this, the child's interest and pride in his mother tongue should be preserved.

A minority of children of 11 years of age can manage only simple reading texts made up of short sentences using common words. They as much as anyone require appropriate reading material on almost all aspects of the curriculum so that they may better appreciate the importance of reading. The great majority of children should learn to use books, fiction and non-fiction, in the sense that they improve their powers of comprehension, that they learn how to find the books they want on the library shelf, and that they learn to use a contents page and an index. The full range of reading skills required by the more able 11-year-olds is much wider than this ...

Learning to read and learning to write go hand in hand, and the majority of children should, by the time they are 8, be able to write stories and accounts of events in their own words. As they go on through the primary school many children should become accustomed to writing which involves presenting a coherent argument, exploring alternative possibilities or drawing conclusions and making judgements. Children should learn, in the course of their work, to spell the words they use, to employ acceptable forms of grammar and sentence structure and to begin to develop styles of writing appropriate to the task in hand.

In mathematics, priority should be given to acquiring familiarity with whole numbers up to 100 by gaining skills in relating them to one another – including the speedy recall of the commonly used addition, multiplication, subtraction and division facts – and by applying them to circumstances that occur in everyday life. But nearly all of the children should go far beyond that. They should begin to appreciate the simpler spatial relationships and they should make a start on work requiring a relatively explicit application of logic as with some popular games and puzzles ...

Over the course of the primary school years children should learn how to observe and to measure with increasing precision. They should also learn to use these skills with common sense; for example, when measuring or weighing, to use a degree of accuracy that is appropriate to the circumstances. They should learn to record – and to interpret and comment on – what they have seen, heard or otherwise learnt. They should gain from increasing control over their nervous and muscular systems so that they can use tools, instruments and a variety of small equipment in drawing, painting, modelling, music-making and games in such a way that they feel a sense of achievement.

CONTENT AND CONCEPTS

A wide range of skills, not least those concerned with the development of good personal relations, are relevant to the education of each child, though each makes progress at a different rate. The skills are learnt in the context of developing concepts and in the acquisition of information ... Some appropriate historical, geographical and scientific concepts are discussed in the following paragraphs.

When topics are being selected for inclusion in the programme a number of factors should be taken into account. These include the characteristics of the children, the knowledge of the teachers and the availability of suitable resources and facilities. The information to be covered should be worth knowing and useful in providing further insights into some more general idea or in improving a skill. There needs also to be some agreement between teachers in a school, with teachers in the secondary schools, and with teachers in neighbouring primary schools so that if a topic is to be studied twice or more in the course of a child's school life, the second and later occasion will build on previous experience.

On the national level it can be said that all primary schools should help their pupils to appreciate that today's world grew out of yesterday's, and to acquire some sense of historical chronology, even if the topics studied are not presented in chronological order. The children should learn to distinguish between fiction and historical fact and some should begin to recognize that historical evidence may itself be partial or biased. The youngest children's introduction to the past might concentrate on the immediate circumstances of their own families and friends and the paraphernalia of daily life. But today's world cannot be understood without some knowledge of Britain's role overseas today and in former years, and reference to this should certainly be included in the later primary school curriculum in a balanced and sensitive way as a means of helping children to understand our multi-cultural society.

The lives of the children and their parents are also conditioned by the geographical circumstances under which they and others live. As they go through primary schools, children need to become more aware of local features, of the formation and characteristics of the earth beneath their feet and of the weather. They need to learn something of the major differences in the conditions under which children live in other parts of Britain and abroad, and of the consequences of those conditions. They should also learn of the importance of routes and other means of communication between human settlements.

Skills of observation, listening and touching need to be developed so that children possess information on which their imaginations can work and be expressed through painting, modelling, music-making, dancing and storytelling. They need to be developed more than is now common in such a way that children are introduced to scientific ideas about stability and change in living things and materials; about reproduction, growth and development in succeeding generations; about forms of energy sources and storage; and about factors which influence personal and community health, including safety. Children should grow to respect and care for living things. In the course of the work they should learn how to observe systematically and carefully, to note similarities and differences and to make reasonable generalizations; they should conduct, and some should learn to devise, simple experiments to test out hypotheses.

Religious education has a statutory place in the curriculum of all maintained schools and the agreed syllabus system makes it possible to provide a framework of advice and guidance for this aspect of the curriculum in county and voluntary controlled schools. However, it is necessary for schools and teachers through their schemes of work to decide how that framework is to be adapted to the capacities and experience of the particular children with whom they are concerned.

Through religious education children can begin to learn something of the characteristic practices and beliefs of Christianity and of other major world faiths, and the influence these faiths have on the life and conduct of the believer. On another level, also important in the growth of attitudes and of an appreciation of human behaviour and achievement, it is necessary to introduce children to suitable examples of literature, drama, music and the graphic arts. Of these, literature offers an especially rich source and the children should be introduced to books by the major authors who have written for, or whose books have been adopted by, children. Some of the books should have been written by authors alive today.

SUMMARY

Current practice is such that discussion on the primary school curriculum does not need to concern itself so much with the total range of the work as with the extent to which parts of the curriculum are developed, especially for the more able children. It is only provision of observational and experimental science that is seriously lacking in many primary schools; and the teaching of French that is sometimes attempted when conditions are not suitable. More extensive discussion is required on the levels to which work could and should be taken, at least for some children, in the various parts of the curriculum; for example, the identification of the skills and ideas associated with geography and history that are suitable for primary school children should help teachers to ensure that the day-to-day programme is organized so that children become acquainted with these skills and ideas, and should help to improve continuity from one class or school to the next – whether or not these subjects are shown separately on the timetable. Working parties of teachers, LEA advisers, inspectors and others have already shown what useful guidelines can be produced for parts of the curriculum, particularly, but not only, in mathematics.

Anxiety is sometimes expressed that maintaining a wide curriculum in primary schools may be possible only at the expense of the essential, elementary skills of reading, writing and mathematics. The evidence from the HMI survey of primary education in England does not bear out that anxiety. A broad curriculum can include many opportunities for the application and practice of the skills of reading, writing and calculating. It should be planned to include them, and every opportunity should then be taken to improve children's abilities in these essential skills.

Appendix C Assessment methods

Standardized tests

The project found widespread use of standardized tests in schools. Despite their prevalence, however, teachers' interpretation of results quoted on records is still fraught with difficulty because of the wide variety of different tests used (see Table 12, listing tests in use, p. 198ff.). This problem arises where tests from different sources are standardized in different ways, producing scores which are presented in different forms and are not directly comparable. For instance, teachers may well be puzzled by having to compare scores on a test recorded in the form of reading ages with another test where scores are presented in terms of a reading quotient, and yet another with results in the form of standardized scores.

It is useful to consider briefly how standardized tests are constructed. The development of these tests follows a well-established pattern involving field trials on a representative sample of children numbering between 2000 and 25 000. Test items or questions are selected for their ease or difficulty and how well they discriminate between the able and less able child. Tables of standardized scores are provided so that an individual score can be compared with a *national* peer group.

Standardized tests are checked for validity, that is, that they are testing what they purport to test. Various factors affecting the validity of a test are illustrated in the section on 'Teacher-made tests' (see below). The reliability of a standardized test is an important factor, particularly when important decisions are to be based on the results. Reliability, usually expressed as a correlation coefficient (e.g. 0·96) indicates to what degree pupils would obtain the same, or nearly the same, score on being re-tested.

Readers interested in the details of standardization procedures should refer to textbooks on educational measurement. Table 12 (p. 198ff.) gives a list of standardized tests used by teachers in our survey ...

Teacher-made tests

Many teachers met during the project used standardized tests in order to obtain data which were reliable and seemingly objective, frequently without considering whether data of this kind were helpful to them in making decisions about pupils'

Reproduced from Philip Clift, Gaby Weiner and Edwin Wilson, *Record Keeping in Primary Schools* (Schools Council Research Studies), Macmillan Education, 1981, pp. 169–82.

| | Placement testing | | | | |
	Readiness pretest	Placement pretest	Formative testing	Diagnostic testing	Summative testing
Focus of measurement	Prerequisite entry skills	Course or unit objectives	Predefined segment of instruction	Most common learning errors	Course or unit objectives
Nature of sample	Limited sample of selected skills	Broad sample of all objectives	Limited sample of learning tasks	Limited sample of specific errors	Broad sample of all objectives
Item difficulty	Typically has low level of difficulty	Typically has wide range of difficulty	Varies with segment of instruction	Typically has low level of difficulty	Typically has wide range of difficulty
When test administered	Beginning of course or unit	Beginning of course or unit	Periodically during instruction	As needed during instruction	End of course or unit
Type of instrument	Typically is criterion-referenced mastery test	Typically is norm-referenced survey test	Typically is criterion-referenced mastery test	Specially designed test to identify learning errors	Typically is norm-referenced survey test
Use of results	Remedy entry deficiencies or assignment to learning group	Instruction planning and advance placement	Improve and direct learning through ongoing feedback	Remedy errors related to persistent learning difficulties	Assign grades, certify mastery or evaluate teaching

Reproduced from N. E. Gronlund, *Measurement and Evaluation in Teaching*, New York: Macmillan, 3rd ed. 1976, table 6.1. This table was adapted from P. W. Airasian and G. F. Madaus, 'Functional types of student evaluation', *Measurement and Evaluation in Guidance* 4, 1972, 221–33.

future learning. Tests made by teachers themselves were often seen to be much more relevant to this latter purpose.

The following questions should be borne in mind when devising a test for pupils. (The term 'test' can include a range of techniques from pencil-and-paper tests to informal observation of pupils during normal activities in school.)

1. Why are you constructing a test? The reasons may be various and are presented in Table 11. (Tests have been given purely to occupy children quietly for a short time!)
2. What are you expecting your pupils to be able to do, or 'know', as a result of your teaching, for which you are setting the test?
3. What kinds of activities or behaviours are you asking of your pupils when taking the test?
4. What kind of test would be most appropriate for gathering information on the activities selected for examination?

Unless the four questions above are considered before devising the test, the results obtained may be invalid. Of the two concepts, validity and reliability, mentioned in connection with standardized tests, validity is the more important for a teacher-made test.

A vital factor to be considered by teachers, when devising questions in either oral or written form, is the choice of words. Lack of precision in using vocabulary may lead to a pupil misunderstanding what is required of him. So, if a pupil gives a 'wrong' answer it may be that he is answering a different question from the one his teacher is asking. Points made earlier in the chapter concerning the wording of objectives are pertinent to the writing of test questions, since ambiguity can affect the validity of tests.

Some factors to be considered in relation to validity are probably best illustrated by listing the most common faults in question construction:

1. Unclear directions as to the kind of pupil response required.
2. Reading vocabulary and sentence structure too difficult for pupils to comprehend.
3. Inappropriate level of difficulty of test items.
4. Poorly constructed test items. Unintentional clues given either within the test item, or a series of items, will reduce the validity.
5. Ambiguity – leads to misinterpretation and confusion, frequently amongst the more able pupils (brighter pupils frequently see more possibilities in the range of answers to a question).
6. Test items inappropriate for the outcomes being quantified. The test attempts to measure higher order reasoning by using wording and question form which is suitable mainly for measuring factual knowledge.
7. Test too short. There is an insufficient quantity of items sampling a particular skill or behaviour, or an insufficient sample of behaviours represented in the test.
8. Improper arrangement of items. Items are usually placed in order of difficulty. Difficult items early in a test can deter the less able pupil and also use up time for trying easier questions later on.

Other factors to be considered:

i When objective tests are being constructed, one needs to try and avoid identifiable patterns of answers emerging. (Such tests have answers – true/false – or a multiple-choice format.) Faults in this category are similar to (4) above.

ii The use of negative words and phrases can make it harder to understand a question. As well as any other skills being tested, all test questions given in a written form will demand a certain level of reading and comprehension skill before a pupil can respond.

iii Where a response in written form is required from a pupil, handwriting capabilities will to some extent affect his test scores. Research studies in the field of examinations have pointed to the considerable effect pupils' handwriting can have on the way examiners allocate marks to essays, regardless of the quality of knowledge and reasoning content.

Should any of these factors be overlooked, the validity of the test will be reduced. The degree to which teachers can ignore the concept of test reliability will depend on the importance placed on the results and the weightiness of decisions likely to be based on them. For general classroom purposes, where erroneous decisions can be speedily rectified, the reliability of teacher-made tests is not so critical.

Records which are used for transfer and transition of pupils were heavily criticized by project teachers for the difficulties of interpretation which they presented. The interpretation of teacher-made test results which appeared on such records could be greatly assisted by the inclusion of the following additional information:

1. the range of scores (marks) obtained by the class on each test;
2. some information on how grades or ratings were allocated: what criteria (or guidelines) were used in deciding the cut-off points between each grade;
3. a copy of the test (where possible) and some details of the conditions under which the pupil was examined or observed;
4. (and perhaps) the conversion of raw test scores into z-scores.

Observational techniques of assessment

Many of the comments written on records by teachers, particularly those concerning pupils' personal, social and emotional development, are based on casual observations over a lengthy period. The evidence for these comments and the situational context within which they were made, were generally not included on the record or report.

Many of the project teachers expressed suspicion about 'subjective' comments. Others tended to avoid reading them lest their own perceptions became prejudiced! For these reasons it was frequently found that comments on a pupil's personal development would be put aside for about a month during which time the new teacher had time to form his/her own opinion. Conversely, the recipients of transfer and transition records complained frequently that information on a pupil's personal and social development was not included. (From the survey and questionnaire on transfer record content, and from informal contacts at project workshops, it was evident that teachers in secondary schools or who had secondary school experience considered this category of information more important than did their primary teacher colleagues.)

Since many teachers appeared to devote considerable time to writing about the personal, social and emotional development of their pupils, it is worth while considering the aspects of these records to which many of the project teachers objected. Consider the following hypothetical, though possibly typical, example as a basis for criticism: 'T—does not work as hard as he should, though he seems a bright child when he tries hard. He can be annoying in class.'

Three main points emerge:

1. There is little factual and useful information contained in this statement.
2. The teacher shows some dissatisfaction with this pupil's work and also some indication is given of the teacher's perception of him.
3. Evaluations of this kind are often based on imperfect memories and may be a summary of a few atypical but memorable incidents. Comments of this kind are frequently written as end of term or year reports at a time when teachers are suffering from fatigue.

This type of summary record was frequently found in infant schools where they were called 'profiles' or 'pen portraits (or pictures)'.

When writing down observations as opposed to opinions, there is a need, then, to consider the following features, identified by Gronlund as characterizing a good anecdotal record.

1. It provides an accurate description of a *specific* event.
2. It describes the setting sufficiently to give the event meaning.
3. If it includes interpretation or evaluation by the recorder, this interpretation is separated from the description and its different status is clearly identified.
4. The event it describes is one related to the child's personal development or social interactions.
5. The event it describes is either representative of the typical behaviour of the child or significant because it is strikingly different from his usual form of behaviour. If it is unusual behaviour for the child, the fact should be noted.

The following advice, synthesized from project teacher group deliberations, is also offered to teachers wishing to improve their observation of children.

1. Determine in advance what to observe but be alert for unusual behaviour.
2. Observe and record enough of the situation to make the behaviour meaningful.
3. Make a record of the incident as soon after the observation as possible.
4. Limit each anecdote to a brief description of a single specific incident. (Limiting each description to a single incident simplifies the task of writing, using and interpreting the records.)
5. Keep the factual description of the incident and your interpretation of it separate. (Use only non-judgemental words in the description. Avoid words such as: lazy, unhappy, shy, hostile, sad, ambitious, persistent, etc.) Interpretations of an incident should be expressed in tentative terms.

6. Record both negative and positive behavioural incidents.
7. Collect a number of anecdotes on a pupil before drawing inferences concerning typical behaviour.

The writing of good anecdotal records appears to require a great deal of practice and skill.

In contrast to the unstructured nature of observations and their summary in anecdotal records, there are occasions where more systematic observations are called for. Amongst the records collected, two main techniques were found for assisting teachers in structuring observations. Both rating scales and checklists were used widely for assessing pupils' social/personal development.

Rating scales
A carefully produced rating scale can be a useful way of structuring one's observations. Such a scale comprises a list of personal characteristics or qualities that are to be judged and some type of scale for indicating the degree to which each attribute is present. These are the main advantages of using this technique.

1. It directs observation toward clearly defined behaviours.
2. It provides a common frame of reference for appraising all pupils on the same set of characteristics.
3. It provides a convenient method for recording the judgements of several observers.

The judgements of the observer can be presented numerically on a scale, e.g. 1–5 or 1–7, etc. A verbal description is usually given to each point on the scale, e.g.

5 outstanding
4 above average
3 average
2 below average
1 unsatisfactory.

Categories such as these were found frequently on records but, to avoid the vagueness of such terms, more specific criteria could be used, e.g. for *cooperation*:

1 refuses to cooperate – usually passive
2 cooperation short-lived, poor concentration
3 cooperates willingly as a rule
4 sometimes offers extra help and assistance
5 wishes to please people and is most willing.

Judgements can also be presented graphically and can allow for a greater degree of freedom in assessing behaviours, as in Figure 8, for *plays with other children*.

| never | seldom | occasionally | frequently | always |

Figure 8 Graphical scale for rating behaviours for the item: *plays with other children*. A mark is put along the line according to one's judgement. As in the previous example, more descriptive categories could be used.

Checklists

These are similar to rating scales except that the kind of judgement required tends to be of the *yes/no* variety. One is asked to judge whether a characteristic is present or absent at the particular time when an observation is made. Unless a checklist is extremely lengthy, the number of behaviours included merely represent a sample of those on which a teacher wishes to focus attention ... This method of assessment was found frequently in infant schools in the form of a 'pre-reading record' and follows a similar pattern to informal reading inventories.

The checklist may be used as a framework for assisting teachers to focus on particular pupil behaviours, traits or development. Whether or not it can be used as a record to communicate meaningfully to other teachers depends greatly on the kind of wording used and the frequency of entries made. Many of the checklist records seen by the project team were criticized by other teachers on the following grounds.

1. They were too lengthy and detailed.
2. There was a lack of criteria on the record to explain what a *yes/no* or a tick actually represented.
3. The instability of assessments (a pupil may be able to perform a task one week but unable to do the same the following week).

Though teachers who had *devised* checklists generally praised their usefulness, teachers who had *received* them from other schools expressed their preference for a summary comment. This preference highlights the degree of perceived uncertainty in the interpretation of assessments on checklists ... Many teachers tried to overcome this uncertainty by using a three-category system in conjunction with their checklist. The following example was frequently found:

$\sqrt{}$ has been introduced to
× has had satisfactory practice in
* fully understands this work

Despite this refinement, other teachers criticized the last two categories for their relative vagueness.

The recognition by many teachers of the limitations of checklists prompted frequent questions to the project team on how matters could be improved. We found no simple answer, unfortunately, despite some searching amongst assessment literature. Assuming that teachers wish to continue with this approach to assessment, improvement may only be effected through the careful use of words and general agreement on meanings. Euphemisms in use today originally had, perhaps, more specific meanings. However, the common use of 'good', 'poor', 'improving' and 'unsatisfactory' on records and reports weakens this form of recording due to the wide interpretations possible.

Imprecision can be illustrated by two examples taken from checklists collected in our survey:

1. has a concept of conservation of number;
2. knows terms – bigger, smaller, more, less.

The words 'has concept of', 'knows' and 'understands' are usually reserved for general aims or goals but have little use in the writing of objectives. Without wishing to dwell again on the minutiae of objective writing, it is perhaps obvious that the examples above give little in the way of qualitative information about pupils' attainments. The following versions give some concrete information as to the form of assessment used.

1. The pupil can demonstrate with a group of objects his ability to conserve a numerical quantity.
2. The pupil can use the words 'bigger', 'smaller', 'more', 'less' appropriately when comparing groups of objects.

Despite the improvement, there is still no indication of criteria by which a pupil could be judged competent. The number of correct answers or allowable errors remains unclear in these examples. This illustrates the difficulties encountered when assessments are made on a criterion-referenced basis. The lengths one has to go to in making criteria precise enough to avoid ambiguity may not be worth the time and effort spent.

In most of the checklists seen by the project team, several of the important elements, such as competence level, were not made explicit and therefore remained as mere assumptions in the minds of the teachers who compiled the records. When these records were read by teachers from other schools, interpretation of the content was (obviously) found difficult.

Generally, the teachers with whom the project worked found checklists to be a useful way of focusing attention when observing pupils' characteristics. The teachers who had received checklists from other schools expressed the view that, without additional information such as indicated above, this kind of record was of doubtful value. It appears, therefore, that checklists are more successful in communicating the work and topics which a pupil has attempted and experienced than in providing assessment data about achievements.

It was by no means clear what use was made of test results, apart from their being entered on records. It was impossible in the time available to investigate how far teachers habitually diagnosed pupils' learning difficulties from analyses of pupils' responses or behaviours. Most of the project teachers agonized about 'labelling' children, and it would therefore have been interesting to know how results of standardized tests affected teacher expectations of their pupils. In particular, the widespread use of intelligence quotient (IQ) labels may predetermine pupils' futures. It has been suggested that IQs are more often used as excuses by teachers and psychologists for pupils' poor educational performance rather than as an indication perhaps of poor teaching. Neisworth, writing about the irrelevance of IQ in education, suggests that conventional intelligence tests 'can provide fair predictions of school success, assuming we do nothing exceptional to help or hinder certain students and thus destroy the prediction. Prediction *per se* is of little use since we do not use intelligence tests to make selection decisions.'

'One off' sampling of a pupil's performance in making a diagnosis can be likened to relying on a dipstick reading when finding the general running state of a car. Accurate diagnosis of pupils' learning difficulties demands observation and perhaps testing over a wide range of activities.

To sum up: designing and compiling record-keeping systems should come at the final stages of a planning process once answers have been found to the following questions.

1. 'What am I expected to teach, and in what order?'
2. 'What educational purposes is my teaching to serve? What teaching methods are known to achieve these purposes?'
3. 'What standards of achievement am I expected to aim at?'
4. 'How will I discover whether the course I've been teaching has been successful or not?'
5. 'What can I usefully be told about the abilities, interests and attitudes of the pupils I am to teach?'

Table 12 lists the tests that were used in schools visited or contacted by the project. The tests were used as part of the assessment procedures adopted by teachers, and provided data for ongoing record keeping.

Table 12 Percentage use of tests found in schools visited or contacted by the project (*n* = 192)

	% use
READING TESTS	
Graded Word Reading Test (by F. J. Schonell): Oliver & Boyd	32
Reading Tests A, AD (by A. F. Watts), BD: NFER	17
Standard Test of Reading Skill (by J. C. Daniels & H. Diack): Chatto & Windus	17
Neale Analysis of Reading Ability (by M. D. Neale): Macmillan Education, also NFER	17
Burt (Rearranged) Word Reading Test (by C. Burt): Hodder & Stoughton Educational	13
Group Reading Test (by D. Young): Hodder & Stoughton Educational	12
Holborn (Sentence) Reading Scale (by A. F. Watts): Harrap	11
Silent Reading Tests A, B (by F. J. Schonell): Oliver & Boyd	7
Word Recognition Test (by C. Carver): Hodder & Stoughton Educational	6
Redding Comprehension Test DE (by B. Barnard): NFER	5
Southgate Group Reading Tests 1, 2 (by V. Southgate): Hodder & Stoughton Educational	5
Wide-Span Reading Test (by M. A. Brimer & H. Gross): Nelson	4
Get Reading Right (by S. Jackson): Robert Gibson	4
OTHER READING TESTS USED BY A FEW SCHOOLS	
Edinburgh Reading Tests (sponsored by Scottish Education Department and Educational Institute of Scotland): Hodder & Stoughton Educational	

Table 12 (cont'd)

% use

Crichton Vocabulary Scale (by J. C. Raven): NFER
English Picture Vocabulary Test (by M. A. Brimer & L. M. Dunn):
Educational Evaluation Enterprises
Group Reading Assessment (by F. Spooncer): Hodder & Stoughton
Educational
Aston Index (by M. Newton): Learning Development Aids
Reading Level Tests (tests of known readability, using *cloze* technique
which systematically deletes words from passages): NFER
Framework for Reading: checklists for diagnostic purposes (by J. Dean &
R. Nichols): Evans
Swansea Test of Phonic Skills (from Schools Council Compensatory
Education Project): Blackwell
Reading and Remedial Reading: screening procedures (by A. E. Tansley):
Routledge

ENGLISH LANGUAGE TESTS

English Progress Tests (various authors): NFER   12
Graded Word Spelling Test (by P. E. Vernon): Hodder & Stoughton
Educational   6
Bristol Achievement Tests: English Language (general editor: M. A.
Brimer): Nelson   2
Tests of Proficiency in English: listening, reading, speaking, writing:
NFER   1
An English Language Scale (by F. J. Watts): Harrap   1

VERBAL REASONING TESTS

Verbal Tests BC (by D. A. Pidgeon), C, CD (by V. Land), D (by T. N.
Postlethwaite): NFER   26
Non-verbal Tests: Picture Test A (by J. E. Stuart), *Non-verbal Tests* BD
(by D. A. Pidgeon), DH (by B. Calvert): NFER   10
Essential Intelligence Tests: Forms A, B (by F. J. Schonell & R. H.
Adams): Oliver & Boyd   3
Deeside 7 + Picture Test (by W. G. Emmett): Harrap   2
Moray House Picture Intelligence Tests (by M. E. Mellone): Hodder &
Stoughton Educational   2
Oral Verbal Intelligence Test (by D. Young): Hodder & Stoughton
Educational   2
Non-readers Intelligence Test (by D. Young): Hodder & Stoughton
Educational   1
Coloured Progressive Matrices, sets A, Ab, B (by J. C. Raven): H. K.
Lewis, also NFER

Table 12 (cont'd)

	% use
MATHEMATICS TESTS	
Mathematics Attainment Tests A, B, Cl, C3, DE1, DE2: NFER	30
Basic Mathematics Tests: NFER	7
Bristol Achievement Tests: Mathematics (general editor: M. A. Brimer): Nelson	2
Mathematics Grading Tests: Schofield & Sims	2
Nottingham Number Test (by W. E. C. Gillham & K. A. Hesse): Hodder & Stoughton Educational	1
OTHER TESTS IN USE	
Richmond Tests of Basic Skills (by A. N. Hieronymus *et al.*): Nelson	5
Bristol Social Adjustment Guides (by D. H. Stott, N. C. Marston & E. G. Sykes): Hodder & Stoughton Educational	1

Appendix D *Record Keeping in Primary Schools*: Summary, conclusions and recommendations

Overview of the report

The purpose of this report is to help teachers in primary schools to keep better records of the progress and development of the children in their care. The Schools Council project on which it was based started in the autumn of 1976 and lasted for two years. Its brief was:

1. to collect information about the ways in which school records were being kept by primary schools;
2. to collate and analyse this material;
3. to evaluate the collated material in collaboration with teachers in six regional groups;
4. to develop with these groups of teachers ways of improving record keeping practice ...

Conclusions and recommendations

When producing records, the following synthesis of the collective views of the team and the project teachers should be kept in mind.

Design
Record should have:

1. a clear layout;
2. clear, stable printing that will not fade;
3. clear section headings;
4. the pupil's name in a prominent position (official forms generally use the top right-hand corner of a sheet);

Reproduced from Philip Clift, Gaby Weiner and Edwin Wilson, *Record Keeping in Primary Schools* (Schools Council Research Studies), Macmillan Education, 1981, pp. 235–42.

5. sufficient space provided for comments;
6. a prominently placed key (or a user's handbook) to explain the use of abbreviations, symbols and criteria for the assessment of pupils.

Content
Record content should:

1. be relevant to the purpose of the record;
2. be clearly sequenced;
3. give direct indications rather than implications for future teaching;
4. give a clear distinction between entries concerned with pupils' school experiences and those which are assessments of attainment;
5. clearly present assessment information, *stating*:
   a the derivation of norms used when grading or rating,
   b the criteria used when deciding on pupils' competence,
   c details of standardized tests used as a basis for grading or rating,
   d details of other testing techniques used,
   e teacher-made test marks *in a standardized form*, possibly as standardized z scores to indicate the range and distribution of scores. (This is particularly necessary where sets of marks from different sources have to be compared.)

The following *general* recommendations are also made.

1. *The formulation of records should always be a collaborative exercise involving all the teachers within a primary school.* The discipline imposed on teachers by the act of examining their aims, objectives and assessments is a very valuable one in its own right. A case study has been included to illustrate this process. The experience of one such school is hardly likely to be typical of all schools making such an attempt, but it provides useful pointers along the way for those wishing to follow. Satisfaction with, and systematic, even enthusiastic use of, record keeping systems seemed to be guaranteed only in those schools which had produced a record system as a collaborative exercise involving all the staff. Clearly this cannot be a once-and-for-all event. New teaching priorities emerge, and teachers come and go, and the process needs thus to be a dynamic one with the systems produced seen as in a state of continual evolution.

2. When records are also intended to communicate information to the next stage in education, *the scope of the collaboration should extend to the recipients.* All too often during the course of project activities, the team met with the bland rejection of primary school records by secondary colleagues, on the grounds that much of the information offered was not what was wanted and that, where the information was potentially of a useful nature, comparability between different 'feeder' primary schools was impossible. Surprisingly, the same criticism was often voiced at the infant–junior interface, where these were separate schools, in spite of the fact that generally only one of each was involved.

3. Much valuable first-hand information about pupils and their learning habits is lost since time is not immediately available for teachers to make the necessary notes in sufficient detail. Therefore, if record keeping is to be rather more than an end of day or weekly activity, and seen as part of the process of teaching, then *teachers need to be freed of many of the non-teaching and supervisory activities commonly a part of primary school life*. Without time being made available at the point when important observations are made, record keeping of pupils' progress will remain somewhat sketchy. Without time being made available the process of curriculum planning of which record keeping is merely the final stage cannot be undertaken as a collective staff exercise. Without time being made available, the inter-school visiting and collaboration so important to ensuring continuity in the curriculum between stages of education and the creation of a system of records which communicate meaningfully across the 'transition barrier' cannot be achieved.

Appendix E   Summary of HMI Schedules

The following summarizes all the factors referred to in the HMI Schedules for the inspection of the survey classes.

Aesthetic and physical education

i. Art and crafts

1 The extent to which children make use of the following starting points and resources in the development of aesthetic awareness: the immediate outdoor environment, arrangements and displays inside the school and the classroom, natural and man-made objects, a range of media for two- and three-dimensional work, visits to local art galleries, exhibitions or museums, visits by local craftsmen or artists.

2 The quality of the following resources: the arrangements and displays within the classroom including man-made objects, a range of media for drawing and printmaking, materials and textiles, three-dimensional constructional materials.

3 The emphasis given to art and crafts within the whole curriculum.

4 Evidence that children are learning to observe carefully in relation to form, texture, pattern and colour.

5 Evidence that children may turn readily to paint, clay or other media when they have something to express which is personal to them.

6 Evidence of the use of form, texture, pattern and colour in children's work.

7 Evidence that children are learning to select materials with discrimination.

8 Evidence that the children are learning to handle tools, apparatus and materials carefully and safely and with a sense of fitness for their purpose.

9 The use made of drawing and modelling techniques and skills to record observations or information in other areas of the curriculum.

Reproduced by permission of the Controller HM Stationery Office, from Department of Education and Science, *Primary Education in England*, a Survey by HM Inspectors of Schools, HMSO, 1978, pp. 209–19.

ii. Music

10 The extent to which children make use of the following starting points and resources for musical experience: recorded music, television, radio, untuned and tuned percussion instruments, visits to concerts or to hear outside choirs, visits to the school by musicians.

11 The emphasis given to music within the whole curriculum.

12 The extent to which opportunities are taken to develop singing, listening, the learning of notation and creative music-making as aspects of musical experience.

13 The quality of the songs chosen.

14 The extent to which music is related to other areas of the curriculum.

15 The provision for children in the class to play musical instruments.

iii. Physical education

16 The extent to which children make use of the following starting points and resources for physical education: television, radio, gymnastic equipment of all kinds, games equipment and associated small apparatus.

17 The emphasis given to the full range of movement activities within the whole curriculum.

18 The extent to which opportunities are taken to develop gymnastics, dance, games and swimming within the range of physical activities.

19 Evidence that the children are developing skilful performance in gymnastics, skill in games or a games-like context, awareness and sensitivity in the use of expressive movement.

Language and literacy

1 The extent to which children make use of the following starting points and resources to develop and extend their language, whether spoken, written or through reading:

a experiences out of school which have not been planned by the school
b experiences in school including the display of materials and objects, the keeping of animals and plants, imaginative play, constructional activities
c book collections or libraries
d television, radio, cine film, slides, pre-recorded material for listening, tape recordings by the children
e reading schemes and courses, assignment cards, language course kits, textbooks

f stories and poems read or told by the teacher
g visiting speakers
h the immediate outdoor environment, visits and school journeys.

2 The quality of the following: the arrangement of displays, book collections or libraries, pre-recorded material for listening, cine film and slides, assignment cards, stories and poems read by the teacher.

3 The extent to which opportunities are taken to develop the language used in other areas of the curriculum.

4 Evidence that children are being taught to do the following: follow instructions, follow the plot of a story, listen to poetry, comprehend the main ideas and the details in information they are given, follow a discussion or the line of an argument and contribute appropriately.

5 The emphasis given to talking between the children and teachers, and the children and other adults.

6 The emphasis given to informal discussion among children during the working day and the provision of more formal, structured arrangements for discussion and exchange between children.

7 Evidence that children are encouraged to expand their spoken responses, that new vocabulary is introduced, that the use of more precise description is achieved, that children are helped to frame pertinent questions and that children are taught to use alternative and more appropriate structures in their talking.

i. Reading
8 Evidence, where appropriate, that children's own speech is used to provide early reading material.

9 Evidence that the children's own writing is used as part of their early reading material.

10 The emphasis given to reading practice with main reading schemes and supplementary readers.

11 The emphasis given to the reading of fiction and non-fiction related to curricular work and other reading not related to curricular work.

12 The emphasis on the use of extended reading skills and children's comments on the material read.

13 The emphasis on the selection of books by the children themselves.

14 Evidence that children learn to turn readily and naturally to books for pleasure and that they use books with ease and confidence as a source of information.

15 Evidence that the children read poetry and that some of the children discuss books at more than a superficial level.

ii. Writing

16 The emphasis given to self-chosen and prescribed topics for children's writing.

17 The emphasis given to self-chosen and prescribed topics related to other curricular areas.

18 The extent to which the following are used: copied writing, dictation and handwriting practice.

19 The extent to which descriptive, expressive, narrative and expository styles or modes of prose writing are used by the children.

20 The extent to which descriptive, expressive and narrative styles or modes of poetry writing are used by the children.

21 Evidence that the children's writing is used for the following purposes: to share information or experience with other children, as samples of work used by the teacher to monitor progress, as a basis for learning language, spelling, syntax and style.

22 Where French is taught, the number of sessions and total time per week which is spent on this subject.

Mathematics

1 The extent to which children make use of the following starting points and resources in the learning of mathematics:

  a television and radio
  b textbooks, commercial and school-made workcards
  c investigations arising from questions asked by the children or initiated by the teachers
  d practice of skills directed from the blackboard.

2 Evidence of sustained work on any mathematical topic.

3 Evidence of profitable links with other areas of the curriculum.

4 The emphasis given to the following aspects of mathematics during the current school year:

a qualitative mathematical description; unambiguous description of the properties of number, size, shape and position

b recognition of relationships and logical deduction applied to everyday things, geometrical shapes, number and ordering

c appreciation of place value and recognition of simple number patterns (e.g. odds and evens, multiples, divisors, squares, etc.)

d appreciation of some broader aspects of number (e.g. bases other than 10, number sequences, tests of divisibility)

e use of various forms of visual presentation (e.g. three-dimensional and diagrammatic forms, statistical charts, tables of data, networks, etc.)

f use of models, maps, scale drawings, etc.

g use of algebraic symbols; notations such as 'box' and arrow diagrams

h sensible estimation and use of measurements of length, weight, area, volume and time

i understanding of money and sense of values regarding simple purchases

j quantitative description; sensible use of number in counting, describing and estimating

k practical activities involving the ideas of $+$, $-$, $\times$ and $\div$

l suitable calculations involving $+$, $-$, $\times$ and $\div$ with whole numbers

m examples involving four rules of number including two places of decimals (as in pounds and pence and measures)

n calculations involving the four rules applied to the decimal system

o use of fractions (including the idea of equivalence) in the discussion of everyday things

p competence in calculations involving the four rules applied to fractions.

Science

1 The extent to which children make use of the following starting points and resources in learning science:

a children's experience out of school

b experience of materials, plants and animals in school

c television and radio

d reference books, textbooks, commercial and school-made assignment cards

e the immediate outdoor environment.

2 Quality of the overall provision of resources for scientific investigation.

3 The emphasis given to science within the whole curriculum.

4 The quality of assignment cards, reference books and materials available for scientific investigation.

5 Evidence of investigations arising from questions asked by the children.

6 Evidence that the children are using description arising from direct observation.

7 Evidence that the children are learning about the following:

a notions of stability and change in relation to living things and materials
b knowledge of some of the characteristics of living things including differences and similarities
c reproduction, growth and development in succeeding generations
d forms of energy sources and storage
e factors which influence personal and community health, including safety
f respect and care for living things.

8 The extent to which children are encouraged to identify significant patterns (e.g. the way plants react to light, the way materials react to heat, bird migration, the position of leaves on a plant stem, etc.).

Social abilities

i. Social, moral and religious education
1 The extent to which situations are planned to encourage the development of moral and ethical values in the following aspects:

a the use of initiative and making informed choices
b the exercise of responsibility and self-assessment in behaviour and work
c emotional development and sympathetic identification with others
d respect for other people
e respect for plants and animals
f respect for things
g contribution and participation as a member of a group
h the exercise of qualities of leadership.

2 The extent to which most children appear to be involved in the development of religious ideas and moral or ethical rules and values during the school assembly.

3 The extent to which children learn about man's attempt to frame religious and moral or ethical rules and values in the following aspects of their work:

a history and geography
b the Old and New Testament
c writings of other religions
d myths and legends
e other literature and drama.

ii. Geography and history
4 The extent to which children make use of the following starting points and resources to develop historical and geographical awareness:

a the memories of people known to the children
b artefacts, historical documents and the use of historical aspects of the local area
c historical programmes on television and radio
d history textbooks, workcards or assignment cards
e stories with an historical setting
f history reference books
g weather study
h use of geographical features of the local area
i geographical programmes on television and radio
j geography textbooks, workcards or assignment cards
k stories with an interesting geographical setting
l geography reference books.

5 The quality of the content of school-made assignment cards for history and geography.

6 The quality of history and geography reference books.

7 The emphasis given to developing children's awareness and appreciation of the past.

8 The extent to which children are becoming aware of historical change and the casual factors in relation to people's material circumstances, the way people behaved and the things people believed in the past.

9 The degree to which children are engaged in the following activities:

a understanding the nature of historical statements
b developing sympathy with the predicament of other people
c developing an awareness of the need for evidence.

10 The emphasis given to geographical aspects of children's learning within the whole curriculum.

11 The degree to which the following geographical aspects were included in children's work during the current academic year both within and outside the locality:

a population and settlements
b agriculture and industry
c transport
d geographical land features
e natural resources.

12 The extent to which the children's work reveals an appreciation of man's dependence on natural phenomena and resources.

13 Evidence that children are becoming familiar with maps of the locality, atlases and globes.

Organization and methods of working

1 The emphasis given to cognitive, social, emotional and physical development as judged by the quality of the children's work.

2 The degree to which posts carrying particular organizational or curricular responsibilities influence the work of the school as a whole.

3 The extent to which didactic and exploratory approaches to teaching were observed in the survey classes.

4 Evidence of effective interaction between the basic skills of numeracy and literacy and the more imaginative aspects of the children's work.

5 Evidence that children are encouraged to follow a sustained interest in the course of their work.

6 The extent to which a quiet working atmosphere is established when this is appropriate.

7 The degree of control over the children's use of resources in the classroom.

8 The degree to which the content of the children's work is prescribed by the teacher.

9 Evidence that satisfactory educational use is made of spontaneous incidents which may arise.

10 The attention given to creating an intellectually stimulating environment inside and outside the school.

11 Evidence that vandalism outside school hours limits the creation of an aesthetically pleasing environment.

12 The extent to which the accommodation facilitates or inhibits the children's work.

13 The extent to which the adequacy of resources facilitates or inhibits the children's work.

14 Type of catchment area and whether there is evidence of marked social difficulties.

References

Introduction: the year 2000
1. Carl Sagan, *The Dragons of Eden*, Coronet, 1979.
2. *Planning One-year 16–17 Courses: a Follow-up to 'The Practical Curriculum'* (Pamphlet 21), Schools Council, 1983.

Chapter I. A primary school's aims: contrasting approaches
1. DES Circular 6/81.
2. R. G. Mager, *Preparing Instructional Objectives*, Fearon Publishers, Palo Alto, California, 1962.
3. Department of Education and Science, *Children and Their Primary Schools*, a report of the Central Advisory Council for Education (England), HMSO, 1967, vol. 1, p. 186.
4. Schools Council, *The Practical Curriculum* (Schools Council Working Paper 70), Methuen Educational, 1981, p. 14.
5. Department of Education and Science/Welsh Office, *A Framework for the School Curriculum*, HMSO, 1980, p. 3; Department of Education and Science/ Welsh Office, *The School Curriculum*, HMSO, 1981.
6. *The Practical Curriculum*, p. 15.
7. Schools Council Science 5/13 Project, *With Objectives in Mind*, Macdonald Educational for the Schools Council, 1972, pp. 23–5, 26.
8. Vera Southgate, Helen Arnold and Sandra Johnson, *Extending Beginning Reading*, Heinemann Educational for the Schools Council, 1981, p. 45.
9. Guidelines for Review and Institutional Development in Schools (GRIDS), a Schools Council Programme 1 activity based at the University of Bristol School of Education: this was Maldon County Primary School.
10. GRIDS: Dee Road Infants School, Clwyd.
11. Philip H. Taylor, Gail Exon and Brian Holley, *A Study of Nursery Education* (Schools Council Working Paper 41), Evans/Methuen Educational, 1972.
12. Patricia Ashton, Pat Kneen, Frances Davies and B. J. Holley, *The Aims of Primary Education: a Study of Teachers' Opinions* (Schools Council Research Studies), Macmillan Education, 1975.
13. The Cambridgeshire/Schools Council Self-evaluation Project.
14. *Education in Schools: a Consultative Document* (Cmnd. 6869), HMSO, 1977, p. 41.
15. *Education in Schools*, p. 41.

Chapter II. Describing the curriculum

1. Department of Education and Science, *Primary Education in England*, a survey by HM Inspectors of Schools, HMSO, 1978, 8.23.
2. *Primary Education in England*, 8.29.
3. Department of Education and Science, *A View of the Curriculum* (HMI Matters for Discussion Series), HMSO, 1980. The excellent chapter on the curriculum in primary schools is quoted in full in Appendix B.
4. Department of Education and Science, *Education 5 to 9: an Illustrative Survey of 80 First Schools in England*, HMSO, 1982.
5. *Education 5 to 9*.
6. Schools Council 5/13 Project, *Early Experiences: a Unit for Teachers*, Macdonald Educational for the Schools Council, 1972.

Chapter III. Science

1. *Science in Primary Schools*, a discussion paper produced by the HMI Science Committee, DES, 1983, p. 18.
2. *Science in Primary Schools*, p. 4.
3. *Science in Primary Schools*, p. 4.
4. *Science in Primary Schools*, pp. 9–11.
5. *Science in Primary Schools*, p. 5.
6. Assessment of Performance Unit, 'Science at age 11', a paper for teachers based on the results of the 1980 and 1981 surveys of children aged 10–11 (draft), March 1983.

Chapter IV. Mathematics

1. Department of Education and Science, *Mathematics 5–11: a Handbook of Suggestions* (HMI Matters for Discussion Series), HMSO, 1979, p. 4.
2. Department of Education and Science, *Mathematics Counts*, report of the Committee of Inquiry into the Teaching of Mathematics in Schools under the Chairmanship of Dr W. H. Cockcroft, HMSO, 1982, p. 1.
3. *Mathematics 5–11*, p. 5.
4. Department of Education and Science, *A View of the Curriculum* (HMI Matters for Discussion Series), HMSO, 1980, pp. 27–8.
5. *Mathematics Counts*, p. 4.
6. Brenda Denvir, Chris Stolz and Margaret Brown, *Low Attainers in Mathematics 5–16: Policies and Practices in Schools* (Schools Council Working Paper 72), Methuen Educational, 1982, pp. 66–8.
7. *Low Attainers in Mathematics 5–16*, pp. 70–71.
8. Assessment of Performance Unit, *Mathematical Development: Primary Survey Report No. 1*, HMSO, 1980, p. 99.
9. *Mathematics in Primary Schools* (Schools Council Curriculum Bulletin 1), HMSO, 4th edition, 1972.

Chapter V. Language and literacy

1. *Routes to the Way Ahead*, an analysis of the 5–13 school curriculum by teachers in Jersey, Education Department, Jersey, 1980.

2. Joan Dean, *The Literacy Schedule*, The Centre for the Teaching of Reading, University of Reading School of Education.
3. *Routes to the Way Ahead.*
4. *The Literacy Schedule.*
5. Derived from *The Literacy Schedule.*
6. Derived from *The Literacy Schedule.*
7. Department of Education and Science, *Education 5 to 9: an Illustrative Survey of 80 First Schools in England*, HMSO, 1982.
8. Margaret Mallett and Bernard Newsome, *Talking, Writing and Learning 8–13* (Schools Council Working Paper 59), Evans/Methuen Educational, 1977, pp. 230–31.

Chapter VI. The study of people past and present
1. Department of Education and Science, *Education 5 to 9: an Illustrative Survey of 80 First Schools in England*, HMSO, 1982, pp. 31–2.
2. Schools Council Environmental Studies Project, *Case Studies*, Hart-Davis Educational for the Schools Council, 1972, pp. 22ff.
3. Schools Council Environmental Studies Project, *A Teacher's Guide*, Hart-Davis Educational for the Schools Council, 1972, pp. 75, 76.
4. Schools Council, *Environmental Studies 5–13: the Use of Historical Resources* (Schools Council Working Paper 48), Evans/Methuen Educational, 1973, p. 11.
5. *Case Studies*, pp. 65–73.
6. See, for example, *Case Studies*, pp. 83–8.
7. Professor Alan Blyth and others, *Place, Time and Society 8–13: Curriculum Planning in History, Geography and Social Science*, Collins/ESL Bristol for the Schools Council, 1976, p. 86.
8. Schools Council Environmental Studies Project, *Starting from Rocks*, Hart-Davis Educational for the Schools Council, 1973, p. 75.
9. *Place, Time and Society 8–13: Curriculum Planning*, pp. 134, 136.
10. Schools Council, *The New Approach to the Social Studies: Continuity and Development in Children's Learning through First, Middle and High School*, Schools Council, 1981, pp. 102–3

Chapter VII. Imagination, feeling and sensory expression
1. Department of Education and Science, *Primary Education in England*, a survey by HM Inspectors of Schools, HMSO, 1978, 8.29.
2. Department of Education and Science, *Education 5 to 9: an Illustrative Survey of 80 First Schools in England*, HMSO, 1982, 3.2.8–3.2.9.
3. *Primary Education in England*, 8.27, 8.15.
4. Schools Council Art and Craft Education 8–13 Project, *Children's Growth though Creative Experience*, Van Nostrand Reinhold for the Schools Council, 1974.
5. *Children's Growth through Creative Experience.*
6. 'Development and progress in art and design', an unpublished paper prepared by Joan Dean, Chief Inspector, Surrey County Council.

7. *The Arts in Schools: Principles, Practice and Provision*, Calouste Gulbenkian Foundation, 1982, p. 51.
8. *Children's Growth through Creative Experience.*
9. Reproduced in Michael Laxton, *Using Constructional Materials* (Schools Council Art and Craft Education 8–13 Project), Van Nostrand Reinhold for the Schools Council, 1974, p. 83.
10. Assessment of Performance Unit, *Physical Development*, DES, March 1983, pp. 5, 6, 7.
11. Tom Stabler, *Drama in Primary Schools*, Macmillan Education for the Schools Council, 1979, pp. 27, 31.
12. Margaret Hope-Brown, *Music with Everything*, Frederick Warne, 1973, pp. 1–2.
13. *Music with Everything*, pp. 2–3.
14. *Music with Everything*, p. 38f.
15. *Music with Everything*, p. 39.
16. *Music with Everything*, p. 40.
17. *Music with Everything*, p. 46.
18. *The Arts in Schools*, pp. 51–2.

Chapter VIII. Personal and social development

1. *Discovering an Approach*, Macmillan Education for the Schools Council, 1977.
2. *Discovering an Approach*, p. 43.
3. *Agreed Syllabus of Religious Education*, Hertfordshire County Council, 1981, p. 5.
4. *Putting Principles into Practice: Three Case Studies*, Macmillan Education for the Schools Council, 1979.
5. *Putting Principles into Practice.*
6. *Putting Principles into Practice.*
7. *Discovering an Approach*, pp. 58–9.
8. Kenneth David, *Personal and Social Education in Secondary Schools*, report of the Schools Council working party on personal and social education (Schools Council Programme Pamphlets), Longman, York, 1983, p. 80.
9. Schools Council, *The Practical Curriculum* (Schools Council Working Paper 70), Methuen Educational, 1981, p. 20.
10. Charles Bailey in *Personal and Social Education in Secondary Schools*, p. 83.
11. Adapted from John Wilson, Norman Williams and Barry Sugarman, *Introduction to Moral Education*, Penguin, 1967, p. 405. Much of the thinking in this chapter is derived from this most helpful book.

Chapter IX. Cohesion through topic work

1. Schools Council, 'Developing pupils' thinking through topic work: teacher self-report package', unpublished report.
2. Schools Council Religious Education in Primary Schools Project, *Discovering an Approach*, Macmillan Education for the Schools Council, 1977.
3. M. Bassey, *900 Primary Teachers*, NFER, 1978.
4. 'Developing pupils' thinking through topic work'.

5. Philip Clift, Gaby Weiner and Edwin Wilson, *Record Keeping in Primary Schools* (Schools Council Research Studies), Macmillan Education, 1981, pp. 224–5.
6. Joan Dean, *Organising Learning in the Primary School Classroom*, Croom Helm, 1983.

Chapter X. Assessment and records: progression and continuity

1. Joan Dean, Chief Inspector, Surrey County Council, contributed much of the information in this paragraph.
2. Judith Whyte, *Beyond the Wendy House: Sex Role Stereotyping in Primary Schools* (Schools Council Programme Pamphlets), Longman, York, 1983.
3. Department of Education and Science, *Curricular Differences in Boys and Girls* (Education Survey 21), HMSO, 1975.
4. *Beyond the Wendy House*.
5. Cited in *A Language for Life*: report of the Committee of Inquiry appointed by the Secretary of State for Education and Science under the Chairmanship of Sir Alan Bullock, FBA, HMSO, 1975, p. 209.
6. Assessment of Performance Unit, *Language Performance in Schools: Primary Survey Report No. 1*, HMSO, 1981.
7. *A Language for Life*, p. 100.
8. Department of Education and Science, *Education in Schools: a Consultative Document*, HMSO, 1977, 2.3(ii).
9. Department of Education and Science, *Education 5 to 9: an Illustrative Survey of 80 First Schools in England*, HMSO, 1982, 3.27.
10. Brenda Denvir, Chris Stolz and Margaret Brown, *Low Attainers in Mathematics 5–16: Policies and Practices in Schools* (Schools Council Working Paper 72), Methuen Educational, 1982.
11. W. K. Brennan, *Curricular Needs of Slow Learners* (Schools Council Working Paper 63), Evans/Methuen Educational, 1979.
12. *Education 5 to 9*, 3.28.
13. Programme 2: Diagnostic Assessment of Pupils' Social Knowledge and Awareness.
14. *Low Attainers in Mathematics 5–16*, pp. 22, 23.
15. Eric Ogilvie, *Gifted Children in Primary Schools* (Schools Council Research Studies), Macmillan Education, 1973, p. 51.
16. Graeme Clarke, *Guidelines for the Recognition of Gifted Pupils* (Schools Council Programme Pamphlets), Longman, York, 1983, p. 19. Reproduced with acknowledgement to Essex County Council Education Department.
17. *Guidelines for the Recognition of Gifted Pupils*, p. 20. Adapted from a 'Rapid Checklist' produced by Joan Sigler of the Carleton Board of Education, Ontario, Canada.
18. Vera Southgate, Helen Arnold and Sandra Johnson, *Extending Beginning Reading*, Heinemann Educational for the Schools Council, 1981.
19. Department of Education and Science, *Local Authority Arrangements for the School Curriculum*, report on the Circular 14/77 Review, HMSO, 1979.

20. *Low Attainers in Mathematics 5–16*, pp. 128–9.
21. *Low Attainers in Mathematics 5–16*, p. 130.
22. Philip Clift, Gaby Weiner and Edwin Wilson, *Record Keeping in Primary Schools* (Schools Council Research Studies), Macmillan Education, 1981.
23. Adapted from *Record Keeping in Primary Schools*, p. 240.
24. *Low Attainers in Mathematics 5–16*, pp. 80–81.
25. *Local Authority Arrangements for the School Curriculum*.
26. Maurice Galton and John Willcocks (eds.), *Moving from the Primary Classroom*, Routledge & Kegan Paul, 1983.
27. Martin Creasey, Frances Findlay and Brian Walsh, *Language across the Transition: Primary/Secondary Continuity and Liaison in English* (Schools Council Programme Pamphlets), Longman, York, in preparation.
28. *Local Authority Arrangements for the School Curriculum*.
29. Patrick Whitaker, *The Primary Head*, Heinemann Educational, 1983.

Chapter XI. Organization: making the most or finite resources

1. *Education*, 5 March 1982.
2. Brenda Denvir, Chris Stolz and Margaret Brown, *Low Attainers in Mathematics 5–16: Policies and Practices in Schools* (Schools Council Working Paper 72), Methuen Educational, 1982, p. 102.
3. *Low Attainers in Mathematics 5–16*, pp. 91–4.
4. Department of Education and Science, *Primary Education in England,* a survey by HM Inspectors of Schools, HMSO, 1978, 8.43.
5. *Education*, 5 March 1982, referring to the ORACLE study.
6. Assessment of Performance Unit, *Science in Schools: Age 11: Report No. 1,* HMSO, 1981.
7. *Self-evaluation and the Teacher*, an annotated bibliography and report on current practice, by Gordon Eliott, Lecturer in Curricular Studies, University of Hull, 1980, Part 2.
8. R. A. Howells, *Curriculum Provision in the Small Primary School: a Study of the Problems and Possible Solutions to Them* (Cambridge Occasional Paper), Cambridge Institute of Education, 1982.
9. Letter from the Chief Education Officer, Gloucestershire, to heads of schools in the LEA, 15 September 1980.
10. *Curriculum Provision in the Small Primary School*.
11. Schools Council Committee for Wales and Programme 1, 'Curriculum and organization of primary schools in Wales: the small rural school', progress report, September 1982.
12. Schools Council Art Committee, *Resources for Visual Education 7–13* (Occasional Bulletins from the Subject Committees), Schools Council, 1981, pp. 19–20.
13. *Resources for Visual Education 7–13*, pp. 17–18.
14. *Resources for Visual Education 7–13*, pp. 37–8.
15. Adapted from *Resources for Visual Education 7–13*, pp. 23–4.
16. Anita Straker, *Mathematics for Gifted Pupils* (Schools Council Programme Pamphlets), Longman, York, 1982, p. 4.

17. Vera Southgate, Helen Arnold and Sandra Johnson, *Extending Beginning Reading*, Heinemann Educational for the Schools Council, 1981.
18. E. Lunzer and K. Gardner (eds.), *The Effective Use of Reading*, Heinemann Educational for the Schools Council, 1979.
19. M. Mobley, *Evaluation of Curriculum Materials*, Schools Council, 1982. Further units describing this systematic approach to assessing the suitability of curriculum materials are currently in preparation by the Evaluation of Curriculum Materials Project.
20. Frank Whitehead and others, *Children and their Books* (Schools Council Research Studies), Macmillan Education, 1977.
21. Gillian Klein, *Resources for Multicultural Education* (Schools Council Programme Pamphlets), Longman, York, 1982, pp. 14–15.
22. Kathleen Hartley and Michael Newby, *How to Help a Child at Home*, Home and School Council, Sheffield, 1979.
23. Dr Elizabeth Hunter-Grundin, case study on Parent Involvement in Education, London Borough of Haringey, a multi-ethnic project as part of the Council for Cultural Cooperation's Project No. 7, The Education and Cultural Development of Migrants.
24. Information received from Mrs Nancy Elliott, Senior Inspector, Newcastle upon Tyne.
25. *Helping your Child with Reading*, Stevenage Teachers' Centre.
26. The Mansfield First Schools Curriculum Development Project Home–School: Language Links (1981–2): an Evaluation Report (unpublished).
27. *Home/School Relations*, Section 1, Primary and Middle Schools, National Union of Teachers Education Department, 1983.
28. Anthony Wood and Lena Simpkins, *Involving Parents in the Curriculum*, Home and School Council, 1980, pp. 12–13.
29. Department of Education and Science, *Education 5 to 9: an Illustrative Survey of 80 First Schools in England*, HMSO, 1982.
30. *Curriculum Provision in the Small Primary School*.

Chapter XII. Could we be doing better?

1. Brenda Denvir, Chris Stolz and Margaret Brown, *Low Attainers in Mathematics 5–16: Policies and Practices in Schools* (Schools Council Working Paper 72), Methuen Educational, 1982.
2. C. M. Hunter and J. B. Harrison, 'Talking with books', a Schools Council-supported collaborative research project, interim report, 1982.
3. *Low Attainers in Mathematics 5–16*, p. 138.
4. Teacher–Pupil Interaction and the Quality of Learning (Schools Council Programme 2): 'Some problems of understanding in the reception class', Wendy Hunter and Carol Jones, Grove Primary School, Cambridge, March 1982.
5. Schools Council Programme 2: Surrey LEA.
6. John Nicholls, 'Beginning writing enquiry, report no. 2', a paper presented in the School of Education, University of Bristol, 2 December 1978.
7. Schools Council Programme 2: Networks – Northamptonshire Teaching and Learning Project.

8. *Making INSET Work – Myth or Reality?*, edited by Peter Chambers for the Curriculum and Educational Development In-service Network (CUED-IN), Faculty of Contemporary Studies, Bradford College.
9. Jean Rudduck (ed.), *Teachers in Partnership: Four Studies of In-service Collaboration* (Schools Council Programme Pamphlets), Longman, York, 1982.
10. *Teachers in Partnership.*
11. The above two examples come in a paper from Peter Baker, Centre for Educational Technology, Leicester.
12. D. Oldroyd, N. Smith and J. Lee, *A Handbook of School-based Staff Development Activities*, materials for school-based staff development project, Avon/Schools Council, 1982.
13. *A Handbook of School-based Staff Development Activities.*
14. *Making INSET Work – Myth or Reality?*
15. 'Self-evaluation and the teacher', an annotated bibliography and report on current practice compiled by Gordon Elliott, Lecturer in Curriculum Studies, University of Hull, 1980.
16. 'A school looks in the mirror and evaluates itself', Northamptonshire LEA primary schools in-service discussion paper, 1981.
17. Department of Education and Science, *Primary Education in England*, a survey by HM Inspectors of Schools, HMSO, 1978.
18. Department of Education and Science, *Education 5 to 9: an Illustrative Survey of 80 First Schools in England*, HMSO, 1982.
19. Guidelines for schools which wish to make such a start are to be published by Longman for the Schools Council Guidelines for Review and Institutional Development in Schools (GRIDS) Project.
20. The Cambridgeshire/Schools Council Self-evaluation Project.
21. Morley Victoria Junior and Infant School, Leeds.

Recommended reading

1. *A View of the Curriculum*
   HMI Matters for Discussion Series
   HMSO, 1980 (£1.50 paperback)
2. *The School Curriculum*
   DES/Welsh Office
   March 1981 (£2.00)
3. *Primary Education in England*
   A survey by HM Inspectors of Schools
   DES
   HMSO, 1978 (£3.50 paperback)
4. *Education 5 to 9: an Illustrative Survey of 80 First Schools in England*
   DES
   HMSO, 1982 (£3.50)
5. *Record Keeping in Primary Schools*
   Schools Council Research Studies
   Philip Clift, Gaby Weiner and Edwin Wilson
   Macmillan Education, 1981 (£7.95 paperback)
6. *With Objectives in Mind*
   Guide to Science 5–13
   Macdonald Educational, 1972 (£3.50)
7. *The Practical Curriculum*
   Schools Council Working Paper 70
   Methuen Educational, 1981 (£3.50)
8. *Mathematics Counts*
   Report of the Committee of Inquiry into the Teaching of Mathematics in
   Schools under the Chairmanship of Dr W. H. Cockcroft
   HMSO, 1982 (£5.75)
9. *Mathematics 5–11: a Handbook of Suggestions*
   HMI Matters for Discussion Series
   HMSO, 1979 (£3.50 paperback)
10. *Mathematics for Gifted Pupils*
    Schools Council Programme Pamphlets
    Anita Straker
    Longman, York, 1983 (£2.95)
11. *Low Attainers in Mathematics 5–16: Policies and Practices in Schools*
    Schools Council Working Paper 72
    Brenda Denvir, Chris Stolz and Margaret Brown
    Methuen Educational, 1982 (£5.50)
12. *A Language for Life*
    Report of the Committee of Inquiry appointed by the Secretary of State for

Education and Science under the Chairmanship of Sir Alan Bullock, FBA, HMSO, 1975 (£7.00 paperback)

13. *Extending Beginning Reading*
Vera Southgate, Helen Arnold and Sandra Johnson
Heinemann Educational for the Schools Council, 1981 (£5.50 paperback)

14. *Education for a Multiracial Society: Curriculum and Context 5–13*
Schools Council, 1981 (£5.50)

15. *Resources for Multi-cultural Education: an Introduction*
Schools Council Programme Pamphlets
Gillian Klein
Longman, York, 1982 (£1.95)

16. *Social Studies 8–13*
Schools Council Working Paper 39
Evans/Methuen Educational, 1971 (£3.25)

17. *Art in Junior Education*
DES (prepared by a group of HM Inspectors of Schools)
HMSO, 1978 (£1.95 paperback)

18. *Resources for Visual Education 7–13*
Schools Council Art Committee
Spring 1981 (out of print)

19. *Environmental Studies 5–13: the Use of Historical Resources*
The report of a working party of the Schools Council Committee for Wales
Schools Council Working Paper 48
Evans/Methuen Educational, 1973 (£5.75)

20. *Evaluation of Curriculum Materials*
M. Mobley
Schools Council, forthcoming

21. *Self-evaluation and the Teacher*
An annotated bibliography and report on current practice, 1980
Gordon Elliott, Lecturer in Curriculum Studies, University of Hull
(4 parts, 1–4 £7.90) (1. £1.30, 2. £2.00, 3. £1.60, 4. £3.00)

22. *Curriculum Planning in History, Geography and Social Science*
Professor Alan Blyth, Keith Cooper, Ray Derricott, Gordon Elliott, Hazel Sumner and Allan Waplington
Collins–ESL Bristol for the Schools Council, 1976 (£4.50)

23. *The Primary Head*
Patrick Whitaker
Heinemann Educational, 1983 (£5.95)

24. *The Saber-Tooth Curriculum*
J. A. Peddiwell
McGraw-Hill, 1939 (£2.50)

25. *Discovering an Approach: Religious Education in Primary Schools*
Macmillan Education for the Schools Council, 1977 (£4.50)

26. *Science in Primary Schools*
A discussion paper produced by the HMI Science Committee
DES, 1983

Sources of information

British Catalogue of Audiovisual Materials
1st experimental edition (1979), £15. Supplement (1980), £12.50. Supplement (1983), £12.50. A directory of materials for use in education.

British Education Index
Quarterly, every fourth issue being an annual cumulative volume. A list and analysis of the subject content of all articles of permanent interest in the field of education from nearly 300 periodicals. £27 per annum.

These two publications are available in reference and academic libraries, or by subscription from Sales and Subscription Section, The British Library, Bibliographic Services Division, 2 Sheraton Street, London W1V 4BH. The information contained in both directories is also available on-line from BLAISE, a computer-based service to which major libraries subscribe.

Children's Books. An Information Guide
A directory describing sources of information and advice. £1.70 post free from the Centre for Children's Books, at the National Book League, Book House, 45 East Hill, London SW18 2QZ. The Centre houses a comprehensive collection of contemporary children's books other than textbooks, also a reference library for teachers which is open to visitors Mon.–Fri., 9.30–5.00. The National Book League also offers a general Book Information Service. The direct line is 01-874 8526.

Education Year Book
This contains extensive information on all UK local education authorities and Boards, together with lists of senior staff, and addresses of secondary schools, F & HE establishments, educational publishers, subject associations, educational suppliers, charities, and much else. It is published by the Councils and Education Press and is available from booksellers.

5001 Hard-to-find Publishers and Their Addresses
New edition due 1984. Available direct from Alan Armstrong and Associates Ltd, 2 Arkwright Road, Reading RG2 0SQ.

Treasure Chest for Teachers
This is the NUT guide to materials and services available from societies, industry,

embassies, etc.; places to visit; educational publishers and suppliers. The Teachers Publishing Co. Ltd, 1980–83 edition, £3.50 from booksellers.

Voluntary Organisations. An NCVO Directory
Latest edition 1982/83. Published by Bedford Square Press/National Council for Voluntary Organisations. Available from booksellers.

Where to look things up. 'An A–Z of sources on all major educational topics'
3rd edition 1983. £3 including postage from Advisory Centre for Education, 18 Victoria Park Square, London E2 9PB.

The National Reference Library of Schoolbooks and Classroom Material is based at the University of London Institute of Education, Bedford Way, London WC1. It is a comprehensive collection of contemporary books and materials for classroom use. It is open from 9.30 to 5.30 on Monday to Thursday and 9.30 to 5.00 on Friday, but it is wise to check beforehand if a visit is planned during the university vacation. The telephone number is 01-636 1500.

Members of the Working Party

P. L. Griffin (*Chairman*)	Windsor Clive County Junior School, Ely, Cardiff
J. Brand	Hipper Teachers' Centre, Chesterfield, Derbyshire
Miss J. C. Davenport	Woodhouse Park Infant School, Wythenshawe, Manchester
Mrs A. J. Dean	Chief Inspector, Surrey County Council
D. Denegri	HM Inspectorate of Schools
H. Dowson	Earl Marshal School, Sheffield
R. D. Ellis	St Peter's C. of E. Middle School, Farnham, Surrey
P. Highfield	HM Inspectorate of Schools
C. Morris	Kippax North Junior School, Leeds
A. Noonan	Holyrood RC Junior Mixed School, Watford
A. M. S. Poole	Western Middle School, Mitcham, Surrey
K. H. Wood-Allum	Deputy County Education Officer, Northamptonshire
Mrs J. Yeomans	National Confederation of Parent-Teacher Associations

Schools Council staff

J. Mann	Secretary
R. C. Abbott	Director, Programme 1, Purpose and Planning in Schools
K. Storey	Secretariat